THE CULTURES OF PREHISTORIC EGYPT

II

THE
CULTURES OF PREHISTORIC EGYPT
II

BY

ELISE J. BAUMGARTEL

M.A., DR. PHIL. (KOENIGSBERG I. PR.)

Published on behalf of the

GRIFFITH INSTITUTE

ASHMOLEAN MUSEUM, OXFORD

by the

OXFORD UNIVERSITY PRESS

LONDON   NEW YORK   TORONTO

1960

Oxford University Press, Amen House, London E.C. 4

GLASGOW NEW YORK TORONTO MELBOURNE WELLINGTON
BOMBAY CALCUTTA MADRAS KARACHI KUALA LUMPUR
CAPE TOWN IBADAN NAIROBI ACCRA

Printed in Great Britain
by T. and A. CONSTABLE LTD., *Hopetoun Street,*
Printers to the University of Edinburgh

CONTENTS

PREFACE TO VOLUME II

IT is again my pleasant duty to record my gratitude to all who made it possible for me to write the second volume of *The Cultures of Prehistoric Egypt*. As the revised edition of Vol. I and Vol. II were written at the same time it remains to add to my thanks to the persons and institutions mentioned in the preface of Vol. I, revised edition, my gratitude and thanks to those who gave me their help especially with Vol. II.

To all my colleagues in the United States, where I have been living since 1955, who have helped me so liberally not only with their advice but also with their permission to publish in Vol. II valuable material in their keeping as well as to those elsewhere I tender my grateful thanks. To Mr. J. Cooney of the Brooklyn Museum of Arts, Mr. W. Hayes of the New York Metropolitan Museum, Mr. P. Delougaz and Miss H. Kantor of the Museum of the Chicago Oriental Institute, Mr. W. Smith of the Museum of Fine Arts at Boston, Miss W. Needler of the Royal Ontario Museum, Toronto, Mr. I. E. S. Edwards of the British Museum, Mr. D. B. Harden then of the Ashmolean Museum, Oxford, Mr. C. Winter of the Cambridge University Museum, Mr. A. J. Arkell of the Flinders Petrie Museum, University College, London, my acknowledgements are due for the permission to publish photographs of objects from the Museums under their care. I shall never forget the kindness of M. Raphael of the Cairo Museum without whose help I would not have been able to make the photographs of objects in the Cairo Museum which were used for some of the reproductions in Vol. II.

To Mr. G. A. Wainright who undertook the thorny task of correcting my grammar and, at the same time let me profit from his great knowledge of Ancient Egypt, and to Miss Lucy S. Sutherland, Principal of Lady Margaret Hall, Oxford, who by offering me hospitality at Lady Margaret Hall made it possible for me to stay in Oxford during the summer of 1957 and prepare my typescript for print I offer my grateful thanks.

A sequence of unforeseen events caused Vol. II going to press much later than was anticipated. Mr. Harden's resignation from the Ashmolean Museum and, in consequence from the secretaryship of the Griffith Institute, and his subsequent leaving Oxford for London, and my own change of domicile from Oxford to Chicago were the main reasons for the long delay. As during the years from 1955 to 1959 no excavations in the field of predynastic Egyptian archaeology were undertaken, no need arose to alter the fundamental course of my book, or even, to add to the facts published in it. It is still my great hope that an excavation may be undertaken in a favourable spot, such as Koptos which would put the early history of Egypt on a safer foundation than the one it is resting on now.

It has not been possible for me to add to Vol. II the catalogue of tombs of Petrie's excavation at Naḳāda, still the fundamental source of our knowledge about pre- and protodynastic Egypt. As I had to assemble the card index single handed, it took a long time to complete. Even now the material in the University Museum at Philadelphia, Pa., is not fully included. However, with the help of R. Anthes in whose keeping the Museum now is, I hope that this will be put right in the near future. To arrange this material in tables which could be published was more than I could undertake without at least the help of a secretary, and this was not forthcoming. As soon as the catalogue will be finished it will be deposited in the library of the Hebrew University at Jerusalem. Until that time I shall be glad to answer any question which the catalogue may be able to answer.

ELISE J. BAUMGARTEL.

CHICAGO, *February*, 1959.

LIST OF ILLUSTRATIONS IN THE TEXT

(The scale of Figs. 1-14 is 2 : 3)

ABBREVIATIONS USED IN REFERENCES

ADDENDUM

Abbreviation	*Full Title*
Abydos	Petrie, W. M. F., *Abydos* vols. 1-3, 1902-4.
Bull. Inst. D'Eg. . .	Bulletin de l'Institut d'Égypte.
Cat. Gen. . . .	Catalogue Général des Antiquités Égyptiennes du Musee du Caire.
Cairo, E. J. . .	Cairo Museum, Entrance Journal.
Cem. at El-Maḥāsna .	Ayrton, E. R. and Loat, W. L. S., *Pre-Dynastic Cemetery at El-Maḥāsna* (1911).
Das Re-Heiligtum .	Von Bissing, F. W., *Das Re-Heiligtum des Koenigs Ne-Woser-Re (Rathures)*. Bd. 1 *Der Bau* von L. Borchardt. Bd. 11 *Die kleine Festdarstellung* von Bissing und Kees. (1905-28).
El Amrah . . .	Randall-MacIver, D. and Mace, A. C., *El Amrah and Abydos* (1899-1901).
Gerzeh . . .	Petrie, W. M. F., Wainright, G. A. and Mackay, E. *The Labyrinth, Gerzeh, and Mazguneh* (1912).
Ḥor-Aḥa . . .	Emery, W. B., *Excavations at Saqqara 1937-1938*. *Ḥor-Aḥa* (Service des Antiquités de L'Égypte. 1939).
J.N.E.S. . . .	Journal of Near Eastern Studies. Chicago.
Maḥāsna . . .	Garstang, J., *Maḥāsna and Bêt Khallâf* (1903).
Manuel . . .	Vandier, J., *Manuel d'Archéologie Égyptienne* (1952).
Tarkhan . . .	Petrie, W. M. F., Wainright, G. A. and Gardiner A. H., *Tarkhan I and Memphis V*. Petrie, W. M. F., *Tarkhan II*.
Untersuchungen .	Sethe, K., *Untersuchungen zur Geschichte und Altertumskunde Aegyptens* (1912 ff.).

LIST OF PLATES

(Plates I-XIII at end)

x

INTRODUCTION

THIS second, concluding Vol. of the *Cultures of Prehistoric Egypt* was written ten years after the first part. During the intervening time I was able to consult the literature which had been inaccessible to me during the war years, and, more important, was given the opportunity of visiting Egypt and also the United States. I can now, therefore, base my theses on a much wider range of material than that used for the first part, and this has altered somewhat my outlook on the problems with which I had to deal and the way in which I tried to clarify them. I found it premature in many instances, before we knew the inventory in Egypt itself, to follow up the connexions with countries outside Egypt which certain objects suggested. Vol. II, therefore, is largely concerned with correlation and critical study of the different types of metal, flints, ivories, etc., and also houses and settlements, so that, after having reduced the chaos to some order, we may see what we can learn of the cultural, political, economic and religious situation in predynastic Egypt. As in Vol. I, I have based my deductions mainly on excavated pieces, taking into account antiquities bought from dealers only where I was reasonably sure that they were authentic, for that is the first question one has to settle when dealing with such material. I have also avoided wherever possible basing conclusions on material which I have only seen in illustrations, because they may be very misleading. When I have not seen and handled a piece I have said so. On the plates, quite a number of long since familiar objects will be found photographed for the first time, or photographed from a new angle.

When dealing with the more spiritual aspects of these ancient civilizations my conclusions cannot but be conjectural, and therefore open to dispute. I have founded my views on the known facts (nobody appreciates more than I how scanty they often are), and have avoided drawing conclusions merely from literary sources of later date. These were adduced only where they showed a survival from authentic facts observed during predynastic times. Nothing, for example, can be more misleading than to take a chapter from the Pyramid Texts and project it backwards. I am not sure that in the present state of our knowledge we can say with certainty which of the chapters go back to predynastic periods, as some, no doubt, do. This makes the observations on the earliest Egyptian gods appear rather scanty. There must have been many more than are to be found among the predynastic remains, but as long as no sign of them has been forthcoming, or only very dubious ones, as with Seth, the verdict for me is "unproven".

I would like to conclude these introductory remarks by reversing an oft-quoted sentence from the pen of a distinguished Egyptologist, expressing it thus: "This is not written to be believed, but to be argued about, and, especially, corrected where I have misrepresented the facts, or overlooked some evidence. Only in that way, to my mind, can we acquire some safer knowledge."

CHAPTER I

METAL

THE questions where man first discovered how to use metal and whether gold or copper was the first metal he exploited have often been discussed, but without definite results.

In Egypt no gold has so far been found before Naḳāda I, whilst copper occurs in Badārian times. As this may be due to the accidents of preservation rather than to the actual absence of gold during the earlier period—for the precious metal must have been more coveted than anything else by tomb-robbers—Egypt does not necessarily supply the answer to these questions.

Neither gold nor copper occurs in the Nile Valley proper, but both are mined in the mountains between Egypt and the Red Sea, and copper ores also in the Sinai Peninsula. It is not known whether any of these mines were worked in predynastic times. There is, however, an indication that gold was mined during this early period. The ancient name of one of the most important settlements, Naḳāda, is Nub. t—"gold"—written with the hieroglyph of a necklace. That suggests the assumption that the exploitation of the precious metal was the reason for the name, and that the gold-mines in its neighbourhood were known at least as early as the periods of Naḳāda I and II.

The discovery of copper and of its value to man can only have been made in a country where it was available either in its native form or in an ore reducible by the processes which primitive men were able to achieve. It is not known whether native copper ever occurred in Egypt. But even if it did, it would not prove that it was in Egypt that the use of copper was first discovered. We have seen that the Badārians used inferior desert flint as raw material for their tools, though much better material existed in the cliffs near which they were living. Vast quantities of native copper are found on the shores of Lake Superior, blocks of the pure metal weighing several tons. Yet the indigenous inhabitants of those parts never discovered the art of copper casting, but treated the small nodules, which alone they used, as if they were stone.

Malachite, which is one of the copper ores most frequently found in the mountains east of Egypt, is easily reduced to metallic copper. It was used as a cosmetic by the Badārians, and also for glazing steatite beads to make them resemble turquoise, a stone they highly valued. Lucas [1] maintains that metallic copper was first discovered as a by-product of the glazing process, which he thinks older than the knowledge of metallic copper; he believes that the invention of glazing as well as the discovery of metallic copper was due to the ancient Egyptians. These for the time being are only attractive hypotheses.

The earliest sign of Egyptians having frequented copper-mines was found in Wadi Magharah in southern Sinai. King Semerkhet of the middle of the First Dynasty left a relief there showing him three times over, once slaying an enemy. We do not know whether this early king went to Sinai on a punitive expedition against some troublesome neighbours or whether he went to take possession of the mines, the products of which might have been traded to him by these neighbours. Nor can it be ascertained whether it was the copper ore which attracted the Egyptians to the Sinai mines or the highly-valued turquoise found in the same places. Thus, even in Sinai with its

[1] A. Lucas, *Ancient Egyptian Materials and Industries*, pp. 228 ff.

A

comparatively well-documented history we cannot be sure when copper mining started; it is still less possible to ascertain the age of the mines between Egypt and the Red Sea, about which travellers' reports are all we possess.

BADĀRIAN AND NAḲĀDA I

The earliest metal objects so far excavated in Egypt are of copper and were found by Brunton at Badāri. In the "quite untouched" grave of a child,[1] two copper beads were discovered forming part of a necklace, of blue-glazed steatite or turquoise beads, two cornelian beads, and a shell, still on its original string. They were of "metal ribbon wound round spirally to form rings".

In t. 5112 Brunton unearthed a copper object which he describes as a small pin or borer. It is a thin bent rod (now at University College, London),[2] the original purpose of which is difficult to guess. T. 5112 is a plundered grave, but what is left of its content is Badārian, and there is no reason to doubt the contemporaneity of the copper rod.

These two finds do not teach us much about the Egyptian copper industry of their time. The beads are hammered and so is the rod. Nor is there much to be gained from the study of the following period of Naḳāda I. Copper utensils are still very rare. The characteristic type of the period is a copper pin (pl. III, 14). Those found are between 5 and 10 cm. long, pointed at one end, with heads made by turning one end of the pin back so as to form a loop. These pins have been explained either as dress pins, which would hold a garment together, or as prick pins used for some purpose of the toilet. We do not know of an Egyptian garment which was fastened with pins, nor have enough copper pins, or pins of other materials, been found to make such a fashion likely. Those of ivory or bone are nearly all long and fragile. Most of them were hairpins, some being found *in situ* in the hair. Thus "prick pin" so far seems the most likely explanation.

A copper finger-ring made of a strip of copper foil and decorated with a punched zig-zag pattern was found in Naḳāda, t. 1552, S.D. 35 (?), from which a fragment of a copper pin was also recovered. The ring is bent round so that its ends overlap. The ascription of the tomb to Naḳāda I is doubtful,[3] and the two "rings of copper" from El-'Amrah, t. a 67, which Petrie dates to Naḳāda I on the strength of a "clay male doll (broken)" [4] which was found in the same grave, as well as a small chain of copper, do not dispose of the difficulty of the dating. None of the objects is reproduced, nor can I trace them; Petrie's ascription could not be substantiated, especially as there is no pottery known from the grave. The excavators date t. a 67 to before S.D. 41 on account of the shape of the grave, which they reckon among their class I, "round shallow grave", but add that it was 6 feet deep. Dating from the shape of predynastic graves has not succeeded so far; poorer graves even in later times keep to the simplest types. Thus the ascription of the grave and its ring to Naḳāda I seems somewhat doubtful. Copper rings do not appear in well-dated tombs till Naḳāda II.

No sign of copper casting has been found from Naḳāda I. If we had adequate excavations

---

[1] *Bad. Civ.*, p. 12, t. 5413, pl. L, 86 W 3.

[2] *Bad. Civ.*, p. 33, pl. XXVI.

[3] Ring and fragment of pin at University College, London. The ring is 0·7 cm. high, 0·9 cm. diam. From its slate palette, which is rectangular with incised border type 97b, it seems protodynastic.

[4] *El Amrah* p. 16. W. M. Flinders Petrie, *Prehistoric Egypt*, p. 27.

in settlements the picture might be different. One could hope to find moulds, or crucibles, or other debris from copper working. Copper must have been of great value in these early days, and, if deposited in tombs, it would have been the first item which plunderers would remove. Tomb-robbing was as common during predynastic times as later on.

Therefore, with the limited material at our disposal we cannot make sure whether copper working was practised by the people of Naḳāda I. There does not seem to have been much progress in the types since Badārian times. It may be that copper was imported in small quantities from abroad, or that the little pins were imported ready made. Pins of this primitive type do not belong to Naḳāda I only; they are found in the earliest layers throughout the Near East. They occur in Sialk I,[1] Hissar I, 6,[2] and Shah Tepe.[3]

Since some copper beads were found in the preceding period, it is most likely mere chance that none has survived from Naḳāda I and that the little pins and perhaps one copper finger-ring are all that has come down to us from that time.

Two gold beads are mentioned from El-Maḥāsna, t. H 17,[4] and that is all the gold I have been able to trace from Naḳāda I. Until more work has been done in the field, the chapter on earliest Egyptian metallurgy must remain very unsatisfactory.

NAḲĀDA II

In keeping with its other achievements, Naḳāda II has a much greater variety of copper tools than is known from the previous epochs in the Nile Valley. It is also in possession of a metal unknown so far from the earlier periods, namely silver. Gold, from the few pieces preserved, must have been plentiful, and the skill of the goldsmiths was admirable.

1 Gold

A narrow gold wire curved into several untidy circles of a diameter of 0·7 in. was found in Naḳāda, t. 723, S.D. 46-52. The same grave contained a polished-red pot, type P 16, a small ivory bird from the top of a hairpin, several strings of beads made of clay and shell,[5] and some small shapeless lumps of malachite and agate. The gold wire, which may have been a finger-ring, contrasts oddly with the otherwise rather shabby contents of the grave.[6] A cylindrical gold bead was found together with beads of lapis lazuli, glazed steatite, glazed composition, and cornelian in Naḳāda, t. 667.[6] A plain cylinder of lapis, 0·7 in. long, and a "spindle-whorl" of black and white porphyry, which is more likely to have been a bead, add to the elegance of the outfit. I could trace only one of the pots that must once have belonged to the furniture of this tomb. It is a bowl of smooth reddish clay of Petrie's "late" type L 17a.[7] A rough and thick flint flake completed the list. The grave was not sequence-dated by Petrie, but it belongs to the later part of Naḳāda II.

---

[1] R. Ghirshman, *Fouilles de Sialk près de Kashan*, I, pl. LII, 53.
[2] E. F. Schmidt, *Excavations at Tepe Hissar*, p. 57. "The head (of the pin) was formed by bending over the top."
[3] *Shah Tepe, Swedish Archaeological Expedition to Iran*, Acta Arch., fig. II, 64.
[4] *Pre-dynastic Cemetery at El-Mahasna*, p. 11. Present location not known to me.
[5] I cannot trace the gold beads Petrie mentions. See *Preh. Eg.*, p. 27.
[6] The contents of these graves are at University College, London.
[7] This bowl now belongs to the Museum of the Oriental Institute in Chicago.

A tubular gold bead, 3 cm. long, comes from Naḳāda, t. 36. It is made of a thin gold leaf rolled together and reinforced in the middle by a shallow knob. T. 36 is a rich grave with many interesting features. Of its two stone vases one is of the "shouldered" type, the other of serpentine and bird-shaped. Four pots and a pot-stand (type L 86) are also known from it. One is "decorated", type D 21H, and of two others which are "fancy", one, a very rare specimen, is barrel-shaped with the mouth on the long side (type F 34b), and the other boat-shaped. A rough pot (L 50A) has a strainer inside its neck.[1]

A gold pendant from Ballas, t. 172 (?), dated S.D. 59, of thin gold foil is pear-shaped, and is bent over at the top to form a horizontal suspension tube. The whole of the front is decorated with punched dots. It measures just over 2·5 cm.[2]

Of gold beads from predynastic cemeteries other than Naḳāda the most noteworthy are those which Wainwright found in t. 67 at Gerzeh, for they belong to the same necklace on which some of the famous iron beads were found. The gold beads are cylindrical in shape, as are the iron ones. The iron beads are unique, and, as I shall not come back to them later, I would like to recall here that the iron used in their manufacture is native, i.e. meteoric, iron, not smelted from the ore. They were made (as were the gold beads) by bending a thin plate of metal over a rod which was afterwards removed.[3] Iron beads were also found in Gerzeh, t. 133. As the two graves are contemporaneous (S.D. 53-63 and 60-66), Wainwright assumes that all the beads were made from the same find of iron. No other iron objects have been found among the relics of predynastic Egypt. It seems a chance in a million that the little iron beads should have survived.

To return to gold beads, some more interesting ones were found in t. 55 at Gerzeh, sequence-dated S.D. 65-72 and therefore probably early dynastic. Wainwright calls them "spiral" shaped, which may be somewhat misleading. They are made of a thin gold foil into which ridges spiralling round the bead were punched. Two of these beads were on a short string shown on pl. V of the publication. At the bottom of the plate they are shown enlarged to double their size.

Petrie mentions a tube of "apparently a gold-copper alloy" from Naḳāda, t. 1247.[4] It joins two broken pieces of lapis lazuli tubes. A similar object, a lapis lazuli tube with a gold sheath drawn over one end, is in Cairo. The gold part is cut off at one end and forms a sort of nib. It is impossible to say whether it was originally joined to another lapis lazuli tube like the one from Naḳāda. It seems that the use of these contraptions was to conceal damage done to the lapis lazuli tubes, for they are chipped or broken.

Two small horn-shaped caps and some beads were found by G. Möller in two different graves at Abuṣīr el-Meleḳ, their joints soldered together.[5] The beads are from an early dynastic grave,

[1] The gold beads and the stone vases are at University College, London, the decorated pot was in the Berlin Egyptian collection. The other pots are in the Ashmolean Museum, Oxford. This grave must be dated very late in Naḳāda II, or perhaps even early dynastic.

[2] W. M. Flinders Petrie and J. E. Quibell, *Naqada and Ballas*, p. 15, t. 23 (*sic!*), pl. LXV, t. 172 (this number agrees with that given in *Preh. Eg.*).

[3] W. M. Flinders Petrie, G. A. Wainwright and E. Mackay, *The Labyrinth, Gerzeh and Mazghuneh*, pp. 15 ff. For proof of their meteoric origin see *id.* in *Journal of Egyptian Archaeology*, 18, p. 3.

[4] *Naq. Bal.*, pp. 27-8; *Preh. Eg.*, p. 27. Now in the Ashmolean Museum, Oxford. It is of gold with a high copper admixture.

[5] Schaefer, Möller and Schubart, *Aegyptische Goldschmiedearbeiten. Mitteilungen aus der Aegyptischen Sammlung, Berlin* (1910), p. 13.

the little caps from a plundered grave cited as "probably predynastic". The difference in time between the two graves in any case seems negligible. These are the earliest known instances of soldering so far recorded from Egypt.

Two gold objects in the Cairo Museum are generally ascribed to our period. One was among the objects which in May 1896 came to the Cairo Museum from a place called Homra Doum, Gebel Tarif, "en face de Naq Hammadi"; the other was bought. They are handles fastened to flint implements, and are much larger than any gold object of the time from regular excavations. One [1] is the handle of a ripple-flaked flint knife which must be dated to S.D. 55-65. It is one of a group of ripple-flaked knives which have preserved their handles, and the only one with a gold handle. It was published by Quibell. Since the handle is slightly too big for the knife, Quibell assumes that a leather lining must once have existed to make it fit. The two sides of the handle, made of very thin gold foil, were sewn together with a golden thread. Each bears a different decoration. On one, of which very little is preserved, two serpents are entwined around rosettes; one of these seems to have been a repair, for it was made of a separate piece, and is too large for the space into which it was fitted.[2] The other side is divided into four panels, each containing two animals which attack each other. On the uppermost a leopard is attacking a gazelle from behind; on the next a lion attacks a gazelle. The third panel has what looks like a big dog falling upon an animal which does not seem to fit into any known species; and on the bottom panel a quadruped with a huge pair of wings assails another gazelle. A similar monster with wings is known from the animal palette of Hierakonpolis,[3] to which, as Helene Kantor has shown, the knife handle is closely related in style.[4] There also we find fights between pairs of animals, though not arranged in the orderly fashion of the gold handle but fitted into the available space as best they could be, crowding the picture; where there was no room for two fighting animals, a single one was squeezed in. The artist of the gold handle has no love for empty spaces either. He fills them with small rosettes. The use of this conventional emblem is in keeping with his style, which is much more schematic and tidy than that of the master of the slate palette, but it does not attain the latter's movement and liveliness.

It was pointed out long ago that the motifs of the entwined serpents, the winged monsters and the two animals, one of which attacks the other from behind, are borrowed from Mesopotamian art, where they occur during the periods of Uruk and Jemdet Nasr. The orderly array in panels on the knife handle points in the same direction. The strong feeling for structure, a characteristic of Mesopotamian art, had led to the dividing of a space into geometrical patterns at a very early date.

The other handle from Cairo, of much heavier gold, was also published first by Quibell.[5] He points out that the flint fish-tail to which it is now attached, as if it were a dagger "but not hitherto recognized as being a dagger", made the object somewhat doubtful. The three rivets which "as it seems" pass through the handle and the tang of the dagger are another "suspicious

[1] J. E. Quibell, *Archaic Objects, Cat. Gén.*, no. 14265.

[2] Of the side with the entwined snakes a few fragments is all that remains. For other objects with the same provenance see below, pp. 8-9.

[3] J. E. Quibell and F. W. Green, *Hierakonpolis*, II, pl. XXVIII.

[4] H. Kantor, "The Final Stage of Predynastic Culture, Gerzean or Semainean", *Journal of Near Eastern Studies*, III (1944), pp. 110 ff.

[5] Quibell, "Flint Dagger from Gebelen", *Annales du Service des Antiquités de l'Égypte*, 2 (1901).

fact". Lastly Quibell states that the two plates which form the handle are joined by soldering, which, as he says, "is also new to me in the archaic period".[1] A look at the dagger will show that the handle grips the fish-tail too far down, and does not cover the edges left unfinished because the handle should overlie them. The decoration of the handle shows some strange features also, which have prototypes on the "decorated" pots. On one side a ship with two cabins and branches in the bow is engraved, the rather wide lines filled in with some black substance. One cabin is furnished with a pole on which the emblem is an untidily-drawn Z sign; on top of the other is a curious animal with scarcely any legs, and, as it seems, three horns. The narrow ship follows the upper outline of the dagger, and the many oars, for which there was no room left on the side, are put on top of the handle, where they are met by the oars of the ship drawn on the other side. Two parallel lines on one side, and one of the fan-shaped objects ending in a loop, complete the picture on the obverse. On the reverse, in a boat provided with oars, but with no cabins or any of the other usual features, are three women in a row, and they, too, show marked divergences from the style of the "decorated" ware. Perhaps the different way of rendering the bodies may be explained by the different techniques of painting and engraving, but this would not explain the snake-like arm of one of the women, who holds a "fan", nor the fan itself, which seems to be a misunderstood tree. Add to this the unusual heaviness and solidity of the metal and the colour, which is not the usual colour of predynastic gold, and the authenticity of the object becomes too doubtful for the handle to be taken into consideration here.

A third knife with a gold handle [2] is in the Royal Ontario Museum at Toronto (pl. II, 6 and 7). It is of the time of King Djer, and somewhat later than those mentioned before. The type of the flint knife, well made but not ripple-flaked, with a narrow handle set sharply back from the cutting edge, is of the early First Dynasty. The gold handle is decorated with a *sereḫ* of King Djer and a falcon on a perch inside a rectangular enclosure. The handle is made by wrapping a piece of gold foil tightly round the flint handle. To obtain better adherence a thin layer of glue was spread over the flint and the gold pressed or hammered down on to it. This procedure may explain the rather crumpled state of the handle. However, a tight fit was achieved, and the gold ends in a straight line obliquely across the base of the knife. The fastening of the gold foil to the handle by wrapping and glueing is the most primitive method so far met.

To those finds must now be added the strips of embossed gold foil recently retrieved by Professor Emery from the tomb of King Djet of the First Dynasty at Saḳḳāra. This shows how great the resources of gold must have been during this period, if twelve pilasters, each 1 m. long and 1 m. wide, could have been hung with gold strips, each 1 cm. wide and spaced 1 cm. apart.[3]

2 *Silver*

The finds of silver are surprisingly more substantial than one would expect. Gold, though not found in the Nile Valley proper, was extracted from rocks in the country between Egypt and the Red Sea. Silver, however, must have come from afar. If we knew the source of

[1] Against this see note top of p. 5. The handle was inspected for me by Dr. Zaki Iskander and Mons. Victor Girgis from the laboratory of the Cairo Museum. They share my doubts about the authenticity of the piece.

[2] W. Needler, "A Flint Knife of King Djer", *JEA*, 42 (1956), pp. 41 ff.

[3] W. B. Emery, *The Illustrated London News*, 23 May 1953, p. 840; *Great Tombs of the First Dynasty*, II, pp. 14 ff., pl. XIII.

predynastic Egyptian silver it would cast some light on foreign connexions and trading, and perhaps even on the source of the Naḳāda II culture. Moreover, while gold is found in its natural state, silver has to be smelted from the ore.

Petrie mentions among the metal finds of the Naḳāda cemeteries a thin silver ring from t. 1770; and hollow, globular beads and a jar cap of silver from t. 1257.[1] The silver ring I could not trace. In my card index t. 1770 is represented by a polished-red pot (type P22 B) and a copper "forehead" pendant.[2] As Petrie sequence-dates the tomb to S.D. 61, there must have been more pottery, perhaps now hidden in some small museum, together with the silver ring. The silver lid and some silver beads from the rich tomb 1257 are now in the Ashmolean Museum. Of the beads only small fragments remain, and the jar cap also is in a somewhat dilapidated state. It is circular, with a diameter of about 6·3 cm., and is provided with a narrow, straight rim. In the same tomb an unusual spoon was found. Its bowl is made of slate with a tubular extension into which its handle of copper wire is cemented. Disc-shaped beads are threaded upon it, alternately slate and steatite. It is about 11·8 cm. long. A few steatite beads may have come from the same string as the silver ones. There were also two stone vases, barrel-shaped, one of them of basalt and the other of porphyry, a pear-shaped mace-head of limestone,[3] and two small slate palettes, one of which is in the form of a fish (type 40d) 5 cm. long, with a suspension hole, and the other rectangular, 6·3 cm. long, with a triangular notch at one end and a suspension hole at the other (type 60).[4] Of the pottery, only the extraordinary fragment D 52 could be traced.[5] A few lumps of malachite and other minerals complete the known contents of the tomb. The date is S.D. 42.

Fragments of a globular silver bead together with one of cornelian were found in Naḳāda, t. 1547.[6] Three black-topped vases and the fragments of a fourth with a pot-mark are known from the grave. Petrie dated the grave to S.D. 38, the beginning of the Naḳāda II period.[7] This, so far, is the earliest known occurrence of silver in Egypt.

A silver spoon with a circular bowl and a "twisted" handle mentioned by Petrie[8] vanished before it could be drawn. He dates it to S.D. 57-64, but does not mention the number of the grave in which it was found.[9] A small spoon with a silver bowl was among the finds in t. b 233 at El-'Amrah. It had a copper stem, but no further description or illustration is given, so that we do not know how the bowl and stem were joined.[10] Silver and gold beads were recovered from the large but partly plundered grave H 41 at El-Maḥāsna[11] dated "before S.D. 56". The excavators describe them as: "A string of silver beads. They are very thin shells, and may have

[1] *Naq. Bal.*, p. 45. The analysis of the lid proved it to be nearly pure silver.
[2] Now at University College, London.
[3] Now in the Ashmolean Museum, Oxford.
[4] Now at University College, London.
[5] Now in the Ashmolean Museum, Oxford. The pottery fragment is of a ring pot.
[6] Now at University College, London. I could not trace the solid gold bead which Petrie mentions from this tomb in *Preh. Eg.*, p. 27.
[7] Two of the vases, type B 25d and B 53a, were in the Berlin Collection; the third, type B 35b, and the sherd with the pot-mark *Naq. Bal.*, pl. LII, 51, are in the Ashmolean Museum, Oxford.
[8] *Naq. Bal.*, p. 46.
[9] *Preh. Eg.*, p. 27.
[10] *El Amrah*, pp. 24 and 46.
[11] *Pre-dyn. Cem. at El-Mahasna*, pp. 16 and 30, pl. XVI, 3.

been originally formed over some composition; they are in a fair state of preservation, though much oxidized. A string of gold beads and pendant. The pendant is solid, but the beads, like the silver ones, are thin shells." [1] As far as can be seen from the illustration, the silver beads are of different shapes. Barrel, ring and conical forms occur. Some are considerably larger than the gold ones, all of which seem to be barrel-shaped. The pendant, which is 1·2 cm. long, is oblong and perforated at one end.

Most of the beads of precious metal are made over a core of plaster or other composition and are hammered from very thin metal foil, but a few solid beads have survived which give some idea of what the personal ornaments of the richer graves must have been. Those I have seen are made in the same technique by hammering, only the sheet of gold was thicker, so that the rod over which they must have been formed could be withdrawn after their fabrication, as the material was strong enough to withstand the use to which it was being put.

A far more substantial silver object was recovered by Quibell at Ballas. It is an adze, 17·1 cm. long, 3·7 cm. at its greatest width. Its sides are slightly convex, the cutting edge curved and somewhat spreading, bevelled on one side. It had passed for copper until, on the instigation of Professor Glanville, it was sent for cleaning from University College, London, where it is kept, to the research laboratory of the British Museum. After the corrosion was removed it appeared a white silver. Though Petrie published this adze both in *Naqada and Ballas* [2] and in *Tools and Weapons*,[3] no tomb number is known. This, though quite in keeping with the confusion which characterizes all the records about Ballas (how fortunate we are that Naḳāda was left in a much better state), nevertheless leaves a slight doubt. It seems certain that the piece was found at Ballas, or Petrie would not have stated the fact twice. Its type is characteristic of its period, and therefore I feel justified in including it among the silver of Naḳāda II.

An interesting lot of gold and silver objects, now in the Cairo Museum, also has a somewhat doubtful provenance. The *Cairo Museum, Entrance Journal* states that during June 1896 a number of objects came into the possession of the Museum which were all found in the same grave at Homra Doum "en face de Naq Hammadi", which consisted of a round shaft 2 m. deep. Since in May 1896 large numbers of objects dating from Naḳāda I to Early Dynastic times were registered as having come from "Sahel el Baghlieh, Homra Doum, Gebel Tarif en face de Naq Hammadi", one will have to assume that an early cemetery there was plundered and that some of the finds were acquired by the Museum. Only in the case of the objects from the tomb with the "round shaft" was an effort made to keep the furniture of a grave together. More than two dozen objects from it are registered, but the pottery that must have belonged to the grave is sadly missing. A rich and very peculiar furniture had been buried with this dead person. He took with him a number of finely-polished stone tools. Eight of them seem to have been pounders, between 5 and 10 cm. high, for, different in form though they are, each has a flat end which shows signs of use. One piece, thinner than the rest, may have been a spatula; and the only damaged one, squarish, with sides 5 to 4·5 cm., of fine green schist, looks rather like a weight. An oblong pendant (6·5 by 3·4 cm.) of a black stone with some brown marks (Psitom) is perforated near the top. It is interesting to find a well-made dark diorite axe (12·4 cm. long) (pl. I, 1) pecked and with a ground cutting edge among the tools of igneous rocks. The two copper adzes belonging

---

[1] *Pre-dyn. cem. at El-Mahasna*, p. 30, G.   [2] p. 14.
[3] p. 16, pl. XVI, 65.

to the grave will be discussed below (pp. 12-13). A ripple-flaked flint knife, 6·4 cm. long and broken in two, looks like the upper part of what was once a much larger tool. The receding and rounded tang which it now possesses seems to have been made later, for it is of inferior workmanship to that of the fluted knife and has destroyed the lowest part of the fluting. Three much narrower fluted fragments must have belonged to two different knives. These ripple-flaked knives give an indication of the date of the tomb, namely S.D. 55-56. Three small flint blades, one a mere splinter, the other two with slight retouching, were also found in the grave.[1] Of the two slate palettes which the register mentions, and which are described in the *Catalogue Général*, only one could be identified in the Cairo Museum. It is of the double-bird pattern, with a wide bridge between the heads, one of which is broken. The other palette was fish-shaped. A pear-shaped mace-head of grey limestone has a wide perforation. Of the four stone vases mentioned in the *Entrance Journal*, two have disappeared. They seem to have been of the shouldered type with lug handles. Still on exhibition is a cup-shaped vase with a flat base made of blue and brown veined limestone. The largest and most elegant piece is a squat pot of dark porphyry 22 cm. in diameter and 14 cm. high (pl. I, 4). The lip is deeply undercut, the lug handles are overlaid with gold, and through their openings silver rods are pushed, their ends curved back elegantly. Gold again was used to make a rather peculiar object from the same grave. A piece of gold foil was wrapped round with a sheet of thin silver. It is oblong in form, narrower at the top than at the bottom, with rounded corners, two of which are perforated twice. The length is 6·7 cm. and the width 3·5 cm. There is no obvious use for such a contrivance. The perforations at the top tend to show that it was meant to be suspended. It may, therefore, have been worn round the neck as an amulet (pl. II, 8).

What is left of a silver knife[2] is 12 cm. long and 3·3 cm. wide. It curves symmetrically from a square tang to a rectangular blade and belongs to the type which Petrie has called "double-edged" (pl. II, 3).[3] No exact parallel to this type of knife is known to me. The nearest type in copper has sides which curve symmetrically towards a rounded tip, but are not parallel like those of the silver knife.[4]

The fourth object of precious metal from the treasure-trove of Homra Doum, and the last object of the group to be mentioned, is a silver dagger-blade (pl. II, 4). One of its sides is in perfect condition, the other has been badly eaten into by corrosion. It is 17·9 cm. long and 5·1 cm. at its widest. The blade is triangular with a midrib on each side, and is surmounted by a semicircular grip-plate. A single rivet hole at its top is all that is provided for the fastening of the handle, which is lost. The only other silver dagger of the period known to me was found under well-attested circumstances in El-'Amrah, t. b 230 (S.D. 40-64, about 50 after Petrie).[5] It has hitherto always been published as being of copper (pl. II, 1 and 2), but recent cleaning in the laboratory of the Cairo Museum revealed it to be silver. The dagger was found broken in two and with its tip corroded to the handle, but they have now been separated, so that the piece can

[1] *Cairo Museum, Entrance Journal*, 31548-55. Quibell, *Archaic Objects*, 14163, 14200, 14245, 14251, 14256-62, 14315, 14341, 14384, 14426, 14511-12, 19514-16. L. T. Currelly, *Stone Implements*, 64625, 64633, 64635-6, 64638-40, 64642, 64743-4.
[2] *Cairo E.J.*, 31562. Quibell, *Archaic Objects*, no. 14515.
[3] W. M. Flinders Petrie, *Tools and Weapons*, p. 27. See *ibid* p. 26 for copper knives of this type.
[4] *Tarkhan I*, pls. IV, 1, 2, 7; VI, 1.
[5] *El Amrah*, p. 23, pl. VI, 1 and 2. Petrie, *Tools and Weapons*, p. 28, pl. XXXIII, 1. *Cairo E.J.*, 35158.

be well studied. The blade is triangular with a midrib on each side. The break in its upper half, underneath the grip-plate, which is of a high trapezoidal shape, is slightly rounded at the top and with a single rivet hole. The hilt of this remarkable dagger is preserved, though somewhat damaged. It is of a single piece of ivory with a slot at the bottom to take the blade.

From a flat, semicircular pommel, part of which is missing, sprouts a flat, elongated handle widening towards the blade. Two prongs, their tips now broken off, rest on the blade. From the reproduction in the original publication [1] one can see that once they must have formed nearly a full circle. The length of the dagger when whole was about 16·6 cm., its width 4·1 cm.

As the two silver daggers are of similar type, they will be roughly contemporaneous. The sequence-date of the El-'Amrah piece would agree with the date suggested by the ripple-flaked flint knives from the Homra Doum grave, though that grave may perhaps be somewhat later.

3 *Copper Daggers*

Copper daggers from Predynastic Egypt are very rare. One perfectly preserved specimen corresponds in type to the silver daggers. It was found at El-'Amrah, t. a 131,[2] S.D. 56-64 (Petrie, *Tools and Weapons*, S.D. 61-62). The triangular blade is topped by a roughly semi-circular grip-plate and both together measure 15 cm. in length. It has a midrib on both sides which stops about half an inch below a single rivet hole at the upper extremity of the grip-plate (pl. I, 9). The midribs, which it shares with the silver daggers, pose the question as to how these daggers were made. If they were produced in an open mould, then the ribs must have been achieved by hammering.

The hilt of the El-'Amrah copper dagger, now lost, left a mark on the grip-plate and on the upper part of the blade in the form of a full circle pushed up a little at the lower end where it crosses over the midrib. As the silver dagger from El-'Amrah has preserved the greater part of its handle, we know the shape of the hilt which left such curious marks. It could well have caused an impression similar to that on the blade of the other weapon. Remembering the technique with which the handle of the Toronto knife was fixed, one wonders whether here also glue was not used to give a somewhat firmer hold to the handle than a single rivet could effect, and whether it was not this glue rather than the ivory which left such an ineradicable mark.

A copper dagger of a much more advanced pattern was excavated by Petrie at Naḳāda (pl. II, 5). He found it himself in t. 836,[3] and recognizing at once its importance took great care with the documentation of his discovery. It lay across the hip bones of the skeleton, which it had stained green. The other furniture of the grave is by no means outstanding, with the exception perhaps of the beads, strings of large cornelian, lapis lazuli and other stones, which had been laid round the skull and also round the neck. Along the fingers were parallel lines of beads which must have formed a "beadwork mitten". The grave was undisturbed and is dated to S.D. 63. The dagger is 26·2 cm. long, and narrow like a rapier, measuring only 3·6 cm. at its widest part where it meets the grip-plate, which is trapezoidal (pl. II, 5). Its very prominent midribs and hollow faces on each side make it nearly quadrangular at the tip. The only primitive features left

---

[1] *El Amrah*, pp. 23 and 48, pl. VI, 1 and 2. Cairo Museum, no. 35158.
[2] *El Amrah*, p. 20, pl. X, 5. Now in the Ashmolean Museum, Oxford.
[3] *Naq. Bal.*, p. 22, pl. LXV, 3. The dagger is in the Ashmolean Museum, Oxford.

on this weapon, features which relate it to the triangular type, are the midrib flattened out below the rivet holes and the flimsy attachment for the hilt. The two rivet holes are right at the top of the grip-plate, providing only a poor hold for the handle which was hardly safer than the one provided on the triangular daggers. The developed shape of the weapon made it conspicuous from the moment it was found. Its technical achievements cannot be equalled by any other copper product of its time.

Another dagger must be mentioned, though only a tale about it has come down to us. It was found by G. Möller at Abuṣīr el-Meleḳ, t. 54 e 10. Möller died before he could publish, and A. Scharff, who took over, found only a small piece of corroded metal with a few strips of wood adhering.[1] From Möller's notes he mentions that the excavator found the dagger, which had a wooden hilt, stuck through several small armlets (which are preserved) on the left humerus of the skeleton of a young person. There was no photograph or drawing. The other furniture of the grave consisted of an "ordinary pot" and a bracelet of beads (cornelian, lapis lazuli and small rosettes of faience). The skeleton was covered with a mat. All this is not enough to date the grave. The only interesting feature to remember is the position in which the dagger was found. It was evidently worn on the left arm, and Scharff mentions a few more examples of this fashion.

As we cannot include this Abuṣīr dagger in our collection of existing predynastic Egyptian daggers, we are left with four specimens. Three of them, the silver one from Homra Doum and the two from El-'Amrah, are of the same type—a broad triangular blade with midrib, and a triangular or semicircular grip-plate with a single rivet hole at the upper extremity; the fourth is narrow and long with midrib and hollow faces and trapezoidal grip-plate and two rivet holes at its upper extremity. As far as we can tell from the somewhat vague descriptions in El-'Amrah and Petrie's more exact dating, the three excavated daggers have to be placed roughly between S.D. 50 and 63; the one from Homra Doum will be contemporary.

4 *Spear-Head*

A leaf-shaped spear-head of copper with midrib was found at Tarkhan, t. 474, S.D. 79, or a little earlier. It is interesting not only because it is unique, but also because it is another instance of the struggle to find a solution for a technical problem which the artisan of the period had not yet mastered, namely to find a secure hafting for a metal weapon. The spear-head ends in a flat tang, the lowest part of which is now bent nearly at right angles. This must be an accident, for as it stands it could not have been slipped into a wooden shaft. Surrounding the butt end of the spear-head and the wood into which the tang was inserted was a metal tube most of which is now lost. Although about a quarter of the tube nearest to the head, still filled with the remnants of the wooden shaft, remains, this is too little to enable us to say with confidence how the tube was made, but presumably a piece of copper was bent together and hammered on to the spear-head and the wood, after the tang had been inserted. The spear-head itself seems to have been cast. (The present length of the spear-head is about 17 cm., its width about 3 cm.[2])

---

[1] G. Möller (ed. A. Scharff), *Die Archaeologischen Ergebnisse des Vorgeschichtlichen Gräberfeldes von Abusir El-Meleq*, p. 49.

[2] *Tarkhan I*, p. 21, pl. IV, 6. The spear-head is now at University College, London.

5 *Adzes*

The little silver adze was dealt with above,[1] so it now remains to discuss the copper adzes of similar type. They are not quite so rare as the daggers. Petrie mentions five from Naḳāda [2] and Quibell two from Ballas, one of them broken.[3] Two were in the grave with the round shaft at Homra Doum and two were found at Abuṣīr el-Meleḳ,[4] one of them so corroded that it could not be salvaged. Although measured—19 cm. long and 3·5 cm. wide—it was neither photographed nor drawn, and we therefore can not be certain whether it was of the type with which we are here concerned. This is the more regrettable as it was found in position in Abuṣīr, t. 14 g 9. The dead man clutched it in his hand, which seems to indicate that it had no handle.

Petrie divides the five adzes from Naḳāda into two types. Type I is rectangular with thin straight neck, straight cutting edge bevelled one side, and parallel sides. Four of this type were found in Naḳāda, tt. 702, 1298, Q 600, and ["smaller"] in 400. That from t. 702 is at University College, London, and seems to be the prototype of Petrie's drawing in *Naqada and Ballas*. It is 15·2 cm. long, 2·5 cm. wide and perfectly rectangular. That from t. 1298 was (or is) in Berlin,[5] the one from Q 600 I could not trace (unless it is the silver one), and the last, from t. 400, is at Manchester. It is 12·4 cm. long and 2·2 cm. wide. As it has a somewhat splayed cutting edge and slightly concave sides, it approaches type II.

The only adze that is preserved from Abuṣīr el-Meleḳ, t. 1037, is truer to type. It is larger than the others and seems heavier (23·5 cm. long, 3·75 cm. wide). From the other contents of the grave it must be early dynastic in date. Another adze similar to the one from Naḳāda, t. 400, was found by Quibell at Hierakonpolis. It is in the Manchester Museum and is also rather larger than those of which the predynastic origin is beyond doubt. It measures 19·6 cm. in length, 3·1 cm. in width and is 0·4 cm. thick. With it in the Museum are two other pieces from Hierakonpolis, an adze with semicircular neck, and a square and heavy copper chisel, 18·7 cm. long, 1·1 cm. wide and 1·3 cm. thick, curved through use by being hammered on its square butt. Quibell mentions an "archaic" grave [6] in which he found two chisels and one adze, but whether one of the three Manchester pieces belonged to that particular grave cannot be ascertained. The last two pieces are certainly dynastic. One of the adzes from Homra Doum, 17·7 cm. long and 3·3 cm. wide, must be included in this type. It has a straight neck and straight sides, and the cutting edge is slightly splayed (pl. I, 7).

Petrie's type II has concave sides and a splayed cutting edge bevelled from below. At Naḳāda it was found once only, in t. 39. This adze (now in the Ashmolean Museum) is 14·4 cm. long and 3·8 cm. wide at its cutting edge. To this type belongs the silver one from Ballas. Of the other Ballas adze nothing is known beyond its existence. Quibell does not mention its tomb number, nor does he describe it, and I have failed to trace it. It may be identical with the one Petrie calls Q 600.

The second adze from Homra Doum (pl. I, 6), 11·7 cm. long and 2·6 cm. wide, has a straight

---

[1] p. 8.   [2] *Naq. Bal.*, p. 48.
[3] *Naq. Bal.*, p. 14.   [4] *Abusir*, pp. 46, 258 and 259 second half.
[5] *Staatliche Museen zu Berlin. Mitteilungen aus der ägyptischen Sammlung*, Bd. 4 and 5. A. Scharff, *Die Altertümer der Vor- und Frühzeit Ägyptens*, pp. 71-2, b. 131. Berlin 13099. On p. 71 a printing mistake gives the tomb number as 1258, but it is correctly stated with the S.D. on p. 72.
[6] Quibell and Green, *Hierakonpolis*, II, p. 26.

neck, concave sides and a splayed cutting edge. It differs from all the pieces mentioned under these two types, for its cutting edge is bevelled on both sides. This makes it doubtful whether it and the other tools described under this heading were really adzes, especially if we remember that one was found in the hand of a skeleton and had had no handle. They are sometimes called chisels; but their straight and thin necks are not suited for chisels, and never show traces of hammering. In early dynastic times the necks of these "adzes" become semicircular, which also speaks against their use as chisels.

As far as can be seen, all the adzes mentioned were cast and then hammered.

6 Axes

Copper axes are much rarer than the adzes or even the daggers. Until not very long ago not a single axe from Naḳāda II was known, and this gave rise to some conjecture as to why the ancient Egyptians did not use these tools.[1] Through recent excavations we have learnt better. A heavy copper axe was found by Brunton at Matmar, t. 3131, S.D. 38-46,[2] and an axe of similar style was excavated by Mustafa Amer at Ma'adi which is early dynastic.[3] T. 3131 at Matmar was plundered in antiquity. It contained a wooden coffin, parts of its sides still upright when found, and four pots in position at the north and east sides of the grave. "Under the wooden floor of the coffin at its north or foot end lay the large copper axe-head." Its position under the coffin hid it from the plunderers. Here, as with the lost adze from Abuṣīr el-Meleḳ, the position of the tool as it was excavated is exactly described. And here also the tool does not seem to have had a handle. Of course, the handle of the Matmar axe may have perished, but the wooden coffin was very well preserved, which makes such an assumption somewhat difficult. Wooden handles for tools are preserved from the First Dynasty.[4] The Matmar axe is 16 cm. long, 11 cm. at its widest, and nearly 0·9 cm. thick, weighing 3 lb. 7 oz. It is trapezoidal with bulging surfaces. The neck is square, slightly curved and rough, as from heavy battering, the sides splayed, the corners of the cutting edge deeply rounded. It seems to be a carpenter's axe for roughing out a piece of furniture, or the planks of the very coffin under which it was found, out of the tree trunk or block of wood, the rounded corners ensuring a smooth cut without sharp edges. The device of the deeply-rounded corners occurs here for the first time and is yet another technical achievement. It was carried even further in the axes used during the Old Kingdom, where we see them on reliefs of mastabas in the hands of shipbuilders. Brunton suggests, as an alternative, that it may have been a battle-axe.

The analysis of the metal was made by H. C. H. Carpenter.[5] It proved to be 97·35% copper, 1·28% nickel, 0·49% arsenic, 0·17% lead, 0·15% iron, 0·6% manganese, and about 0·5% not

1 *Tools and Weapons*, p. 5.

2 *Matmar*, p. 16. *Cairo E.J.*, 59136.

3 Brunton cites it, *Matmar*, p. 21. Mustafa Amer, *Bulletin of the Faculty of Arts*, Cairo University, vol. II, part II, p. 177. Illustration in *Excavation of the University of Cairo at Maadi*, 1930-35 (in Arabic), fig. 16a. The piece has since been lost. Another axe, a faulty cast, also from Ma'adi, is of the rectangular type with thick neck known to be early dynastic.

4 Emery, *Great Tombs of the First Dynasty*, I (Cairo, 1949), pp. 24 ff.

5 H. C. H. Carpenter, Letter in *Nature*, 130, no. 3286, 22 Oct. 1932, pp. 625-6. The object is now in the Cairo Museum.

accounted for (nearly all oxygen). Carpenter also stated that the axe had been cast and then hammered, but did not specify whether it was made in an open or a closed mould.

This is not a primitive axe, an imitation of an older flint or stone model, but is a sophisticated tool made by a skilled coppersmith. Though perhaps somewhat older, it helps to put the Naḳāda dagger [1] in its right place, because it is another example of a highly-developed copper technique at so early a time. The question remains: where was it evolved? Can we assume its existence in Egypt? Brunton himself thinks that the axe might be an importation, on account of the high percentage of nickel contained in the copper, "which is a much higher percentage than found in the analysis of other early Egyptian objects with the exception of the statue of Pepy I from Hierakonpolis".[2] It reminds Brunton of the copper-nickel admixtures at Ur and Kish. He adds that a vase "strange both in form and ware", which was found with the axe, may point in the same direction.

Towards the end of the predynastic period and the beginning of the First Dynasty copper axes become more frequent; they differ, however, in type from the Matmar axe, which seems more developed than any of the later ones. In tombs at Tarkhan,[3] at Hu [4] and in the "Tombs of the Courtiers" of the First Dynasty heavy, rectangular axes occur,[5] some nearly square, with either straight or slightly curved cutting edges. Some, like the axe from Hu, t. 74, or the one from Tarkhan, t. 122, have concave necks. This must have been a device thought to facilitate the hafting, though it seems difficult to imagine how it may have worked. Another attempt to solve the hafting problem was made on an axe found in the tomb of a courtier of King Djer, by the name of Ka-hetep.[6] It has two small square lugs, one perceptibly larger than the other. Petrie says[7] that this is the earliest lug axe so far known from Egypt, and that "such square lugs were barely reached in the VIth Dynasty". "The form is scarcely Egyptian in its feeling, and it seems as if it had been imported. . . ." Its length is about 10 cm., its width including the lugs 7·3 cm. It was analysed by J. Sebelien and was found to consist of 98·3% of copper.[8] A similar axe has since been found at Ezbet el Walda (Helwan) in the large early dynastic cemetery there. It is about 10 cm. long, one lug is somewhat larger than the other, and it has a perforation in the middle of the upper part just below the lugs.[9]

The great treasure-trove of copper tools which Emery found in Saḳḳāra, t. 347, is of the time of King Djer. No axes were included, unless what he calls "copper plates" were meant to represent them. Similar pieces found at Tarkhan and Diospolis Parva were termed axes by Petrie, and Emery himself thinks it is the most likely explanation for these thin and roughly-made specimens. They were useful as tomb furniture only, for which models were sufficient. If this is the correct explanation, it would be the beginning of a custom widely practised during the Second Dynasty, when hundreds of token copper implements were deposited in important tombs, with very few real tools among them.

[1] Above, pp. 10-11.
[2] *Matmar*, p. 21. For another object with a high nickel content see below, p. 18. The Pepy statues are of the Sixth Dynasty.   [3] Petrie, *Tarkhan I*, p. 8, pls. V, 25-27, VI, 7-9. Now in Manchester.
[4] W. M. Flinders Petrie, *Diospolis Parva: The Cemeteries of Abadiyeh and Hu*, p. 36, pl. VII, bottom right.
[5] W. M. Flinders Petrie, *Tombs of the Courtiers*, pl. V, 7.
[6] *Tombs of the Courtiers*, pl. V, 21.   [7] *Tombs of the Courtiers*, pp. 5, 8 top.
[8] J. Sebelien, "Early Copper and its Alloys", *Ancient Egypt* (1924), p. 8. Now at University College, London.
[9] From Zaki Saad's excavations at Helwan. Now in the Cairo Museum.

7 Hoes

It was the late predynastic or the protodynastic period which produced the first copper hoes. One of the earliest was found in Tarkhan, t. 1015.[1] It is 31·8 cm. long, 10·7 cm. wide and 1·1 cm. thick. Its shape is somewhat peculiar. From a wide and thin neck it tapers to a cutting edge which is only about two-thirds of the width of the neck. At about a third of the way from the neck the hoe is provided with a crescent-shaped stop-ridge against which the wooden handle must once have fitted. A second hoe of this type, also from Tarkhan, 30·2 cm. long and 10·1 cm. wide, and now in the Cairo Museum (*Cairo E.J.*, 44009), has the same device for hafting. As far as I know, it was not repeated elsewhere and is another instance of the spirit of invention so characteristic of the time (pl. III, 1).

The hoes from Saḳḳāra and Abydos can hardly be much later. Emery distinguishes three types[2] among his great find in Saḳḳāra, t. 3471: no. 1 with concave sides, slightly flaring towards the cutting edge, and with slender proportions; no. 2 much wider and nearly biconical, splaying towards the cutting edge, with slightly concave neck; no. 3 with parallel sides splaying towards the cutting edge, and straight neck. All three types can have either straight or curved cutting edges. Of these three types only no. 3 is known also from Tarkhan and Abydos, which shows how much is lost where the tomb-robbers have been at work.

The Saḳḳāra hoes had their wooden handles preserved. They are made of two pieces dovetailed into each other. Emery could not find how the joint was secured, but it is clear that the binding which fixed the blade to the wood did not extend over it. If we consider that most of the blades were wider than their handles, so that the binding would be cut by frequent use, the impression is strengthened that because this was a tomb outfit it was not deemed necessary to match the parts so that they could actually be used.

8 Saws

Another interesting invention of the period is the copper saw. The oldest, again, comes from Tarkhan, t. 1917.[3] Its thin blade is 32·4 cm. long and 6 cm. wide. One of its slightly convex sides is denticulated. The teeth are roughly triangular and shallow. The tip of the saw is rounded, its tang narrow and square. The impressions of the wooden handle were still visible when the saw was found. Saws of similar type were found in the "Tombs of the Courtiers", and in Saḳḳāra, t. 3471, there were seven with their stout handles preserved.

9 Knives

Two main types of copper knives have been preserved: the single-edged and the double-edged.

Two sub-types of the single-edged exist: (*a*) a narrow, straight-backed form with tang, like

[1] *Tarkhan II*, p. 9, pls. I and III. Now in Manchester Museum.
[2] *Great Tombs of the First Dynasty*, I (1949), pp. 37 ff. I am following Emery's nomenclature. Petrie takes these tools to be adzes and calls only the later socketed forms hoes.
[3] *Tarkhan II*, p. 9, pls. I and III, 6.

the copper knife from Naḳāda, t. 63 (after S.D. 60), which has lost its tip, but is otherwise well preserved (length now 7·75 cm.) [1];　and (b) the wide blade with square tip, also tanged, as found in grave b 80 at El-'Amrah,[2] which, when found, was hafted in a cloven piece of bone. It is 8·7 cm. long, 4 cm. wide and 0·15 cm. thick at the edge. The knife lay in front of the face just above the hands of the skeleton, and may be a razor. It is classified as "protodynastic". The same date is accorded to another knife of the same type found in the temenos of the temple at Qau.[3]

The double-edged knife curves symmetrically upwards from the tang, sloping towards a rounded tip. The earliest was found at Naḳāda, t. 807, S.D. 49. Part of the tang is broken off, otherwise it is well preserved. It is 10·3 cm. long, 4·1 cm. wide and 0·1 cm. thick at the edge. Similar knives were found in the "Tombs of the Courtiers" at Abydos. At Saḳḳāra there were 31 of them among the treasure in t. 4371. They had baluster-shaped wooden handles. Others were among the finds at Tarkhan, t. 22. The silver one from Homra Doum (pl. II, 3) has already been mentioned (p. 9).

Petrie calls this type "flaying knives". It seems, however, doubtful whether these knives could have been put to this use, long and thin as they are, and this applies especially to the larger ones. The question as to the use to which ancient tools were put will always be difficult to answer. The hoes, adzes and saws can be compared to those actually in the hands of workmen on the reliefs of Old Kingdom mastabas, depicting carpenters and boat-builders at work.[4] The hoes there serve a double purpose. Some are used to deliver a blow and some for scraping the wood, a task in modern times reserved for planes. The carpenter's axe of the time is nearly semicircular, and recalls the axe from Matmar with its deeply-curved cutting edge rather than the more clumsy implements of Tarkhan, Diospolis Parva, etc. As the Saḳḳāra treasure was found in a room which also contained remnants of wooden furniture, it seems that the hoes and adzes were cabinet-makers' tools to serve in case the lord of the tomb wanted new furniture in the hereafter. The knives are more difficult to explain. They may have served in the preparation of the leather needed to make mattresses for the beds and seats for the chairs.

10 Small Tools

Of the smaller tools which are preserved from Naḳāda II, some may also have belonged to the outfits of the woodworker, or of his colleague the ivory-carver. Most of them are variants of the chisel, and many of them have working edges at top and bottom (pl. III, 15). These edges are unlike those of the adzes, sometimes called chisels. They are bevelled on both sides. Where there is only one working edge the other end is often sharply pointed. These little tools are between 8 and 9 cm. long, and similar to modern steel tools used for fine carving in wood or other fine material, only that they are much smaller.

In some rich and well-preserved tombs they occur in sets, e.g. in Naḳāda, t. 1345, about which a few words will have to be said. Petrie dates it to S.D. 34-38, and counts it as still belonging

[1] *Naq. Bal.*, pl. LXV, 23. Now at University College, London.
[2] *El Amrah*, pp. 27, 40, pl. XII, 9. Now in the Ashmolean Museum, Oxford, but without the handle.
[3] G. Brunton, *Qau and Badari*, I, p. 17, pl. XX, 66 and 67.
[4] Wreszinski, *Atlas*, III, pl. 33, tomb of Mereruka; pl. 36, tomb of Ti, both from mastabas at Saḳḳāra.

to Naḳāda I.[1] The three chisels, two of them with a sharp point at the butt end, he mentions as the first and only ones of their period, and he thinks the same of the single-barbed copper and the bone harpoons which were found in the grave together with them.[2] But all the others known are of Naḳāda II date. The pottery on which Petrie bases his sequence-date for t. 1345 I could not trace, but two flint knives now at University College, London, belong to it. One is a narrow blade, unretouched, the other is 16·5 cm. long made of a twisted blade 2·5 cm. at its widest. The back is somewhat blunted, the tip retouched on both sides. These types of flint knives also are otherwise known from Naḳāda II only.[3] With the curved fragment of a pin of angular section and a few scraps of a woven material, presumably linen, this is all I could find of the original contents of t. 1345 at Naḳāda. If one excludes the last two items, which are too fragmentary to allow an ascription to any period, all the rest are familiar from Naḳāda II. Even if we knew what pottery the grave contained I do not think it would greatly alter the situation. As it is, it does not seem possible to ascribe a grave to the Naḳāda I period which so far as we can trace is wholly made up of objects otherwise known only from Naḳāda II. Therefore S.D. 38 seems the earliest possible date, i.e. the beginning of Naḳāda II, but most likely it will have to be put even later and near to another interesting tomb containing a similar set of copper tools. This is Naḳāda, t. 162, which Petrie sequence-dates to 58. He illustrates six little copper tools which he found in this grave, only five of which I could trace.[4] They are a chisel ending in a point, another chisel with a square neck,[5] a square rod ending in a point, a pin with a loop head similar to those already known in Naḳāda I, and a small object 6·25 cm. long which looks like an ear-scoop, for one of its ends is flattened and curved. It is remarkable also by its colour, which is white, for all the other tools mentioned look copper red after cleaning. In addition, t. 162 contains some flint tools, among which is a real graver (burin), and a sharply-pointed blade without secondary retouching. A beautifully-shaped ripple-flaked knife so thin that it is translucent, two flint fragments and a rough flake also belong to it. An ivory comb with a bird top—the head is broken—and some fine pottery make up the contents.[6] The flint graver and the sharp flint point add to the impression that we have here the last resting-place of an artisan who worked in ivory or fine wood, and that the little chisels together with the flints were the tools of his craft. Against this we have to hold that the chisels are the most frequently found metal objects of Naḳāda II, only surpassed by the loop-headed pins which occasionally accompany them in the same grave.[7] This seems to speak in favour of their being toilet implements, as the pins in all probability are. Brunton found a pin at Matmar in a sheath of bone, a dainty thing which seems better fitted for a personal object than for a tool.[8] It also seems somewhat odd that the ivory- or wood-carver should have been the one to take his tools with him to the grave, while implements of other artisans are very rare or totally absent. It is suggestive of their use for the toilet that a chisel similar to the Egyptian ones was found among the objects belonging to toilet-sets found by

---

[1] *Preh. Eg.*, p. 26. The tomb is unpublished, the material is at University College, London, and at Manchester.

[2] Later on Petrie himself must have doubted the correctness of this ascription, for he dates the bone harpoon to the earlier part of the second civilization: *Tools and Weapons*, p. 37.

[3] For the knife, see *Naq. Bal.*, pl. LXXIII, 64.

[4] *Naq. Bal.*, pl. LXV, 9-11, 13-15.

[5] All the metals at University College, London. It was not possible to have them analysed; the little scoop may well be silver.

[6] *Naq. Bal.*, p. 25.

[7] E.g. in Naḳāda, t. 1233, S.D. 61.

[8] *Matmar*, p. 21, pl. XVI, 45.

Speiser at Tepe Gawra.[1] It is there called a spatula. One set consists of "an ear-scoop, tweezers, and a spatula or kohl stick. . . ." Only the tweezers are absent from the Egyptian grave. Tweezers occur only once during our period in an Egyptian grave, namely in El-'Amrah, t. a 104, "a pair of copper tweezers about 2 ins. long".[2] The scoop and the spatula from Tepe Gawra have closely-grooved handles, a detail of decoration which is achieved in other pieces of similar nature by hammering the upper end of the piece into a long wire which is then wound in a close spiral round the stem. Another set from Tepe Gawra consists of four pieces, ear-scoop, chisel or spatula, prick point and paint stick, all with plain handles.[3] In Egypt pins with this coiled top were found twice, once at Naḳāda, where the exact find-place is unknown, and once at Badāri, t. 1647, S.D. 59-61?[4] Both the sets of toilet implements were found in Gawra VI, dated to the later part of the Early Dynastic period of Mesopotamia, and therefore considerably later than the set from Naḳāda, t. 162. This does not imply that these toilet-sets were earlier in Egypt than in Mesopotamia; it would require more material than we have at present to decide the origin of the toilet-sets. The occurrence in both countries, however, is fresh evidence of the connexion which must have existed between them.

If we had more analyses of the copper used, we might see the road along which these connexions travelled. A pin from Naḳāda, t. 218, is undated by Petrie, but of the Naḳāda II age, as the grave also contained a fish-tail of the later type. The metal of the pin disclosed, when analysed, rather an odd mixture,[5] for it contained, in addition to the copper, 2% of zinc, 1-2% of nickel, 1% of arsenic and 0·1% each of tin, lead and silicon. If this is a natural mixture, where did the ore come from, for it certainly did not come from Egypt? If it is an intentional alloy, where, especially, was the zinc ore won?[6] Petrie states in *Naqada and Ballas*, p. 54, that the copper from the pre-dynastic cemetery contained 1·55% of zinc, and therefore is "rather brass than bronze", which shows that the pin from t. 218 is not unique. I could not discover which piece or pieces Petrie had analysed. It was not the pin, which showed no sign of scraping or interference before it was cleaned and analysed in Manchester.

Other copper objects known alike to Mesopotamia and Egypt are sewing-needles (pl. III, 13). They occur in Gawra VIII, which belongs to the end of Uruk and beginning of Jemdet Nasr.[7] At Naḳāda a considerable number of them were found in t. 3, S.D. 66, which also contained a copper bodkin. The needles are of different strength, pointed both ends, and the eyes punched in.

Harpoons as well as fish-hooks of copper are known. Harpoons were used in hunting croco-diles and hippopotami, a subject painted on some decorated vases. On a pot fragment from Badāri,[8] which was made in the form of a hippopotamus, three men are painted each armed with a harpoon on a long shaft to which a coil of rope is attached. The middle one carried a piece of

---

[1] E. A. Speiser, *Excavations at Tepe Gawra I*, p. 111, pl. L.

[2] *El Amrah*, p. 23. I could not trace the tweezers, nor a photograph or description of them. Petrie dates them to "probably about 40", *Preh. Eg.*, p. 26.

[3] *Excavations at Tepe Gawra I*, pl. L, 5 and 6.

[4] *Naq. Bal.*, pl. LXV, 19; now at University College, London. *Bad. Civ.*, pl. LIV, 9.

[5] Now in Manchester, analysis by Prof. Thompson of Manchester University.

[6] R. J. Forbes, "Zinc and Brass in Antiquity", *Jaarbericht*, No. 8. *Ex Oriente Lux* (1942), p. 756, mentions pai-t'ud, a natural Chinese copper-zinc-nickel alloy. If it occurs in China, it may occur elsewhere.

[7] *Excavations at Tepe Gawra I*, pl. XLVIII, 7, 10.

[8] *Bad. Civ.*, pl. XLVIII, 3. Now in the Ashmolean Museum, Oxford.

rope in his free hand, which, though not connected with the harpoon, may well be meant to represent that part of the rope which remains in the hunter's hand after the harpoon has been cast. Many more harpoons decorate the remaining part of the fragment. A part of a ship also remains visible. What is left of the painting on this oddly-shaped fragment is enough to suggest that the painting represents the hunt with harpoons of the very hippopotamus on whose hind-quarters it was painted.

A crocodile pierced by three harpoons is drawn on a decorated vase from Naḳāda, t. 193. Though no hunters are shown, and the harpoons must be imagined as having been thrown, they are represented in exactly the same way as those of the hippopotamus hunt, with their coils of rope wound.[1] All these harpoons have a single barb, as have all the copper harpoons which have survived from Naḳāda II. Considering how puny the half-dozen or so of copper harpoons are which have been preserved, one wonders that such feeble weapons could have made any impression on the skin of hippopotami or crocodiles, and must admire the courage and skill of the early hunters. Unless a harpoon could be thrown into a hippopotamus's mouth, it can scarcely have made much of an impression on the pachyderm, and one understands the numbers of harpoons shown on the vases. The two smallest known harpoons are no longer than 6·5 and 7·3 cm. respectively, the former being from Naḳāda, t. 1808, S.D. 36-63, the latter from Naḳāda, t. 1345, which also contained the toilet-set mentioned above.[2] The largest known, from Naḳāda, t. T 9, S.D. 54,[3] is nearly 17 cm. in length. The big harpoon and also some others (Naḳāda, t. 1345, now in Manchester; Ballas, t. 99, in Berlin) have triangular stems ending in a knob. The end with the barb is flattened, the barb itself is pointed, but the tip of the harpoon rounded. Scharff [4] is of the opinion that the harpoon from Ballas, t. 99, in Berlin was cast. If so, the others of the same type are also cast, and, as they do not show the flattened sides of objects cast in open moulds, their moulds must have been closed. Other harpoons with a rounded shaft like the one from t. 1808 Naḳāda, or from Gerzeh, t. 67,[5] S.D. 53-63, may well have been hammered from a thick wire. They lack the knob at the bottom of the shaft and end in a sharp point.

Copper fish-hooks are very rare; indeed, Petrie maintains that none is known from the pre-dynastic periods. The one from Ballas, t. 103, he dated to the First or Second Dynasty [6] on account of a clay coffin found in the grave. It is made of a strong wire curved and pointed to form a hook at one end, while the other is turned back in the opposite direction to shape the eye. Another was found in Naḳāda, t. 855, similar to the one from Ballas, 103, but with the eye broken off. Petrie does not mention the Naḳāda hook, and the grave is not sequence-dated. A much more interesting type of fish-hook was excavated by Brunton in the undisturbed grave Matmar, t. 2649. He sequence-dates it "37 (?)". It is somewhat difficult to see how Brunton came to this result, even with a question-mark. Of the four pots which the grave contained, the two black-topped ones are of a common form which has a long range, the two rough ones are new corpus types, which Brunton dates from this very tomb. As long as there is no stronger evidence fixing Matmar, t. 2649, and the fish-hook to Naḳāda I, I shall treat it as undated, and add the fish-hook here. This is a double-barbed specimen with a square shaft and a blunt tip, which is rounded.

---

[1] Vol. I, pl. X, 1.
[2] pp. 17-18.
[3] Now in the Ashmolean Museum, Oxford.
[4] *Die Altertümer*, I, p. 69.
[5] *Gerzeh*, pl. IV, 2.
[6] *Naq. Bal.*, pp. 7-8, pl. III, 14. *Tools and Weapons*, p. 37, pl. XLIII.

Brunton found traces of a thread on the two barbs, which are perforated, and on the shaft. The hook is 3 cm. long and 2 cm. wide.[1] The only known parallel is a fish-hook in the Flinders Petrie Collection, University College, London, of no known provenance.[2]

A hooked tool, labelled by Petrie a "pruning hook", was found together with two other copper objects—a fish-tail and a little oval dish—in El-Maḥāsna, t. H 85, which the excavators date after S.D. 60. Petrie in *Prehistoric Egypt* dates the grave to S.D. 40, for which rather perplexing date he adduces no reason.[3] The hook is about 8·2 cm. long, broken at the bottom and very thin, and was hafted in a wooden handle of which traces remained on the object when found. It has a straight shaft from which the hook springs in a sharp curve. Petrie assumes that the hook was used for pruning vines, but this seems doubtful, the cutting edge being at the outside of the curve. It may have been a cutting-out knife, perhaps for thin leather (pl. III, 5).

The fish-tail resembles in shape the earlier well-known type of flint implement. Its concave top and the adjoining parts of the sides are denticulated as on the flint fish-tails. Through the plain part of the edge a hole runs askew through the metal to the other edge.

The third piece of the group, the little bowl, is oval and shallow, being shaped like a shell with a perforation near the end of one of the longer sides. It is 5·5 cm. long and 3·5 cm. wide. A similar dish, also roughly oval, 7·2 cm. long and 5·1 cm. wide, comes from Naḳāda, t. 1770, S.D. 61. It is perforated near the longer axis. Petrie calls these little dishes "forehead pendants", but it seems doubtful whether this is justified, especially as the piece from El-Maḥāsna has a hole which is eccentric near the curve of one of the long sides.   To me it looks rather like a shell for eye-paint or the like. Scharff, when describing similar little bowls from Abuṣīr el-Meleḳ, t. 1052, reaches the same conclusion.[4] Another copper dish (or is it a lid?) was found at Gerzeh, t. 145, S.D. 55-57.[5] It is circular and has perpendicular sides. The excavator does not mention whether they were made in one piece with the bottom, or soldered to it. The type is that of the silver jar cap or dish mentioned on p. 7 above. G. Möller thinks that similar pieces from Abuṣīr el-Meleḳ, ts. 1094 and 1052, were cast.

The use of copper was not restricted to the making of tools and weapons during Naḳāda II. It kept its place also as a material for personal ornaments, and for strengthening or embellishing furniture.

11. *Personal Ornaments*

Among the personal ornaments, the finger-rings are the most common, together with arm- or foot-rings, and occasionally beads.

The finger-rings are not much different from the one which was mentioned before as perhaps belonging to Naḳāda I. They are made of strips of metal bent together so that the ends overlap. It may be mere chance that those of the later period all taper towards the ends while the one which may be earlier remains the same width throughout. With only one specimen preserved

---

[1] *Matmar*, p. 13, t. 2649, pl. XVI, 39. *Cairo E.J.*, 5ᴀ 327.

[2] *Tools and Weapons*, p. 37, pl. XLIV, 86.

[3] *Pre-dyn. Cem. at El-Mahasna*, pp. 19 and 32, pl. XIX, 5. *Preh. Eg.*, pl. LII, on p. 26; in the text he even attributes it to "before S.D. 40". The pieces are in the Cairo Museum, *Cairo E.J.*, 4128 1-2. No traces of wood are now left.

[4] Scharff in Möller, *Abusir*, p. 45, no. 255.

[5] *Gerzeh*, p. 24, pl. VIII, 24.

from Naḳāda I, and that a doubtful one, no conclusions are admissible. Two rings from Naḳāda, t. 1480, are loosely dated S.D. 33-55.[1] They were found near the knees of the skeleton, and Petrie must have realized only after the publication of *Naqada and Ballas* what they really were, for he had them pressed open and flattened for the reproduction. A similar ring with the same zig-zag pattern from Ballas, t. 244, is not sequence-dated. Rings made of plain bands, "plain broad strip folded over",[2] were found in El-'Amrah, t. b 28, before S.D. 46 (S.D. 44-50 after Petrie); in Naḳāda, t. 1761,[3] one narrow, one wide, both tapering towards the ends; and two fragments in Naḳāda, t. 1248, S.D. 72.[4] Two rings and a small chain of copper, neither described nor reproduced, from El-'Amrah, t. a 67, are dated before S.D. 41.[5] The chain is quite unique, and, as Petrie says, does not occur otherwise before Khasekhemui from the end of the Second Dynasty, nor has any come to light since Petrie wrote *Prehistoric Egypt*. Another ring said by Petrie to be a finger-ring, which came from Naḳāda, t. 1290, S.D. 68, seems rather large for that purpose, and is more likely an arm-ring. Its diameter is 5·5 cm. at the outside, 4·75 cm. at the inside. It is 0·75 cm. wide.[6] This assumption is made likely by the fragments of an ivory armlet stained green from the contact with copper which was found together with it. The copper ring differs completely from all those mentioned before in that it is closed, and most likely cast. It seems nearest in technique to those found at Saḳḳāra, t. 3471, though without the decorations. Other armlets made of wire and open at the ends were in t. B 57, S.D. 47-62, at Abadieh, and t. B 378, S.D. 52, from the same cemetery. This last is still round the wrist of the hand which it once adorned.[7] Three were in the important grave, El-'Amrah, b 62, S.D. 56-64, the wire used for their manufacture being cut from sheets and not drawn. Fragments of two copper bangles were found in Armant, t. 1547, S.D. 46-63.[8] They were very corroded. One of the pieces had a fastening or decoration made of copper wire wound round it. Much farther to the north in Lower Egypt, at Abuṣīr el-Meleḳ, a similar bracelet was excavated, in t. 10 i 10. A copper wire covered the gap where the two ends of the bracelet meet, two more strips were decorations only. Nine copper bangles were in t. 1052 at Abuṣīr el-Meleḳ.[9] Two of them are decorated with animals in high relief, one with three crocodiles, the other with a serpent. The excavator states that they were cast by the "*cire-perdue*" technique.[10] Another piece, probably made in the same way, is a little statuette of a baboon from Tarkhan, t. 1552, S.D. 77.[11] It is not much more than 2 cm. high, and in a poor state of preservation. This baboon is the first of a long row of similar statues found at Abydos and elsewhere, the most remarkable of which is the life-sized animal with the inscription of King Nar-Mer in the Berlin Museum. The Tarkhan ape is the only metal one known to me from such an early date. The *cire-perdue* technique must be counted among the inventions of the Naḳāda II metal-worker, a technique practised in Egypt as long as there was an Egyptian craftsman at work.

1 *Preh. Eg.*, p. 26; *Naq. Bal.*, p. 28, pl. LXIV, 100-1. Now at University College, London.

2 *El Amrah*, p. 18.

3 Now at University College, London.

4 Now at University College, London.

5 See above, p. 2.

6 Now at University College, London.

7 *Diosp. Pa.*, p. 34, pl. VI. Thus preserved in the Ashmolean Museum, Oxford.

8 R. Mond and O. H. Myers, *Cemeteries of Armant*, I, pl. XLIII, 1-4.

9 *Abusir*, pp. 45 and 55, no. 255. All in Berlin.

10 G. Möller, *Metallkunst*, p. 16.

11 *Tarkhan II*, pl. I. Now at University College, London.

Another metal statuette, somewhat earlier than the baboon, comes from Naḳāda, t. 721, S.D. 44-64.[1] It is of silver originally hammered over a core which was probably of wood. Petrie speaks of copper pins with which it was fastened to the core, but these are not preserved. He calls it a falcon and thought it was made of lead, but an analysis proved it to be of pure silver. The technique of hammering metal over a wooden core for the making of statues was still practised at the end of the Old Kingdom and later. The monumental statues of King Pepy and his son from Hierakonpolis [2] were made that way, and for them the technique seems much more adequate than for the small statuette from Naḳāda, which is only about 5 cm. long.

To return to personal ornaments, the last items to be dealt with are copper beads. Copper beads were found only at Badāri, Mustagidda and Abuṣīr el-Meleḳ. It is difficult to say why this is so, unless it be mere chance. They were either cylinder, ring- or barrel-shaped, and come from Badāri, t. 1664, undated, and t. 3730, S.D. 44-50. In Mustagidda, t. 1872, some copper beads were found together with other beads. The grave did not contain any pottery, but only the beads, a bangle of horn or tortoise-shell, and the legs of a statuette which might be intrusive; the grave was disturbed. It is not clear why Brunton ascribes it to Naḳāda I (Amratian). Copper beads occurred in the dated Mustagidda tombs 1604, S.D. 57-58, and 11747, S.D. 58-63. A bead 4·1 cm. long, one 1·3 cm. long and several cast ones are mentioned from Abuṣīr el-Meleḳ.[3]

12. *Copper Fittings*

Copper was also used for fittings of wood or leather during Naḳāda II. The few pieces preserved are, however, not enough to give us much of an idea about their original purpose. Four copper strips about 7 cm. long and 2·75 cm. wide, with four perforations at each end and bent double so that the perforations nearly touch, were found in Naḳāda, t. 1201. The grave is not sequence-dated, but from the pottery (a smooth pot, Corpus type L 16B, another of similar make but polished-red inside, type P 24N, and a third, P 95G), as well as from the pear-shaped mace-head, it must be of Naḳāda II, and from the end of that period. A copper cone, hollow and now in fragments from Naḳāda, t. 264, could have served as the ferrule of a stick.[4] A strip of copper binding from Ballas, t. 111, 8 cm. long and 1·2 cm. wide, bent together into an oblong shape with rounded corners, and now pressed open where the two ends once overlapped, has a parallel in a similar piece found in the town of Nub.t.[5] It may have been the trimming of a leather strap. Emery mentions a leather bracelet with a joint of copper from Saḳḳāra, t. 3471.

Of all the raw materials used in remote antiquity, none were more exposed to the vicissitudes of life than the metals. Precious or not, they were the thing robbers coveted most, and once taken away from their original resting-places were prone to be melted down and their typical shapes for ever lost. Oxidization attacks silver and many of the baser metals and took much of what the robbers left. To trace the native source of a given piece of metal the help of a specialist in metallurgy is needed, and this is not often easily available. All this makes the attempt to trace the

---

[1] *Naq. Bal.*, p. 46, pl. LX, 14. Now in very poor condition, in the Ashmolean Museum, Oxford.
[2] *Hierakonpolis*, II, pp. 46-7, pls. L-LVI.
[3] *Abusir*, p. 59.
[4] Now at University College, London.
[5] *Naq. Bal.*, pl. LXV, 18. All the pieces mentioned are at University College, London, except the piece from Nub.t, which I cannot trace.

history of metal during Egypt's predynastic periods difficult, and, at best, so incomplete that it may well give a distorted picture.

We cannot say at present when metallurgy in its proper sense, namely the working of objects from the raw material, began in Egypt, still less when the Egyptians began to smelt the metal from the ore. The only nugget of copper which may perhaps still date back to predynastic times was found with two copper pins and rubbish of late dynastic or later date underneath the ruins of a temple "of XVIIIth and earlier Dynasties" at Badāri.[1] It is less than 1 in. long, and of irregular shape. Only from Ma'adi during early dynastic periods have we got quantities of copper nuggets which testify to metal-work being done in that place. All the metal objects we know from Badārian times and Naḳāda I are hammered; where the raw material came from is not known. It may have been imported, since the characteristic type, the pin with the head bent back into a circle, is found all over the Near East. That gold was known to both of these cultures is probable, but not proved by any find of this precious metal. It could be picked up in the country between Egypt and the Red Sea; and it gave its name to the town which was the most important during the predynastic period.

Though we have neither nuggets nor moulds from Naḳāda II, we are probably right in assuming that metal was worked during that period. Many of the metal objects when we first find them in Egypt are already removed from their most primitive forms, and no development can be traced in Egypt. Therefore, unless we assume that all the earlier forms are lost, their origin must be looked for elsewhere. Yet, when we first meet them in Egypt, they show what I would like to call "the Egyptian touch". The triangular daggers know the device of the midribs, certainly a technical advance over a dagger made of a flat sheet of copper. But their handles are fastened with one rivet at the top only, perhaps reinforced with glue, and the maker of the sophisticated rapier-like dagger from Naḳāda [2] knows no better than to add a second rivet next to it. This rather ineffectual method of hafting remains characteristic of Egyptian daggers for a long time to come.[3] The flat adzes may be of foreign origin. The one found in the deep layers of the Tell Halaf mound, among others, is too similar in form to the Egyptian pieces to be dissociated from them [4]; and, moreover, the one made of silver at least points to a foreign origin for its raw material. On the other hand, the adzes with the crescent-shaped stop-ridges are of Egyptian invention; and they show once more the advance in technique and the inventive spirit so characteristic of Naḳāda II, and especially its late period.

[1] *Bad. Civ.*, p. 45, pl. LVIII, 6.

[2] See above, pp. 10-11.

[3] V. Gordon Childe, *New Light on the Most Ancient East* (1934), p. 98.

[4] Max Freiherr von Oppenheim, *Tell Halaf*, 1, *Die Praehistorischen Funde*, bearbeitet von Hubert Schmidt, p. 119, pl. CXIV, 23.

CHAPTER II

FLINT AND STONE IMPLEMENTS

THROUGHOUT Egypt's history, and not only in predynastic times, flint and stone have been the raw material for its basic industries. Both were found in abundance and in excellent qualities in the mountain terraces bordering the Nile Valley. The terraces, moreover, are strewn with weathered-out flint nodules.

We had reason to assume that the Badārians used this inferior surface material, but that from the time of Naḳāda I onwards flint was mined.[1] The flint obtained is of various colours, and mostly of the tabular kind. Research on the flint-mines in Egypt has been restricted to those near Maghara on the eastern side of the river, which were discovered by Seton Karr and have since been revisited by me. No excavations were undertaken.[2]

Tools produced from the tabular flint often have remains of cortex on one side; sometimes on both. Only on the best pieces is the cortex wholly removed.

The Badārian flint industry is predominantly a core industry shaping the flint nodule by flaking from both sides. This predilection for bifacial work remained with the Egyptians for as long as they used flint for tools, which means until the New Kingdom, at least. The period during which they made beautiful blade knives, which may reach a length up to 25 cm. for their best pieces, is restricted to Naḳāda II and the early dynasties. Even during this period the craftsman was not really satisfied when he had produced a blade and given it the most regularly-flaked blunted back: he pressure-flaked one side partly or wholly, and provided the sharp cutting edge with the tiniest of denticulations.

Grinding and polishing flint is a technique mainly used in a subsidiary function. We have no example of it from Badārian times. Flint tools wholly produced by grinding are exceedingly rare. Even the axes made of igneous rocks are mostly pecked, and only the cutting edge is sharpened by grinding. The limestone axes, however, which Brunton ascribes to the Badārian culture, are mostly ground throughout.

During Badārian times Egyptian flint working was poor, but by Naḳāda I flint working had reached a remarkable standard of perfection. The fish-tails and especially the double-edged knives up to 41 cm. long and about $\frac{1}{2}$ cm. thick, and provided with a regular denticulation, are so well made that it is difficult to imagine their craftsmanship being surpassed. Yet the succeeding period of Naḳāda II shows an even greater degree of accomplishment in the manufacture of the "ripple-flaked" knives which the Egyptians themselves must have treasured highly, for they set them in handles of ivory and gold.

BADĀRIAN

For the Badārian flint industry we still depend on Caton-Thompson's typology set out in the publication of her classic excavation at Ḥammāmīya. Brunton's researches in the neighbourhood

---

[1] Vol. I, pp. 22, 28.

[2] Seton Karr, *Liverpool Annals*, II, pp. 77 ff. E. J. Baumgartel, *A.E.* (1930), pp. 103 ff.

of Mustagidda have not added to the inventory, so that we still do not know what axes the Badārians used. He found a deposit of seven axes at Matmar,[1] which he claims to be "Tasian". "They lay", he says, "just under the surface, stacked in pairs one over the other, with a rough flint core on top of all. Three of these celts are of grey igneous rock and four of hard whitish limestone; the longest measures 26 cm. or over 10½ in. long." They were found close to but not in the "Amratian cemetery 2700". It is a pity that nothing datable was found with these axes. They are far larger than any I know from predynastic times.

1. *Push-planes*

The most typical Badārian flint tool is a push-plane made of a nodule with a flat base. By removing a few rough, parallel flakes a working end was created, the domed cortex of the upper face being used as a hand grip. The tool, which is very coarse, is thought by Caton-Thompson to have been used in leather tanning. The claim that small knives on flakes of good workmanship belong to the Badārian inventory, about which Caton-Thompson herself is somewhat doubtful, seems to me very difficult to uphold. It is mainly based on a specimen found underneath a Badārian rippled pot not found in her own excavation but in the shallow remains of a settlement of Badārian date in the Qau Bay. The distribution of [2] these little knives at Ḥammāmīya does not bear out the claim for a Badārian age, and their distribution in the settlement of Armant [3] also speaks in favour of a later date for them.

2. *Disc-scrapers and Borers*

Rather coarse disc-scrapers and an occasional borer all give the impression that they were made when the need for them arose, and no more work squandered on them than seemed absolutely necessary.

3. *Sickle-stones and Knives*

Of much better workmanship are the sickle-stones, knives and, especially, arrow-heads, all or most of them found in the graves and not in the dwelling site at Ḥammāmīya.

The sickle-stones are rather heavy, and worked with a shallow retouch from both sides, with a denticulated edge. All are pointed. Sometimes, but rarely, they are pointed at each end, and then they are about twice as long as the simple sickle-stones, and have been claimed as saws. Two sickle-stones with notches at the butt found at Matmar are surface finds, and should not therefore as yet be added to the Badārian types. The same applies to a few other objects collected there, especially to a small adze [4] which in shape is unlike any other known from predynastic times.

Badārian bifacial knives are very rare and mostly found in contexts which cannot with certainty be dated to the Badārian period. One large specimen, heavy, with a square butt and symmetrically curved, was found in Badāri, t. 5739. The grave did not contain any pottery, and none of the other

---

[1] *Matmar*, p. 4, pl. VI, 1.
[2] *Bad. Civ.*, p. 76.
[3] *Cem. Arm.*, I, p. 220.
[4] *Matmar*, pl. VII, 23. The adze seems nearer to Middle Kingdom pieces as found in Lahun than to any other kinds known to me.

objects found in it are exclusively Badārian.[1] The sickle-stone could be of Naḳāda I date or perhaps later, the bone pins of any period, as also the little blade, which is of much better workmanship than any found in closed deposits of the period. The slate palette, rectangular with one curved side, also looks later. A similar knife from Badāri, t. 569, comes from an early dynastic grave with which I have dealt in Vol. I,[2] which contained a few intrusive Badārian objects. The very fine knife from Mustagidda, t. 2228,[3] comes from a grave with a single pot, quite unique, which, with its everted lip and decoration of incised triangles, resembles nothing so far excavated from the Badārian period. I therefore think that for the time being it is safer not to ascribe these knives to the Badārian age.

4. *Arrow-heads*

There can be no doubt that both the winged and the leaf-shaped arrow-heads show Badārian flint work at its best. They were found in graves and also in the settlement at Ḥammāmīya.[4] The best specimens are delicately pressure-flaked on both sides. The winged arrow-heads are of a variety of forms, from the straight-sided with square wing-tips to those with convex sides and pointed wing-tips. Some have short, others longer, wings. One would like to think that the different shapes served different purposes. Some of the leaf-shaped types as well as the winged have serrated edges.

5. *Flakes*

A few rough flakes were found in graves, which shows that they must have been put to some use. Yet it is surprising how little use was made of flakes, which any sort of flint work must have produced as a by-product.

NAḲĀDA I

To define the flint industry of Naḳāda I is difficult. We lack an excavation which would show its beginning, or even one that would show it unmixed with elements of Naḳāda II. The material which is available for its classification comes from Ḥammāmīya, Armant and Naḳāda South Town (Nub. t.). In none of these places can it be safely divided from that of Naḳāda II. Flints excavated from graves are better dated, but there are few of them, and they are not always identical with those from the settlements. The material from the graves is nearly exclusively bifacial, and so is the greater part from the settlements.

As all or nearly all the flint types from the Fayum occur also in the Upper Egyptian settlements, I am adopting Caton-Thompson's typology for them.[5] Of about 25 different flint types from excavations or surface finds which she calls "neolithic",[6] I could identify 20 in Upper Egypt. Of these I have tentatively ascribed to Naḳāda I those that are bifacially worked, which she found *in situ* in the excavations of the Koms W and K. This equation of the two cultures seems to me justified because their similarities seem to me to be greater and more important than their differ-

---

[1] *Bad. Civ.*, pl. XX, 16.   [2] Part I, p. 21.
[3] *Mostagedda and the Tasian Culture*, pl. XXII, 31-35.
[4] *Bad. Civ.*, pls. XXIX, 6; LXXXIII, 166A, 167.
[5] I have deviated from it only in the classification of knives, where I have taken shape rather than pebble butt as the distinguishing mark.   [6] G. Caton-Thompson, *The Desert Fayem*, pp. 19 ff.

ences: both inter their dead outside their settlements, and this sets them apart from the Merimdian. They store their grain in holes lined with matting. They have disc-shaped mace-heads, and use palettes for grinding their cosmetics. The Fayum pottery is much coarser and poorer in shape than most made in the Nile Valley, yet many of the shapes are not foreign there, and if one were to have more settlement pottery from Upper Egypt or some grave pottery from the Fayum the differences might be still less noticeable. But even as it stands, quite a number of the Fayum pots have their equivalent in Petrie's Corpus and Brunton's additions to it. Even the more sophisticated form of the footed vase of Naḳāda I appears in a rather debased shape in the Fayum.

Though it is quite possible and even likely that the Naḳāda I people used some blades in their settlements, I do not yet see how to recognize them. Their typology must be left until proper excavations in settlements have clarified the position.

TYPOLOGY OF STONE AND FLINT TOOLS OF NAḲĀDA I
(The sites of the equivalents in the Fayum Neolithic are given in brackets)

1. *Axes of igneous and sedimentary rocks* (Fayum Kom W and Kom K)

A fragment (the butt end is missing) was found in Naḳāda Town.[1] It is of igneous rock, the curved cutting edge ground and polished, the sides slightly squared. Another of porphyrite (also without the butt) was excavated from the lowest level of Armant.[2] De Morgan collected two stone axes at Toukh.[3] One, of serpentine, is more slender than the Fayum type, and ground all over with a straight cutting edge. The other, pecked with a curved cutting edge, is a "hache à boudin", not known from the Fayum, but found at Merimda. The settlement of El-Maḥāsna provided another, too badly published for any details to be discernible.[4] Brunton found several stone axes at Matmar and Mustagidda, all isolated in holes or accompanied by atypical flints. They cannot be dated. Those from the settlements mentioned cannot be older than Naḳāda I, for these settlements have produced nothing older than that period.

2. *Polished flint axes* (on top but not *in situ* at Kom W)

Three were found on the surface of Fayum Kom W, but none in the excavated strata. One, larger, comes from Naḳāda, t. 1410, dated to S.D. 36-44.[5] This would indicate a somewhat later date than Naḳāda I.

3. *Polished and flaked axes* (Fayum Kom W and Kom K) [6]

These have so far been found in the Fayum, where they are the most characteristic flints, at Merimda, and at Naḳāda Town, where three are known. One of the Naḳāda pieces, already mentioned in Vol. I, p. 28, has a straight cutting edge; the two others, now in the Manchester

---

[1] Now at University College, London.
[2] *Cem. Arm.*, pp. 205-6, pl. LVII, 26.
[3] J. de Morgan, *Préhistoire orientale*, II, p. 80, fig. 90.
[4] J. Garstang, *Maḥâsna and Bêt Khallâf*, p. 6, pl. V, upper right. I was unable to locate this axe.
[5] Now at University College, London.
[6] Vol. I, pl. IV, 3.

Museum, may have been hoes. Manchester, no. 2417, with rounded cutting edge, is transversely
flaked. There are traces of polish on the one side and remnants of cortex on the other, the cutting
edge of which is made with longitudinal flaking. The other, Manchester, no. 2422, also bifacial,
has traces of grinding near the cutting edge. Since they were found at the South Town, these
axes cannot be older than Naḳāda I.

4. *Celtiform* (Fayum Kom W)

These, which range from bifacial ovates to piriforms, and include hoe-shaped bifacials, are
more or less ovoid, some having straight cutting edges. One from Naḳāda Town has a pebble
butt; a hoe-shaped bifacial is roughly tanged. Their earliest possible date there is Naḳāda I.
They are common in the Fayum.

5. *Arrow-heads* (Fayum Kom W and Kom K)

(a) *With Concave bases.* Vol. I, pl. IV, 5, 6, 9; Vol. II, pl. I, 8 and 9.

The four different varieties which Caton-Thompson distinguishes from the Fayum Koms
are all known from Upper Egypt. The narrow, straight-sided type with shallow notch occurs
at Naḳāda Town (Vol. I, pl. IV, 5); the type with the exaggeratedly deep notch is known from
de Morgan's excavations at Zawaideh [1] (Vol. II, pl. I, 8 and 9, and at El-Maḥāsna [2]). The ogival
form occurs at Naḳāda Town (Vol. I, pl. IV, 6), and the convex-sided one at El-Maḥāsna,[2] an
example which has squared wing-tips. The three last varieties are mentioned and figured as from
Upper Egypt by de Morgan,[3] one of his pieces having squared wing-tips. He remarks that they
remind him of Fayum types, as do the triangular ones he figures together with them. Brunton
found all variants of concave-base arrow-heads in his "predynastic" (as distinct from Badārian)
village sites on the spurs of the desert near Badāri.[4] Two concave-base arrow-heads from
Koptos (Vol. I, pl. IV, 9) do not fit in any of the four categories: one is straight-sided, but not
shallow-notched, having two well-developed wings with squared tips; the other, ogival, also with
squared wing-tips, has one wing longer than the other.

Concave-base arrow-heads are so far the oldest known type in Egypt. A narrow, straight-sided
one with shallow notch, a convex-sided one and two ogivals were excavated from the Badārian
strata at Ḥammāmīya,[5] and ogival arrow-heads were also found in the Badārian graves.[6] As our
evidence proves, they were still in use during Naḳāda I, and possibly later.

(b) *Triangular arrow-heads* (Kom W)

Several of these were found at Naḳāda Town. The best, damaged at one side, is thin and
carefully pressure-flaked from both sides, and has serrated edges (Vol. I, pl. IV, 4). Similar
arrow-heads were found at Armant and also at Toukh. Neither at Naḳāda nor at Armant can
they be earlier than Naḳāda I.

---

[1] Now in Brooklyn Museum, published here by kind permission of the Museum.
[2] *Maḥâsna*, pls. III and IV, also as clay models.
[3] *Préhistoire orientale*, II, p. 99, fig. 114.
[4] *Bad. Civ.*, pl. XXIX, 3, 5, 6.
[5] *Bad. Civ.*, pl. LXXXIII, 157.
[6] *Bad. Civ.*, pl. XXVI, 5120, 5112.

6. *Sickle-stones* (Kom W and Kom K)

These are rectangular and worked on both sides, most of them being pointed at one end. They are denticulated along one side. They were found at Koptos (Vol. I, pl. IV, 8), at Armant and perhaps at El-Maḥāsna, though the reproduction is so bad that one cannot be sure.[1] One from Naḳāda Town (Vol. I, pl. IV, 7) with its butt broken off may have been double-pointed like some found in Badārian strata. Their origin goes back to Badārian times, but they persisted into Naḳāda I. They are typical of Fayum A.

7. *Leaf-shaped points, and chisel-ended points* (Kom W)

These vary from long and slender forms (fig. 1) to shorter and wider ones (Vol. I, pl. V, 6). Their butts are carefully flaked and may have been put to some use as well as the points, as some are snapped off. Some have chisel-ends. A leaf-shaped point with broken butt, a point with chisel-end and the fragment of a bifacial knife were found together with a small rhomboid slate palette in Naḳāda, t. 1906, sequence-dated to 34, thus forming a dated group. Other leaf-shaped points come from the undated graves, Naḳāda, 61 and 1370. One was found at Naḳāda Town, at least one at Armant and probably one at El-Maḥāsna,[1] in all of which places they cannot be older than Naḳāda I.

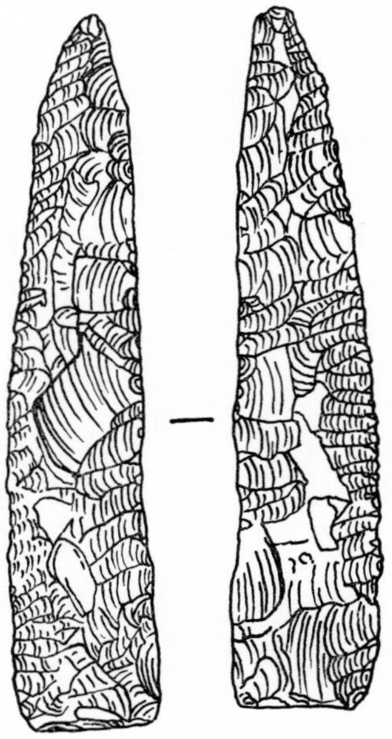

Fig. 1   Leaf-shaped bifacial. Naḳāda t. 1906.

8. *Pebble-butted and pebble-backed tools* (Fayum Kom W)

As the tools of Upper Egypt are generally finer and better than those of the Desert Fayum, pebble-backed and pebble-butted specimens are rare, even though the tools were made of tabular flint. A hoe-shaped bifacial from Naḳāda Town is pebble-butted. A coarse knife from the same place, the butt of which is broken, has remnants of cortex along its straight back, and on both sides, so that it might be reckoned among Caton-Thompson's "tabular flint knives" to which I have not given a special type number here. A side-scraper (see 3 (a) below) is made in the same technique. Quite a number of the fine bifacial knives from Upper Egypt have small remnants of cortex at their butts. They will be dealt with under the heading of bifacial knives.

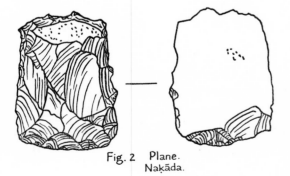

Fig. 2   Plane. Naḳāda.

9. *Planes* (classified as Fayum Neolithic, probably A, certainly B Group; fig. 2)

These are formed of flat pieces of flint, the plane face being either the natural cortex or a flat area of natural fracture. They may have straight or convex cutting edges. Some fine pieces are made of flakes, the bulbar face remaining unretouched, the upper being convex and retouched all over. Planes are common at Naḳāda Town

---

[1] *Maḥâsna*, pl. V, "Hoes and small knives", second from right.

and Armant, and were also found at Toukh. In all those places they cannot be older than Naḳāda I. A fine specimen from Naḳāda Town has its cutting edge resharpened by a transverse blow. This technique, not known with certainty before Naḳāda II, tends to show that the planes continue into that period. They were also found in the Fayum, but not *in situ* in a Kom.

10. *Scrapers* (Fayum Kom W, only those made of split pebbles)

(a) *Side-scrapers* (fig. 3a)

These are heavy bifacial tools, some with remnants of cortex. They are oblong, with curved backs and straight working edges. The largest from Naḳāda Town is nearly 14 cm. long. They are oval in section. Some are made from split pebbles like planes, but the working edges are along the long sides. In Upper Egypt they are so far known from Naḳāda Town only.

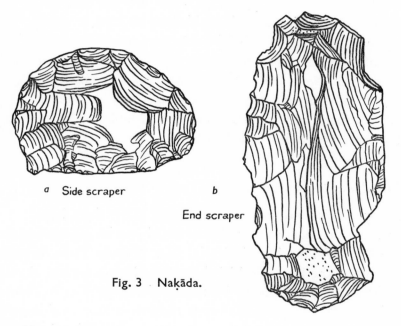

a   Side scraper   *b*

End scraper

Fig. 3   Naḳāda.

(b) *End-scrapers* (fig. 3b)

These are narrow bifacial tools with a steep working edge at one of the short ends. Some have provisions for hafting, or were prepared for a secondary use as hollow scrapers along their sides. They were found at Naḳāda Town and in the Fayum.

(c) *Core-scrapers* (Fayum Kom W)

These are small with a more or less circular base, similar to those found by Caton-Thompson in the Badārian levels at Ḥammāmīya. One was found in Fayum Kom W. They seem to be survivals from the Badārian age. Caton-Thompson calls them carinated core-scrapers. Huzayyin found them at Armant and says they are somewhat coarser than the Badārian. One was found in a grave (B 107) at Abadiyeh not quite securely dated to S.D. 33. Huzayyin mentions [1] that they were also found at Ma'adi. They evidently had a long life.

[1] *Cem. Arm.*, p. 202.

11. *Dibbles or rimers* (fig. 4)

These are made of large nodules, often pebble-backed. They have triangular necks. The best ones are resharpened by a transverse blow. Huzayyin, who describes those found in the deepest stratum at Armant, takes them to be tools for digging the soil. It seems to me somewhat doubtful whether so much care would be wasted on a tool for a purpose that would be better served by a simple digging-stick. They may have been rimers, which follow up the work of gimlets to enlarge holes in wood. Two rather atypical ones, found at Naḳāda Town, do not show remnants of the original pebble. The smaller may have a reshaped butt, roughly flaked from both sides with large strokes.[1] No dibbles are known from the Fayum.

12. *Fish-tails*

These tools (or weapons?), which are often beautifully finished, occur not infrequently in tombs—sometimes several in the same grave. They must have been in daily use also, for Brunton found them among the village rubbish on the spurs of the desert near Badāri.[2] Though fish-tails are quite familiar objects among Egyptian flints, we still do not know what they were used for. They are most commonly thought to be lance-heads.

Fish-tails of Naḳāda I are shaped like elongated triangles with concave bases. These "bases", however, are their working edges. They and the

Fig. 4   Dibble or rimer. Naḳāda Town.

adjacent parts of the sides are finely serrated up to the point where the handle begins. A fish-tail from Naḳāda, t. 1388, was found with a cord wound round it "with two alabaster knobs at the outer end and the whole wrapped in hide".[3] From this Petrie concludes that the fish-tails were lances used for throwing at short distances, and were checked by a cord from flying too far. I wonder whether the cord may not have been for hafting, for the cord on this fish-tail does not seem long enough to have served in the way that Petrie suggests. If the cord was for hafting, then the fish-tail cannot have been a lance-head. A copper fish-tail was found in t. H 85 at El-Maḥāsna.[4] Though the grave is of Naḳāda II date, the shape of the tool is like those of Naḳāda I; it is even serrated like the flint fish-tails. Where the serration ends, a hole is pierced through it somewhat askew from one edge to the opposite. In Armant, t. 1457, a fish-tail was found together with a grinder for red ochre, and tiny specks of a red material are on the edges of two fish-tails from Naḳāda, t. 1676, S.D. 32. More evidence will have to be collected before we can say whether or not this has any significance. The finer of the two fish-tails from t. 1676 is of semi-translucent flint and shows signs of wear inside one wing where it has obliterated the serration. Both are

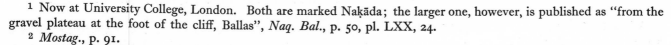

[1] Now at University College, London. Both are marked Naḳāda; the larger one, however, is published as "from the gravel plateau at the foot of the cliff, Ballas", *Naq. Bal.*, p. 50, pl. LXX, 24.

[2] *Mostag.*, p. 91.

[3] *Naq. Bal.*, p. 51. This piece is now in the Ashmolean Museum.

[4] See above, p. 20.

broken. The same grave yielded two large double-edged knives (type 13).[1] The fish-tail is unknown to the Fayum Neolithic civilization.

13. *Double-edged knives with rounded tips* (pl. I, 2)

As far as I am aware, double-edged knives are known from graves only. They are between 27 and 41 cm. long and 4 and 5 cm. wide, and even the longest are not more than about 0·6 cm. thick. Their sides are symmetrically convex and end in rounded tips, and are finely serrated all around except where once covered by the handle. All specimens recovered so far are broken, and, according to Brunton, who found the longest and the shortest in t. 1847 and t. 1854 at Mustagidda,[2] were broken before they were deposited in the graves. Both these graves contained no pottery. Brunton assigns them to Naḳāda I.

The double-edged knives, even more than the fish-tails, show what the Naḳāda I craftsmen could do at their best. How they did it remains unanswered. Did they start from a selected piece of tabular flint which could be reduced from both sides to the required shape, or could such a piece be split into perfectly flat layers which would only need to be shaped and then finished off with pressure-flaking from both sides, or lastly, did they grind them to shape as did the craftsmen of Naḳāda II, and then pressure-flake them? The results of their skill were perfectly symmetrical knives, the denticulated edges being very sharp, but too thin to withstand much pressure or any form of hard usage. What, then, were they used for? They are too rare to have had any general connexions with the ceremonies of burials. They may have been the badge of some office which the owners took with them into the next world. They were not found in the Fayum Neolithic sites, but this may be because they are connected with graves, and the graves belonging to Fayum A still remain undiscovered.

14. *Single-edged knives* (knives are classified as "mainly A group" in Fayum Neolithic)

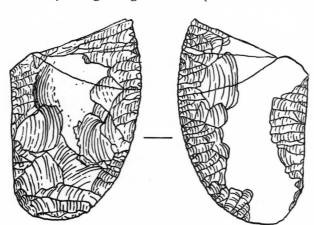

Fig. 5   Straight-backed knife.
Naḳāda t. 1443.

These are asymmetrical, with pointed tips. Their butts may be straight, or rounded, some with remnants of cortex. Two sub-types can be distinguished:

(a) *Knives with straight backs and curved cutting edges* (fig. 5)

This is a common form in graves as well as in settlements. Most of them were broken. The straight back ends in a point to which the cutting edge curves back. Fragments were found at Armant and at Naḳāda Town. A rather coarse one from Naḳāda Town, made of a suitable piece

---

[1] Tomb 1676 is the one mentioned in Vol. I, p. 109, as containing a footed basalt vase and an unretouched twisted blade. Petrie dates it to S.D. 32. I think that the highly sophisticated flint work makes it difficult to ascribe the tomb to the beginning of Naḳāda I rather than to the end of that period.

[2] *Mostag.*, p. 91.

of tabular flint, is pebble-backed and butted. The lower part of one with rounded butt comes from Naḳāda, t. 1443, S.D. 31. It was a very fine knife, 5 cm. wide but only about 0·4 cm. thick, made from a split pebble, with remnants of cortex on one side and of the natural surface on the other. The cutting edge is finely serrated (Fig. 5). Such knives were also found in the Fayum.[1]

(b) *Knives with curved backs and straight cutting edges* (fig. 6)

These knives are constructed so that the maximum pressure can be exerted on the tip. This is formed on the straight cutting edge, and the back is curved. A short way below the point the back is steeply retouched to form a platform on which a finger-tip can rest and press the knife down. The lower part of the back is mainly blunted. Such knives are common in the settlements, but also occur in graves. Two fine pieces were found in Naḳāda, t. 1569, loosely dated to S.D. 35-51, and in t. 100, undated, but probably of Naḳāda II. The knife from t. 1569 is 14 cm. long, 4·8 cm. wide and only about 0·3 cm. thick. The back lacks the steep retouch near the point, and has two small notches for hafting near the butt, on which some cortex is left. On the knife from t. 100 the steep retouch extends fairly far down the back. Its butt also has some cortex left. T. 100 contained two fish-tails of Naḳāda I type.

Curved-back knives remained in use during Naḳāda II, a typical example being found in Gerzeh, t. 135, S.D. 55-57, another in Naḳāda, t. 456, S.D. 56, which also contained some blade knives.

They are not rare in Naḳāda Town, where the preserved specimens are heavier than those recovered from the graves; none seems to have been found at Armant. They are known from surface finds in the Fayum.[2]

Fig. 6   Curved-back knife. Naḳāda S. Town.

15. *Daggers*

These are elongated triangular to trapezoidal and have triangular grips a little wider than the blades, which are serrated. One was found in Hu, t. U 259, dated S.D. 36-40, another in Naḳāda, t. 1410, S.D. 36-44, where the polished flint axe (see above, p. 27) was also excavated. Several more are known from Naḳāda II, but no exact parallels from the Fayum. A dagger from there,[3] a surface find and unique, is much heavier than those from the graves, and lacks the protruding grip. Whether the fragments of what Caton-Thompson calls halberds should be entered here is uncertain, as no complete example exists.

These 15 types of bifacial tools and weapons represent what with more or less certainty we can call the flint industry of Naḳāda I. For a few—too few—we have the confirmation of dated graves. As all the flint tools found *in situ* in the Koms of the Fayum, with one single exception,

---

[1] *The Desert Fayum*, pl. XXXVI, 2 (surface Neolithic).
[2] *The Desert Fayum*, pl. XXXVII, 3 (Fayum Neolithic).
[3] *The Desert Fayum*, pl. XXXVII, 6.

are among these 15 types, I have included the Fayum A culture as part of the Naḳāda I civilization. The one type not yet found in Naḳāda I is the ground point, of which two exist from the Fayum, one excavated in Kom W, the other a surface find.

Many of the 15 types survive into Naḳāda II and even later. Three, the concave-based arrow-head, the bifacial sickle-stones or saws and the small core-scrapers, were already known to the Badārians. The most characteristic of these, the core-scraper, was found once only in Fayum A. This, I think, prevents us assuming that the Fayum had direct contact and was contemporaneous with Badāri.

It remains to describe the two blades which were excavated in Naḳāda I tombs. The smaller one from t. 223, S.D. 34, is 4·8 cm. long and has retouches along three edges extending over the cortex which remains on its upper side. The bulbar end is plain, the tip squared. A fish-tail with shallow curve, and the fragment of what may have been the butt of another, complete the known flint inventory of t. 223. Of pottery, only a black-top pot seems to have survived. The sherds of a white-cross-lined vase cannot be ascribed with certainty to it as two are marked 206 and one 223. The other blade (from t. 1600, S.D. 37) is 10 cm. long, and heavy. The bulb is removed and a chisel-end formed from below, the retouch continuing along half of one edge. The other edge shows remnants of cortex. The edge opposite the chisel is broken off. A fragment of a copper pin and a spatha shell come from the same grave. Both blades are atypical.

Typology of Stone and Flint Tools of Naḳāda II

The period of Naḳāda II shows Egyptian flint work at its best. Good and useful flint tools were produced in Egypt up to New Kingdom times or even later, but never again was the material handled with such mastery to produce pieces of such beauty. Naḳāda II was in many respects one of the great ages of Egypt.

The addition which Naḳāda II makes to the flint industry of Egypt is the manufacturing of blades. They occur quite frequently in graves, small ones by the dozen, and, too, long ones up to about 25 cm., finely retouched not only at the back but over great parts, or even the whole of one surface. This to my mind shows that the flint worker of Naḳāda II, with the strong tradition of good bifacial flint work of Naḳāda I behind him, never quite accepted the new technique, at least for his masterpieces. It may be that a technical detail made him in the end return to bifacial work for all the larger pieces and reserve the blade technique for the small tools. It seems difficult, if not impossible, to detach a large blade from a nucleus so that it becomes truly straight. Where the stroke loses its force the back of the blade will turn and become rounded in outline. The sharp edge will either follow this, or adopt a twist of its own, which has earned these pieces the name of "twisted blades" (pl. I, 3). The worker, for whom during this period no technical problem seems to have been too difficult, corrected this by reserving the straight part of the blade for the working end and flaking away the bulb in order to form the tip of his tool.

For so long as we lack stratified excavations in Upper Egyptian settlements it will be difficult to ascertain which of the bifacially-worked tools were innovations of Naḳāda II. Only where the graves give confirmation can we say that a certain type of bifacial tool belongs exclusively to that period.

1. *Axes of igneous and sedimentary rocks*

We know that axes, pecked and with ground cutting edges, were still made during Old and Middle Kingdom times, when they imitated the rounded copper axes with lugs. They were found at Koptos, Lahun and elsewhere. Whether Naḳāda II developed a special form we do not know.

A red breccia axe, ground and polished all over, was found in t. a 96 at El-'Amrah, dated before S.D. 56.[1] This is a rich grave which contained three pear-shaped mace-heads, five fish-tails of the later shape, gold, lapis lazuli and cornelian beads, and, among the pots, the rare squat one (F 1) with a corrugated surface, as well as two decorated vases. The axe has a square neck and sides and splayed cutting edge, which is slightly damaged. Two holes are bored through it near the neck. The breccia axe can hardly have been of practical value, and may even, as the holes suggest, have been worn suspended from the neck as an amulet.

An axe of dark diorite, 12·4 cm. long, oval in section and with a rounded neck and finely-ground cutting edge, was found in a grave at Homra Doum near Nag Hamadi. This grave, rich in gold and silver, contained eight finely-polished objects of hornblende and similar stones. They are of different shapes; some look like axes but are blunt and show traces of pounding. A squarish one of green schist, 5 by 4·5 by 2·3 cm., might have been a weight. The grave belongs to the end of Naḳāda II[2] (pl. I, 1).

2. *Flint axes* (Vol. I, pl. V, 2)

The flint axe typical of Naḳāda II is the flaked axe resharpened by a transverse blow. It is as yet impossible to ascertain the exact date of its introduction. The technique of resharpening the edge by detaching a single flake with a stroke from the side points to a craftsman accustomed to making blades, and that means a craftsman of Naḳāda II.[3]

The flint axes may be oblong or oval in shape (Petrie calls them "ovates"), and from 6 to 10 cm. long. Some have straight and some have rounded cutting edges. To keep the rounded ones in form after resharpening by a transverse blow they were carefully retouched from the other side. Some have rounded necks, and some pointed ones, obviously shaped for better hafting. In short, there are many variations, but the type remains distinct, and they must have had many uses about the house. They are the most common tool from Naḳāda II settlements.

Dozens were found at Nub. t and at Armant. Though Armant is not a stratified site, and the three levels do not correspond to any of the predynastic periods, the lowest level III, which Myers dates to "S.D. 35-38 or 42", yielded only three flaked axes, whilst level II, dated "S.D. 38 or 41 to 57 or 59", produced 12, and level I, "S.D. 53 or 58 to 72 or 78", had 30. This would agree with my assigning them to Naḳāda II. Another confirmation of their date is their presence in the Naḳāda II layers at Ḥammāmīya.[4]

---

[1] *El Amrah*, p. 19, pl. VII, 1. Can this be Cairo, 64648, Currelly, *Stone Implements, Cat. Gén.* (1913), p. 238, pl. 42, provenance given there as "Upper Egypt"? A similar piece is in the British Museum.

[2] See above, pp. 8-9.

[3] Huzayyin in *Cem. Arm.*, footnote 6 to p. 196, quotes an oral communication by Brunton that these axes were found in village remains of mixed Tasian-Badārian date at Mustagidda. None of the objects from these villages are of more value than surface finds. In his publication of *Mostagedda*, Brunton states that it is impossible to say "which flints should be classified as Tasian and which as Badārian" (p. 31), which is another instance of how unsure he was himself about his Tasian. In spite of this he enumerates on the same p. 31 different flints as Tasian, among them axes. This is pure conjecture, not based on any finds in graves or assured by stratigraphy.

[4] *Bad. Civ.*, p. 77.

3. *Arrow-heads*

(a) *Bifacial, tanged*

These are small, shaped like elongated triangles to which the tang is added. Some are denticulated. One was found in Naḳāda, t. 1856, S.D. 43-56, another in t. 397 at Hu, S.D. 65. They are frequent in archaic times, when they become larger, with bulging sides. Twelve tanged arrow-heads, slightly different in that some of them were winged, were found in an Eighteenth Dynasty grave (D 29) at Abydos. The excavator thinks that they may have been collected from a nearby archaic grave.[1] A somewhat coarse piece, the tip broken, was excavated from the top layer at Ḥammāmīya, where a concave-base arrow-head, made from a blade, was also found.[2]

(b) *On blades, chisel-headed and lunates*

These two types are taken together, because they are both rare. The chisel-headed arrow-head is made from a fragment of a blade the width of which forms the cutting edge. Predynastic examples are so far known from t. 1066 at Abuṣīr el-Meleḳ only, unless the very bad drawing of a tool found in the settlement at El-Maḥāsna [3] represents another. In Abuṣīr, t. 1066, three were found which are triangular, as are so many of historic date in Egypt. The piece from El-Maḥāsna, which is figured together with a somewhat larger concave-base arrow-head, looks rather like a miniature fish-tail, but that may be the fault of the drawing. Even the chisel-headed arrow-heads —typical of blade cultures—did not escape the inveterate inclination of the Egyptian craftsman to fashion them in the bifacial technique, and this produced such strange compositions as those found in the tomb of King Djer at Abydos, where the chisel-end provided with a long stem is attached to a tanged base.[4]

Lunates (Vol. I, pl. V, 7) of red agate come from t. 836 at Naḳāda. This grave with its unusual furniture also contained the narrow copper dagger mentioned on p. 10 (metal). Both, lunates as well as the dagger, are quite unique.

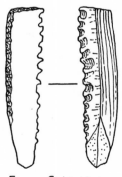

Fig. 7 Sickle blade.
Teeth blunted by use.
Naḳāda t. 626.

4. *Sickle-blades and saws* (fig. 7)

These are slender blades, either squared at both ends or with one pointed and the other squared. The backs are blunted, sometimes from the bulbar side, a technique characteristic of Naḳāda II. The cutting edges, which are denticulated, have in some cases preserved the gloss caused through cutting grain.

They are frequent at Nub. t, Armant, and Ḥammāmīya, and were also found at El-Maḥāsna. A pointed one comes from Naḳāda, t. 1665, which is not dated. Others from Abadiyeh and Hu come from t. B 427, S.D. 45, and t. R 83, S.D. 41.

5. *Points*

Points are made from blades struck from prepared striking platforms. The bulbs are removed with one stroke, which often leaves a deep scar. The sides are retouched. One each was found in

[1] *El Amrah*, pl. XLVIII, 1.   [2] *Bad. Civ.*, pl. LXXI, 66.
[3] *Maḥâsna*, pl. IV.   [4] *Royal Tombs*, II, pl. VI, 13 and 14.

t. 179 and t. 219, neither dated, and in t. 1241, S.D. 52, all from Naḳāda. A similar point was found in t. 5119 at Matmar, S.D. 47-68.

6. *Scrapers*

(a) *Side-scrapers* (fig. 8)

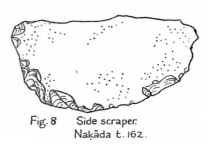

Fig. 8   Side scraper. Naḳāda t. 162.

These rather coarse tools are made from thick flakes, and are roughly semicircular, with the edge either on the straight or the curved side. They were found in the settlements of Nub. t and Armant as well as in graves. One was recovered from the rich grave, Naḳāda 162, which also contained a set of metal toilet tools (p. 17), and one of the most beautiful ripple-flaked knives. It is dated S.D. 58.

(b) *End-scraper and scraping knives on blade* (fig. 9)

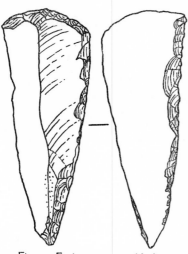

Fig. 9   End scraper on blade. Naḳāda t. 471.

Some of these are made from heavy blades with a steep working end (keel-scrapers); with others the natural turn at the end of many blades is utilized and trimmed to a working end. In addition to the working end some have one blunted and one sharpened side, the sharpening being often done from underneath. The bulb is generally removed. This type is called a scraping knife by Huzayyin.[1] End-scrapers are very common. They were found at Armant, in the upper levels of Ḥāmmamīya, at Nub. t and in some graves. One in Naḳāda, t. 108, is dated to S.D. 43; another from t. 471 forms part of a collection of blades and flakes, some typical, some atypical. It is vaguely dated S.D. 32-48, but certainly of Naḳāda II. The scraper is a "scraping knife" with one edge sharpened from the bulbar side. This may have been a device to make it straight, as the scraper is on a twisted blade.

(c) *Circular and oval scrapers* (fig. 10)

These are made of flakes or blades, the working end being circular or oval. Examples were recovered from Armant, and are frequent in the top layers of Ḥammāmīya. One from a grave, Naḳāda, t. 665, is not dated.

(d) *Hollow or round scrapers*

They are either notched at the tip of a blade or at the side when the tip is fashioned for some other use. They are made to scrape a piece of wood or bone into a rounded shape. De Morgan found them at Toukh, and Petrie at Nub. t.[2]

Fig. 10   Circular scraper on flake. Naḳāda t. 665.

---

[1] Huzayyin, in *Cem. Arm.*, 1, p. 220.
[2] *Préhistoire orientale*, 2, fig. 102. *Naq. Bal.*, pl. LXXIII, 70.

7. Fish-tails

The fish-tails lose nothing of their popularity during Naḳāda II. While the older shape described under Naḳāda I (no. 12, p. 31) is still used, another one is now introduced. It is slender with nearly parallel sides only narrowing where the handle once covered them. They have V-shaped cutting edges, and the wings do not protrude as with the earlier form. Among the typical shapes of the fish-tails of Naḳāda I and II nearly every conceivable angle of the cutting edges exists. Fish-tails generally occur in pairs, or even in series in one tomb, often of different shapes. Their points must have been exposed to the greatest wear, for quite a number have been broken and repaired anciently. A special variety has a long, sharply-receding tang, sometimes notched, to facilitate the hafting with cords (?).

Naḳāda II fish-tails are of beautiful workmanship, even finer than those of the preceding period. With some of them one still can see how they were manufactured. They were first roughly flaked to the desired shape, and then ground to give them thinness; but under this ground surface the scars of the earlier flaking can still be recognized. Finishing was by pressure-flaking, the better pieces being carefully pressure-flaked all over, so that nothing of the ground surface remained, with the others being so worked along the sides, at least, and over part of the ground surface.

The fish-tail was still in domestic use during Naḳāda II, for it was found in the top layers of Ḥammāmīya. It is not known when it developed into the tool used in the funerary ceremony of "opening the mouth". Perhaps the two wings of the V-shaped fish-tail suggested the lips to the ancient Egyptians. Fish-tails are dated by finds in graves: one in Badāri, t. 102, is of S.D. 44-61, and a set of five belongs to El-'Amrah, t. a 96, from which the breccia axe (p. 35 above) was also recovered. More than a dozen were found in different Naḳāda tombs. Where the sequence-date could be ascertained it was of the Naḳāda II period.

8. Knives

(a) Double-edged knives, bifacial

None of the large, double-edged knives (type I, no. 13 above) with rounded tips have so far been traced to Naḳāda II. Instead we find a related but smaller form, pointed, and sometimes with small protuberances where the tang begins. Like the older type, it was discovered in graves only. Several come from Naḳāda.[1] One from Mustagidda, t. 1803, was found with a disc-shaped mace-head and no other furniture. As there were no pots, Brunton could not date the grave, but, probably on the strength of the disc-shaped mace, calls it Naḳāda I (Amratian). The disc mace, however, continues through Naḳāda I into Naḳāda II and into archaic times, so that Mustagidda, t. 1803, cannot be dated from it. A fine piece [2] with serrated edges of an accuracy and smallness which one would not think possible in flint was recovered from the same grave, Naḳāda 1410, as the polished flint axe of S.D. 36-44. The grave must be dated near the end of this period. The fragment of a miniature knife with the tip broken, and now only 8·3 cm. long and 1·7 cm. wide, comes from Naḳāda, t. 1857, S.D. 40-62.

[1] Their length is about 20 cm. or a little more.
[2] Now in the Ashmolean Museum, Oxford.

(b) *Single-edged knives, bifacial*

The innovation which Naḳāda II contributes on single-edged knives is a new technique of pressure-flaking which allows a straight flake to be taken off the flint at exactly the place desired. The pieces so made are known as ripple-flaked or fluted knives. They exist in several sub-types. They can be comparatively wide, about one-quarter to one-third of their length; others are narrow. They are ripple-flaked on one side only, while the other is ground and polished. They have straight backs to which the rounded cutting edges curve up, ending in points at the end of the backs, which are carefully blunted. The fluting is done from a line which runs from the tip to the base, generally somewhat nearer to the cutting edge than to the back. In some pieces the fluting is so exact that nothing is left of the ground surface over which it was executed, and the edges have the finest serration. These knives must have been highly valued when they were made, for we sometimes find them provided with decorated handles in ivory and gold. What their special use was is not known. The Flinders Petrie Collection at University College, London, possesses one that is worn down by use to a fraction of its original width. A fragment of another was found in the top level of Ḥammāmīya reshaped as a scraper.[1] Five ripple-flaked knives were found at Gerzeh, where they range from S.D. 53-64,[2] one at Harageh in t. 457 of S.D. 55-58, and eleven from Abuṣīr el-Melek. This cemetery was not sequence-dated, but belongs wholly to the later end of Naḳāda II and the beginning of the dynasties. Several were recovered from Diospolis Parva, one from the large grave B 408 of S.D. 57, another from B 191 of S.D. 56 (?).

One piece must have special mention, because it is perhaps the finest ever made. Its material seems to be a semi-translucent chalcedony. It is equally well fluted on both sides, no remnant of the ground surface being visible. It is more slender than the other ripple-flaked knives, its width being one-sixth of its length, its straight back turns near the tip to meet the cutting edge, with which it forms an elegant curve. The back is blunted and the edge serrated. This knife was found in the rich tomb Naḳāda 162 of S.D. 58, to which a metal toilet-set also belongs.[3]

The trick of the ripple-flaking dies out with Naḳāda II. One cannot help thinking that it may have been the jealously guarded professional secret of a single workshop.

Another type of the single-edged knife is not so well finished. It is sickle-shaped, but the cutting edge is on the outside, and not the inside as with a sickle. Both surfaces are pressure-flaked all over in a sort of ripple-flaking far inferior to that of the knives described above. The fluting is irregular, the serration of the edge coarser. The backs are blunted. These knives are not quite so thin as the ripple-flaked pieces, with one exception. This, which has no provenance and is in the Ashmolean Museum, is only 13 cm. long, finely ripple-flaked on one side, and ground on the other.

Six of these knives were found at Naḳāda and three at Ballas.[4] One each is from t. 39 of S.D. 56,[5] t. B 99 of S.D. 61, t. 178 of S.D. 57,[6] t. 414 of S.D. 51, t. 1215 of S.D. 49-63, and t. 1203 of S.D. 35-61.[7]

---

[1] *Bad. Civ.*, p. 101, pls. LXXII, 142; LXXXI, 89.
[2] *Gerzeh*, p. 23, pl. VII. No tomb numbers are given.
[3] See chapter on Metals, p. 17. It is now in the Ashmolean Museum.
[4] *Naq. Bal.*, pl. LXXIV, 84.
[5] This knife was in the Egyptian Museum, Berlin.
[6] Now in the Manchester Museum.
[7] Now at University College, London.

(c) *Knives on blades* (figs. 11 and 12) (pl. I, 3)

Several variants of blade knives exist,[1] some narrow and some wide, and some with a prominent dorsal rib which gives them a triangular section. Their backs are blunted and some have very steep retouching. With the large and carefully-made specimens a regular zig-zag pattern is produced along the dorsal rib.

These large and heavy blades offered technical difficulties of their own to the tool-maker (p. 34 above). The blades tend to curve, sometimes the two edges being curved in different directions. The blades are then known as "twisted blades". Whether the twist could be pro-

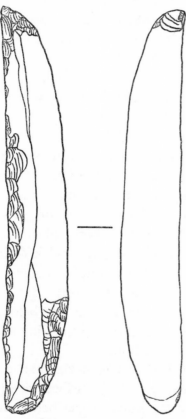

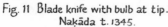

Fig. 11 Blade knife with bulb at tip.
Naḳāda t. 1345.

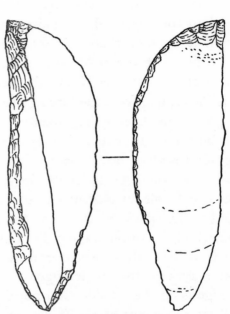

Fig. 12 Blade knife with bulb at tip,
cutting edge retouched from
below. Naḳāda, South Town.

duced intentionally I do not know, but am inclined to believe it is a counter-measure to the simple curving of the blades. These twisted blades are the "leitfossils" of Naḳāda II. As a further corrective—and this applies to the curved as well as to the twisted knives—the craftsman used the straightest part of the blade, that is, the bulbar end, to form the tip of the knife. This necessitated a careful trimming away of the bulb itself, a feature which is usual with most of the blade knives, even if the bulbar side remains otherwise unworked. All the better knives, however, have much secondary flaking. On some the bulbar side is ripple-flaked all over, but the flaking never reaches perfection. For this, it seems, a surface ground completely flat was needed. Often part of the

[1] Miss Caton-Thompson in *The Desert Fayum*, pp. 69-70, distinguished two types, one with little-worked edges and one where the back is worked from the dorsal rib downwards.

upper side is also retouched. Where the bulb is at the butt it is generally taken off with a single stroke, causing a single deep scar. Many of these knives have remains of cortex at the butt end (pl. I, 3a-c).

The amount of secondary retouching lavished on the blade knives goes far to show that, even while adopting the blade technique, the craftsman when producing a fine piece did not feel satisfied until he had provided the knife with a certain amount of pressure-flaking. The bifacial technique must have had very deep roots in Egypt. The making of large blade knives was abandoned soon after the end of Naḳāda II.

During their own period, however, they were frequent. They were found in the upper stratum at Ḥammāmīya, at Armant, at Nub. t and at Toukh. They were recovered from the dated graves Naḳāda 294 of S.D. 47-50, 456 of S.D. 56, two from 1263 of S.D. 34-38, 1791 of S.D. 34-46, 1866 of S.D. 43 and B 99 of S.D. 61; others come from Gerzeh, where they are dated S.D. 53-64; from Diospolis Parva graves B 309 of S.D. 50, B 185 of S.D. 65 and U 396 of S.D. 68; from Mustagidda, 1609 of S.D. 49-53 and 1623 of S.D. 51-53; and from the First Dynasty grave 219 of S.D. 77-80. There are too many to cite them all. They must have been a common household tool.

9. *Daggers and spear-heads*

It is difficult to distinguish the double-edged knives from the daggers, and the daggers from the spear-heads. It would seem that a flint tool would break easily if used with some force as a dagger, and that the thin and carefully-worked pieces are more suited to be lance-heads. They are slender and leaf-shaped. The largest is about 21 cm. long, flaked, ground and then pressure-flaked, with convex sides, perfectly rounded butt, and serrated edges meeting in a sharp point. One was found in Naḳāda, t. 331, S.D. 56, another at Ballas, ? t. Q 753.[1] A related type, smaller, ground, and with the secondary pressure-flaking only along the edges, comes from Naḳāda, t. 414, S.D. 51 (Vol. I, pl. IV, 2).[2] To these must be added the winged spear-head from Merimda, which also has the secondary retouching only along the edges, with the ground surface showing elsewhere (Vol. I, pl. IV).

10. *Gravers* (fig. 13)

Gravers, known as the tools which the Upper Palaeolithic artist used in engraving the caves, were produced in Egypt during Naḳāda II, while unknown in Badārian or Naḳāda I times. The technique remained the same, gravers being made by a single stroke from the tip of a tool. They were found at Armant and at Nub. t. A fine specimen from Naḳāda, t. 162, S.D. 58, is made out of a flake from which several blades had been struck, the bulbar end being thinned to facilitate hafting. An angle-burin from Naḳāda, t. 1846 (Vol. I, pl. V, 1),[3] is not dated. It is also struck from a flake squared at the top from which several blades had been made.

Fig. 13 Graver.
Naḳāda.
t. 162.

---

1 *Naq. Bal.*, pl. LXXII, 56.
2 See above, p. 16, Vol. I.
3 A polished-red pot, Berlin 13072, Corpus type 47a, is all I could trace otherwise from this grave.

11. *Side-blow flakes* (pl. I, 5)

These curious tools, which have their bulbs in the middle of one of their long sides, were first described by Caton-Thompson in *The Desert Fayum*, p. 21, where she found them in surface sites. They were also excavated by H. de Morgan in a grave of Naḳāda II at Zawaideh. The flake,[1] however, differs from those recovered in the Fayum in that the back instead of being blunted shows the natural cortex, thus resembling those from Kharga Oasis, where they are surface finds.[2]

12. *Small blades* (fig. 14a)

The typological difference between the small blades and the blade knives of type 8 (*c*) is not only one of size. While the blade knives have blunted or steeply retouched backs, many of the small blades have two very sharp edges. They are usually between 3 and 8 cm. long and very thin. The edges in some cases show retouching from wear. The bulbar end is thinned from above, which shows that the little blades were hafted. Only rarely is the bulb itself removed by one skilled blow. Very few have blunted backs or the tips sharpened either from above or below. Some have blunted tips. They possess either one or two dorsal ribs. They occur in the settlements at Armant and Nub. t. Caton-Thompson says that a certain type of small knife appears to have existed as early as Badārian times.[3] In some Naḳāda II tombs dozens of them occur, the majority only a little retouched at the butt. At Gerzeh, a cemetery wholly of Naḳāda II, Wainwright found as many as 28 in one grave.[4] There were 18 in Naḳāda, t. 1233, S.D. 61, some nearly symmetrical, others, retouched, with one curved and one straight edge. One, not more than 3 cm. long, is twisted. Five from Naḳāda, t. 294, S.D. 47-50, were struck from the same nucleus, and Petrie was able to join two of them together again. They are nearly 8 cm. long and somewhat coarser than most. The important grave, Naḳāda 162, contained 5.[5] They were also found in graves at Abuṣīr el-Meleḳ.[6] The graves in which they occur are too many for all to be mentioned here, but though they go on into dynastic times none can be attributed to Naḳāda I.

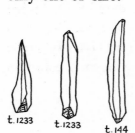

Fig. 14a Small blades. Naḳāda.

t. 1233   t. 1233   t. 144

13. *Borers* (fig. 14b)

These are made of strong blades, one end of which is fashioned into a three-sided borer tip. The long edges of the blades are blunted, and in some the bulb is removed. From Naḳāda, t. 471, loosely dated to S.D. 32-48, comes a fine borer which has its working end where the bulb must have been, the other end being flat. A borer from Nub. t is made on a twisted blade.[7] As so often with the twisted knives, the bulb end of the borer is used as the tip, as the percussion rings clearly

Fig. 14b Borer. Naḳāda t. 1203.

1 Now in the Brooklyn Museum.
2 G. Caton-Thompson, *Kharga Oasis in Prehistory*, p. 178, pl. 120, 4.
3 See above, p. 25.   4 *Gerzeh*, p. 23.
5 See above, p. 17.   6 *Abusir*, p. 1, 42, t. 10 e 2, pl. LIII, t. 56 al, etc., all late Naḳāda II.
7 Now in the Ashmolean Museum, Oxford.

show. The bulb itself has vanished with the making of the three-sided borer. The long sides are carefully blunted, with steep retouching, one from above and one from below. The tool is 15 cm. long and the dorsal rib is removed from the last 3 cm. of the butt end. Another, from Naḳāda, t. 1203, has a butt shaped like a keel-scraper. Borers were found at Armant; they are rare in graves.

14. *Cores*

Cores, unlike those of earlier periods, are primarily for the detaching of blades and not tools in their own right, though some of them have been used finally as scrapers. None has been found which could have produced the long blades used for the manufacture of the large knives. Only one is known to me from a grave, Naḳāda, t. 461, which has not been given a sequence-date, but is presumably from Naḳāda II, since the "Magic Slate"[1] of double-bird type which comes from the same grave does not occur earlier. The core is about 8 cm. high. Cores were also found at Nub. t and at Armant.

Preh. Eg., p. 39.

CHAPTER III

IVORY, BONE AND OTHER SMALL ANTIQUITIES IN VARIOUS MATERIALS

BONE is perhaps the oldest raw material used by tool-making man. It existed in profusion among the remnants of his meals, and can be worked into some shape by mere rubbing. Bone tools and engravings on bone as well as figurines of bone were found among the remains of palaeolithic civilizations, and bone as a raw material has been used until modern times, when the newly-invented plastics have largely superseded it.

Tools made of splinters of bone or the long bones of animals, all of the simplest forms, were found in Badārian graves, and also among the material from the settlements at Ḥammāmīya, where they were excavated from all strata.[1] If we had more excavations in settlements, this list could probably be extended to far into the historical periods. These little tools have not attracted interest in Egypt, because from Badārian times onwards people in Egypt produced much more sophisticated objects, and not only in bone but in a much more beautiful material, namely, ivory.

It seems that all the Badārian ivories were of elephant ivory, for Brunton does not mention anything else. During the later predynastic periods the tusks of hippopotami were also used. As very few of the objects have been studied by experts, the identification of the material must often remain uncertain, and objects of both kinds of ivory as well as of bone are here treated together, as I unfortunately do not possess the necessary knowledge to make identifications myself and only in very rare cases was I able to avail myself of the help of an expert.

As well as using the simplest form of bone points, the Badārian civilization produced needles of bone or ivory which are provided with eyes. Some of them are curved like modern carpet-needles, others are straight, and are evidently the forerunners of the copper sewing-needles which were used during later predynastic periods.[2] Some of the needles show some decoration. One from Mustagidda, t. 1259, has slight lines engraved on its shaft, two of which cross each other above the eye. Another from Mustagidda, t. 1215, thicker but not quite so long as the first, has its head carved in the shape of six discs of diminishing sizes superimposed on each other.[3] This carved part takes up nearly a quarter of the length of the needle, and, in consequence, the eye is fitted low down on the shaft. The little tool calls to mind some of the much later metal toggle-pins rather than anything known from the early periods.

It is from Naḳāda I onwards that, as Petrie says,[4] we find the long and elegantly-decorated pins which he calls hairpins because he once found them stuck through the well-preserved hair on a skeleton. He states that the plain ivory pins were in use from S.D. 31-72. These graceful pins, 15 to 20 cm. long, are generally found in pairs or multiples of pairs and might well be knitting-needles. I know of no occurrence earlier than Naḳāda II, nor does Petrie give an example from Naḳāda I. The most common type of needles have their tops decorated with the figure of

---

[1] *Bad. Civ.*, pl. XX, t. 5739; pl. LXX, 29. See also *Cem. Arm.*, pl. XLVI, 1209B.
[2] See chapter on Metal, p. 18.　　　　　　　　　　　　　　　　[3] *Mostag.*, pl. XXIII, 6.
[4] *Preh. Eg.*, p. 51.

a small bird which, though it commonly occurs as decoration during the predynastic periods, yet cannot be identified. Petrie allows a duration from S.D. 31-70 for the bird-headed pins. The earliest example he quotes is from Naḳāda, t. 1774, which he assigns to S.D. 31. In the list of sequence-dated graves from Naḳāda,[1] t. 1774 is not mentioned. All I could trace from it are the pin in question,[2] which has lost its tip, another much more elaborate pin with the ears and horns of the fertility-goddess forming its head,[3] a rhombic slate palette (type 90D) with one end broken,[4] an oblong pendant of agate, a mamilla shell, and a small figurine of a bird of "green glaze on a sand core".[5] No pottery could be traced, so that the date is somewhat doubtful. While the little bird statuette seems to be fairly naturalistic, the one on top of the pin is what Petrie calls a "simplified bird". It looks rather like a hook. A similar pin comes from Naḳāda, t. 1658, S.D. 33. A roughly rhomboidal slate palette and a black-topped pot are also known from the same grave.[6] A somewhat unusual pin was found in t. H 45 at El-Maḥāsna.[7] From its round shaft a head grows roughly in the shape of an elongated triangle. Out of its curved base sticks what might be the head of a snake. The illustration is too bad to see whether this is broken, and I have not handled the original. T. H 45 is a rich grave with several more ivory objects. Among its pottery is a white-cross-lined bowl. Ayrton and Loat date the grave to before S.D. 41, Petrie to S.D. 33-37.

One of the most interesting pins was excavated by Brunton in t. 1854 at Mustagidda.[8] It shows the upper part of a human figure with arms raised. Small holes over the flat body probably indicate necklaces. Brunton calls the pin "Amratian" (Naḳāda I), and dates it to S.D. 37-45. It is not quite clear how he arrives at this conclusion, for t. 1854 did not contain pottery on which sequence-dates are based. A fine double-edged knife with rounded tip and a syenite disc-shaped mace-head together with the pin made up its furniture. It can hardly be earlier than the time of transition from Naḳāda I to II. To the same time will have to be ascribed the first pins which have naturalistically-shaped birds as tops. In Badāri, t. 1670, two bird-headed pins were recovered, and a third with a head in the shape of a gazelle, also the earliest of its kind. The date is again not secure, as this grave also had no pottery in it. A cup made of an ostrich egg and the three pins were all its furniture.[9] More naturalistically shaped bird pins are known from Naḳāda II, though they remain rare. One, with the pin broken off, comes from Naḳāda, t. 723, in which the ring of gold wire was also found. The pin typical of Naḳāda II is the plain one,[10] while the "simplified bird" remains in fashion. This suggests to me that the "simplified bird" was originally a hook which had some utilitarian purpose. The faint resemblance to a bird may have occurred to the predynastic carver, and may have induced him in a few cases to replace it by a real bird. That it was not a stylistic peculiarity or a lack of skill is shown by the occurrence of two pins, one with a "simplified", the other with a naturalistic, bird head in one and the same grave, Naḳāda, t. 350, which is undated.[11] This grave also contained a quantity of beads, mostly

---

[1] *Preh. Eg.*, pl. LI.
[2] Now at University College, London.
[3] Now in the Ashmolean Museum, Oxford.
[4] Now in the Chicago Natural History Museum.
[5] The first two at University College, London, the bird not traced.
[6] The pin and the palette at University College, London, the pot in Berlin.
[7] *Pre-dyn. Cem. at El Mahasna*, pl. XIII, 4.
[8] *Mostag.*, pl. XLII, 59. Now in the British Museum.
[9] *Bad. Civ.*, pls. XXXIV, 4; LIII, 20, 32.
[10] *Naq. Bal.*, pl. LXII, 36. In Naḳāda, t. 1212, four plain ivory pins were found.
[11] Both in the Ashmolean Museum, Oxford; the rest of the furniture at University College, London.

of clay, and the shapeless fragment of a slate palette; a bifacial flint axe, its cutting edge broken, was in the filling.[1]   A pin with a head in the form of a little falcon from Naḳāda, t. 74,[2] is probably early dynastic.

The pins which are provided with scratch combs are also very rare.   Petrie found three at Naḳāda and one at Diospolis Parva.   Of the three from Naḳāda, the one which Petrie puts earliest, at S.D. 39, from t. 289, may not even have been the top of a pin.   The comb has rounded shoulders and shows a break in the middle of its top.   This may indicate a now missing pin or a handle, for combs with handles occur.[3]   T. 289 also contained a potsherd with a mark, and a pot, F 81c.[4] The pin-comb from Naḳāda, t. 147, S.D. 60-61, has a long pin attached to it.   Its tip is broken, as are all of its teeth, of which there seem to have been many.[5]   The comb is square-shouldered, as are the other two which Petrie mentions.   The piece from Diospolis Parva, t. B 378, S.D. 52, is dated.   One little comb from Naḳāda, t. 1614, S.D. 33, may perhaps belong to the pin-combs. A small broken piece remains of its top, which may have had either a pin or a handle.   It differs from all the others so far mentioned in that it has three comparatively long teeth.   No other object from the grave is known to me.   A single object, and of doubtful purpose at that, seems too little evidence on which to contradict Petrie's assumption that pin-combs belong to Naḳāda II only.

It is not very safe to follow Petrie's ascription of the pins decorated with incised criss-cross lines to a period as early as Naḳāda I.   His view is based on a single object, namely, the piece with the ears and horns of the fertility-goddess already mentioned from Naḳāda, t. 1774, and the date of that grave is not secure.   All the other incised patterns at present known, be they parallel circles or spirals around the shafts, are of Naḳāda II.

The result of this short survey of pins does not agree with the more commonly held views about them.   Decoration of their heads with quadrupeds is not characteristic of the pins of Naḳāda I,[6] for the only dated one—that with a gazelle—is from the time of transition to Naḳāda II. Nor do the more naturalistically shaped bird-headed pins belong to the earlier period.   With this Petrie's favourite theory of the deterioration of style from the more naturalistic and careful work of Naḳāda I to the schematic and coarse work of Naḳāda II is once more shown to be erroneous. If we can speak of a development at all, it seems possible that what began as a hook for some utilitarian purpose during Naḳāda I was sometimes fancifully changed into a bird which the silhouette of the hook may have vaguely suggested to the artists of Naḳāda II.   The hooklike top survived into Naḳāda II.[7]

More care and love was spent on the making of the flat hairpins than on any of the round ones.   Some of them are most attractive specimens of applied art.   The bird-headed variety is the favourite, but how different is the little creature on the flat pin of Naḳāda, t. 1503, S.D. 36,

[1] At University College, London.

[2] The pin and the unusual pot D 70 in the Ashmolean Museum, Oxford, a retouched flint blade at University College, London.   No S.D.

[3] *Preh. Eg.*, pl. XXX, 1.

[4] The comb and the sherd with mark, *Naq. Bal.*, pl. LVI, 504, at University College, London; the fancy pot in the Ashmolean Museum, Oxford.

[5] The pin-comb, 2 flint blades, a squat stone vase, a spatha shell at University College, London; a comb and slate palette in the Ashmolean Museum, Oxford; a wavy-handled pot in the Oriental Institute, Chicago; a bowl, P 22B, in the Museum of Fine Arts, Boston.

[6] J. Vandier, *Manuel d'archéologie égyptienne*, p. 388.

[7] E.g. Naḳāda, t. 867, S.D. 49-66; t. 1216, S.D. 52-69.

from the hooklike birds of Naḳāda I round pins. It is shown in the moment of alighting with its wings lifted.[1] Though severely stylized and without any details, it conveys a lively idea of the movement which it represents. The pin, which is 15 cm. long, is further decorated with two pairs of knobs along its stem. Quite another bird adorns the flat pin of t. H 29 of El-Maḥāsna.[2] The excavators call it an ostrich, with its triangular head, rounded body and long legs. This pin is short and thick in contrast to the long and elegant one from Naḳāda, t. 1503, and was found together with the fragment of another one at some distance from the skeleton. The fine piece with the serpent head has already been mentioned in Vol. I (Naḳāda, t. 1654, S.D. 34).[3] It may be mere chance that none of the flat pins with the ears and horns of the fertility-goddess are known from Naḳāda I and that all we have are of Naḳāda II. One fragment with the head on a notched stem, from Naḳāda, t. 1578, is vaguely dated to S.D. 31-56. The only other things I know from this grave are a plain comb,[4] a type which begins in Naḳāda I and carries on into Naḳāda II, and a pebble. Naḳāda, t. 293, S.D. 61-72, has a well-preserved flat pin with the horns on top and pairs of knobs underneath, the top pair of which may represent the ears. The grave also contained a copper pin, a comb, decorated with a sort of fringe at its top not unlike the one on a slate palette found at Badāri,[5] and three black-topped sherds with pot-marks. This grave belongs to the time of transition from Naḳāda II to protodynastic times. While two of the round pins were actually found in the hair of the bodies to which they once belonged, and some at least near their heads, it is different with the flat pins. Brunton, therefore, is somewhat doubtful whether they can have been hairpins at all, and not rather "amulets or fetishes of some kind".[6] The pin from Mustagidda, t. 1832, which aroused these suspicions, is in a special class. It is in the shape of a woman, very stylized, without arms and ending in a peg, and resembles the pot-bearers from Naḳāda, t. 271.[7] Four of these in a row were placed upright along the east side of the grave. They were certainly not pins of any sort, but women bearing offerings, and their peg-like ends served to keep them standing in the sand. I am inclined to take the woman from Mustagidda, t. 1832, for a similar object, even though she lacks the pot on her head. Her thickness alone should make her unsuitable as a pin to fasten in the hair. Whether the other much thinner and lighter objects, with which we have been dealing, were or were not hairpins will be difficult to prove. Their shape seems to indicate that they were meant to be stuck into something, and the hair seems the most likely place. This does not exclude the possibility that they also had some amuletic value.

Though none of the rare Badārian combs were found in the hair or even near the head, they are believed to be hair ornaments. The large piece from Badāri, t. 5130, was found in a disturbed grave. Its rounded top has two corresponding protuberances at the outside which remind Brunton of birds' heads. It had many short teeth, nine of which, though loose, are preserved. A very charming figurine of an ibex, which may once have been the decoration of an ivory spoon handle, found in the same grave, shows how well the Badārian artist was able to

---

[1] Tomb 1503 also contained another flat pin, its head broken, the fragment of a copper pin, 3 hair combs, about 17 bracelets in ivory and tortoiseshell, a large number of beads, the claws of a lion (?), the pots F and F 17a. They are in University College, London, the Ashmolean Museum, Oxford, and the Berlin Museum.

[2] *Naq. Bal.*, pl. LXIII, 61.   [3] Vol. I, pl. IX, 1.

[4] In the Ashmolean Museum, Oxford.

[5] *Bad. Civ.*, pl. LII, 11; see also chapter on Palettes, p. 83.

[6] *Mostag.*, p. 87.   [7] Vol. I, p. 35.

represent the characteristic features of animals in a simple and abbreviated way, if he so desired. I therefore think it unlikely that the projections on the top of the comb were meant to be birds. A smaller comb, also with rounded shoulders, was found in Mustagidda, t. 428. Its short head is crowned by the figure of a long-necked bird, possibly a goose. The comb has six long teeth, wide apart. It comes from an undisturbed grave, and had been deposited at the feet of the skeleton, underneath the covering mat. The two bone combs from Badari, t. 5390, are of a totally different type. They have plain, triangular tops and a large number of very small teeth. T. 5390 also was undisturbed, the combs and two ivory vases being recovered from near the hands of the skeleton. Brunton thinks they may have been used to produce the ripple pattern of the Badārian pottery. They may just as well have been scratch combs.

Plain hair combs with square shoulders are known to us first from the period of Naḳāda I. Our material recovered from Badārian times is too scanty to state with certainty whether this is a change in fashion—from the round-shouldered to the square-shouldered—or an accident of preservation. Combs of all types seem to have become more necessary to the predynastic Egyptians, for their increase in number after the Badārian period is greater than would be warranted by the mere increase in the number of the known and excavated Naḳāda I graves. At the same time the decoration on their tops become more diversified, though birds remain in favour. A rather clumsy comb with bird top comes from Naḳāda, t. 1505, S.D. 31.[1] While with most of the combs the decorating feature is separated clearly from the comb itself, here the body of the bird is merged with that part of the comb from which the teeth project. There are five of them. The front of this "body" is straight, and from it a strong neck curves back with a head that must have been very small, even when it was still complete. On the opposite side the body curves out beyond the teeth to give it a resemblance to that of a swimming bird. The comb was found together with fragments of a flat ivory hairpin, and sherds of a white-cross-lined pot.[2] A comb which in some respects resembles the one from Naḳāda, t. 1505, was found by Brunton in Mustagidda, t. 1867, which he dates to Naḳāda I (Amratian). The comb is rather badly preserved, and shows the more orthodox division into ornamented top, plain middle piece and teeth. The bird on top is of the same clumsy type as that from Naḳāda, with the straight front and bulging back. The strong neck is also sharply curved back, but where one would expect the head, the piece from Mustagidda has, surprisingly enough, a little wing. After this the neck, which has become much more slender, turns upwards and ends in a head which looks towards the back of its own body. From the same grave at Mustagidda two more combs were recovered; one has the ears and horns of the cow-goddess, the other, very damaged, has lost its top.

The combs with quadrupeds as their decoration are generally considered to be the most characteristic of Naḳāda I, though they are hardly more common than those with which we have dealt so far. Some very attractive pieces belong to this category. A slender and elegant giraffe forms the top of a comb from Naḳāda, t. 1497, S.D. 33 (pl. III, 10). With the minimum of detail the artist who created it understood how to produce a finished and even sophisticated representation. The comb to which it belongs is square-shouldered. It has lost all its teeth.[3] An equally successful little work of art is the gazelle which crowns a comb from Naḳāda, t. 1687,

[1] Now at University College, London.
[2] The comb and the pin at University College, London; the sherds of the pot in the Oriental Institute, Chicago.
[3] Now in the Ashmolean Museum, Oxford.

S.D. 35 (pl. III, 9). Again with the simplest of means the artist has produced a characteristic image, and, especially, the alertness of the little animal, while, at the same time, making it an integral part of the comb into which its feet merge. The comb, which has barely marked shoulders, once was provided with five long teeth.[1]

If the animal which is perched on one corner of a comb from Naḳāda, t. 1562, S.D. 35, is a hartebeest, as its horns suggest, then it is rather an unusual one, for neither its head nor its feet are marked. It seems to overbalance the comb towards one side and to draw its surfaces out of the vertical.[2] The plain piece between the animal and the teeth of the comb is longer than its seven teeth. Of similar proportions is a comb from Mustagidda, t. 1880. It has the long, plain middle piece, and the comparatively short teeth. The ibex which is carved at its top is a much more successful attempt at portraiture than the hartebeest from the Naḳāda comb. It also is set to one side, its hind legs continuing the straight edge of the comb, and its front legs set at just about the middle of the base. The comb, which is of wood, is dated by Brunton to Naḳāda I.[3]

The little "Seth" animal from El-Maḥāsna, t. H 29, seems to have belonged to a comb of similar type, for it probably formed the head of a fragmentary comb from the same grave on which small remains of front and back legs, also set to one side, are still left. The comb has the long, plain middle piece; its teeth are too broken to assess their original lengths.[4]

An interesting addition to our knowledge of combs was made recently by Miss Kantor of Chicago. She published two white-cross-lined bowls painted with what can only be animal-topped combs. On one, now at Princeton, she sees Seth animals, each one standing on a line from which a number of teeth descend. The animals have slender cross-lined bodies with big heads filled in with white. The heads have small beaks and enormous ears. It is not clear from the reproductions whether they have tails.[5] These are not realistically-drawn combs, for they lack the plain middle pieces which would give them stability, and to which in the real objects the teeth would be attached. Each of these curious comb creatures is attacked by a dog, which adds to the unreality of the scene, and makes one think of a fairy tale. The two groups are separated from each other by a vertical row composed of pairs of short, parallel strokes and large triangles hanging from the lip of the vessel, their points towards the bottom. The way in which the dogs are painted reminds Miss Kantor of the style used in the decorated pottery of Naḳāda II, and, in consequence, she dates the bowls to the time of transition from Naḳāda I to Naḳāda II. Brunton has already suggested that the white-cross-lined pottery continued into Naḳāda II.[6] This is another indication of how gradually these periods merge into each other, and how difficult, if not impossible, it is to discriminate between the end of Naḳāda I, the time of transition, and the beginning of Naḳāda II.

The other bowl published by Miss Kantor is from the Boston Fine Arts Museum. The comb

[1] Now in the Ashmolean Museum, Oxford.

[2] Now in the Ashmolean Museum, Oxford. Tomb 1562 also contained the palette in the form of a sheep, see Chapter IV, p. 84.

[3] *Mostag.*, pl. XLII, 46.

[4] *Pre-dyn. Cem. at El-Mahasna*, pls. XI and XII. My Vol. I, p. 34

[5] H. Kantor, *Prehistoric Egyptian Pottery in the Art Museum. Record of the Art Museum, Princeton University*, XII (1953), 2.

[6] *Bad. Civ.*, pl. XXXVIII. Bowl C 3828 is dated S.D. 44, which is well inside Naḳāda II; others have dates which also extend into that period.

animals, again in juxtaposition on the inside of the vessel, are by themselves, enclosed between two sets of pairs of short strokes. As on the Princeton vase, so here the two combs are separated by cross-hatched hanging triangles. The animals on the Boston piece are ibexes characterized by their long and curved horns. Their bodies merge into the plain middle parts of the combs, which, compared with the long teeth, are short. Combs with combined animal tops and plain middle pieces are known in ivory from Naḳāda I and II. Nearest in style to those on the vase is a comb from Naḳāda, t. 260, S.D. 40-43, with a top formed like a long-necked bird, perhaps an ostrich (pl. III, 7). Its body is in one with the middle piece, which once was provided with nine short but strong teeth.[1] The resemblance of the comb from Naḳāda, t. 260, to those represented on the bowl in Boston confirms the rather late date of the vessel.

Naḳāda II carries on the excellent tradition in ivory combs which started with the Badārian period, and some of the finest pieces belong to it. To the motifs of decoration known from earlier periods are added some fresh ones. All this goes far to show that it was not a period of decadence, but was one of the liveliest and most inventive in the long history of Egyptian civilization. A quadruped, its head broken off, formed the head of a comb from Naḳāda, t. 1649, S.D. 38. It may have been a hippopotamus with its stout body and short legs. Like the quadrupeds on the earlier pieces it is set to one side of the comb, which has a very long, plain middle piece. Not one of the teeth is preserved to its full length. From the same grave came a fish-hook of shell, and a black-topped pot (B 76a) of rather advanced shape.[2] Most of the other animal-topped combs from Naḳāda II prefer the decoration in the middle rather than towards one side of the tops, and this may indicate a change in fashion. A very elegant and well-preserved hartebeest is mounted on the centre of a comb from Naḳāda, t. 1586, vaguely dated to S.D. 33-46 by Petrie (pl. III, 6).[3] The grave also contained a polished-red pot with knob handles and a necklace of three incised rows of dots around the mouth, a decoration which does not occur during Naḳāda I. A second comb, also from t. 1586, was topped by the double bird with a tall middle piece or handle between the heads. This motif is more common in slate, where it can be dated. It is doubtful whether even its simpler forms, where more of the bodies is left, ever occur during Naḳāda I. The exaggerated shape, with the body having dwindled away and the two birds seem to be joined by their necks, while the centre piece has grown so as to become the main feature of the composition—we are clearly in Naḳāda II. Both combs are well and carefully made little masterpieces. The one with the hartebeest in the middle of the top has sloping shoulders which gives the illusion of the animal standing on a hill. Its plain middle piece is long and narrow, and the five prongs, of which only the top of one is broken, are strong and not too short. The comb with the double-bird top has a small knob between it and the wide and long middle piece, which has square shoulders. The top is centred, the seven strong teeth are perfect.

The decoration of the comb from El-Maḥāsna, t. H 41, was most likely a giraffe. The long and slender legs stand at equal distances from the edges, and support a small body. Part of the neck and the head are missing. T. H 41 belonged to a woman, and was a rich interment. It is dated to "before S.D. 56".[4]

---

[1] Now in the Ashmolean Museum, Oxford.
[2] The comb at University College, London, the rest in the Ashmolean Museum, Oxford.
[3] Now in the Ashmolean Museum, Oxford.
[4] *Pre-dyn. Cem. at El-Mahasna*, pl. XVII, 2.

Some of the best bird-topped combs were preserved to us from Naḳāda II. Three excellent examples were found at Naḳāda itself. The one which Petrie dates earliest is from Naḳāda, t. 1465, S.D. 38. It bears a duck, its slender legs touching the centre of the comb's middle piece, forming only a very thin link between them. It is this, perhaps, which makes the bird look more naturalistic than any with which we have had to deal so far. The comb is straight-shouldered, its plain middle piece somewhat shorter than its eight strong and well-preserved teeth.[1] As in so many instances, this grave contained more than one comb. The other has a plain square top; most of its teeth are missing.[2]

Of a totally different type is the comb from Naḳāda, t. 1419, S.D. 44. While in all the other combs the figure on top is subordinated to the main working part of the comb, and is much smaller than even its plain middle part, in the comb from t. 1419 the bird is the dominating feature. It is larger than the middle piece and its teeth taken together. The comb resembles in its proportions the small plain ones which are first met with during Naḳāda I. The bird, perhaps a goose, with its long, gracefully-curved neck and small head, stands in the centre of the plain middle. Its body is sharply divided from its legs, which are one with the sloping shoulder of the comb, the other shoulder being square. Grave 1419 also once possessed two combs,[3] but I could not trace the second. The comb from Naḳāda, t. 1411, is of a similar pattern (pl. III, 7). The bird which crowns it seems even larger in proportion to the rest of the object than that on the comb from t. 1419, because the teeth are missing. There were once many and as they were very narrow we are reminded of the short teeth of the scratch combs so that, in our mind, we restore the comb with these minute teeth. The plain middle piece is wider than its height, and on the middle of its upper edge crouches the large bird, perhaps an ostrich, its wings lifted as if starting to run. The body merges into the top of the comb and there are no legs. The whole, though very summarily rendered, conveys a vivid impression of movement. Two more combs were found in t. 1411. One is a plain one, rather narrow and high with all but one tooth missing. But the third is of more than usual interest, for it has as its decoration a double-faced human head, and, engraved on the middle part, commonly left plain, three concentric rows of necklaces.[4] It once had eight teeth. Through the extension of the decoration to the middle part of the comb this is given the function of the body of the person, and makes it comparable to one of those block figures which are an invention of Naḳāda II. The two faces have the same semicircular skull and triangular lower face which have earned these figurines the name of bearded men, though they are as often women as men.[5] Possibly because the figure on the comb is more carefully worked out than most of this type, and perhaps also on account of the necklaces, it gives me the impression of a woman, or at least one of its two faces does. The circular eyeholes must once have held some inlay, and the sickle-shaped eyebrows also. Two small ears serve for both faces, but neither mouths nor noses are indicated. The chins seem somewhat more rounded than is usual with this type of figure and just touch the body, giving the illusion of a neck. I know of

[1] The comb and a fancy pot, F 27, in the Ashmolean Museum, Oxford.
[2] The plain comb, a black-topped sherd with mark, some beads, pieces of wood, perhaps from a throwing-stick, at University College, London.
[3] See *Naq. Bal.*, p. 28. The bird comb is at University College, London.
[4] *Naq. Bal.*, p. 28. The bird comb and a polished-red pot, P 36a, in the Ashmolean Museum, Oxford; the other combs, the fragments of a horn vase, armlets and miniature pots at University College, London.
[5] Cf. Vol. I, p. 34.

no other bifacial figure found in an excavation, and the meaning of this one remains obscure. A rather similar object, but much coarser and with one face only, was found in Naḳāda, t. 1561, which has no sequence-date. Whether this too was a comb also is not certain; for the plain piece, which is decorated with necklaces, is broken at the bottom so that no trace of the teeth remains.[1] Another object, with one face, but certainly a comb, comes from Naḳāda, t. 268. It is a much more sophisticated piece than the other two. Though superficially it seems little at variance with the others, yet the artist has tried somehow to humanize the stiff block figure. The head has come down on to the plain middle piece and the pointed chin has become a long, pointed beard. The curve of the skull has been made to resemble a human skull, the eyes are incised, and so are the nose and mouth. Lastly, the plain middle piece narrows towards the bottom, giving it somewhat the appearance of a waist. Petrie dates t. 268 to S.D. 50; but I wonder whether it may not be early dynastic. The grave contained the polished-red pot P 87a, which has a long life; two fancy pots, one in the shape of a goose, F 69a, the other belonging to those curious tall vases with wavy outlines ; and a small alabaster tag pierced at the top.[2] The publication of *Naqada and Ballas* mentions a slate elephant, an alabaster vase found in front of the knees containing the human-headed comb, and a disc-shaped mace-head, but what has happened to them I do not know.

Along with these elaborately-decorated combs simpler ones were also in use. There is the plain comb with square top, mostly of modest dimensions, oblong and with seven or eight strong teeth. In at least one case even the curved top of Badārian times turns up again; which shows how difficult it is in ancient Egypt to date a tool otherwise than *post quem*, and how tenaciously forms once acquired were preserved. The round-topped comb was found in Naḳāda, t. 1858, S.D. 40. Some combs have flat knobs as decoration, either one in the centre or several next to each other. This design, as Petrie has already pointed out,[3] resembles the decoration of some slate palettes, and he concludes that it looks "like a magic or amuletic design". The motif of the ears and horns of the fertility-goddess lent itself to countless variations, some so fanciful that their origin is much obscured. The development is much the same as with the similar motif on the slate palettes. There it seemed likely that what originally were horns were turned eventually into birds looking in different directions.[4] Some combs with heads in the form of the sign of the cow-goddess from graves of Naḳāda I carry horns of such exaggerated type that they look more like birds than any headgear a cow could be supposed to boast. A comb from Naḳāda, t. 1503, for example, is fitted with ears and two such heavy horns, and there is a similar one from the same grave which has no ears, but long, straight horns which have sprouted small birds at their tops (one of which is now missing).[5] Perhaps in order to counteract this ambiguity between horns and birds some combs, and slate palettes also, instead of representing the cow-goddess with the large and double-curved horns, such as she has on the fine vase from Naḳāda,[6] replace them by a pair of simple, inward curved horns, which even a lively imagination cannot mistake

---

[1] Now in the Ashmolean Museum, Oxford. A rough potsherd with a mark is at University College, London.

[2] The stone tag is at University College, London, the rest of the traceable objects in the Ashmolean Museum, Oxford.

[3] *Preh. Eg.*, p. 29.

[4] See below, p. 86.

[5] Both combs and a large plain one are at University College, London. The grave also contained the flat pin with bird top, see above, p. 46.

[6] Cf. Vol. I, pl. III.

for birds. No representation of this simpler form is known to me which can be attributed with certainty to Naḳāda I. A good example of it was found in Naḳāda, t. 1417,[1] a grave which Petrie ascribes to S.D. 35-41. As it contained three flint blades, one of them twisted, it must be near to S.D. 41 and be of Naḳāda II date. The inward-turned horns also do not escape transformation. Sometimes they meet forming a ring in which a notch at the top shows that originally there were two separate horns. In Naḳāda, t. 1852, S.D. 50, a comb with such a decoration was found which also seems to have two pairs of ears. This multiplying of the ears and treating them as if they were ornaments will be met again on the slate palettes decorated with the symbol of the cow-goddess.[2] On the comb from t. 1852 the decoration looks rather as if it were meant as a handle. It sprouts from a middle piece which is wider than it is high, and once had eight strong teeth.[3] Whether the ring motif on a comb from Naḳāda, t. 260, goes back also to the horns seems difficult to decide. If it does, then the ears have travelled to the top of the horns, and between them grows a notched rod.[4]

Both forms of horns remained associated with the cow-goddess for a long time. Her horns on the Nar-Mer palette have the simple, inward-curved shape. On the triads from the temple of Mycerinus's pyramid, perhaps the loveliest images ever made of her, she is crowned with the old impressive double-curved horns.

In spite of the elaborate decorations of some of the combs, it seems to me unlikely that they were meant to be worn in the hair. Most of them are rather top-heavy, the ornamented tops together with the plain middle pieces can be three to four times as long as the teeth and that would give them a rather unstable grip on the hair, so that they would easily fall out. Whenever the position of the combs within the graves was observed, they were not in the hair, or near the head, but near the knees or even the feet of the skeleton. What we know of the hair fashions at the time comes from the figurines found in the graves. In t. 1546 from Naḳāda, S.D. 37, two wigs were preserved which show an elaborate arrangement of curls.[5] The combs just described seem well suited to arrange and keep tidy curls like these.

Another type of comb is the scratch comb, which perhaps we have met already in the Badārian period, and also as the top of some of the hairpins.[6] It is usually plain and small, and is fitted with a row of very small teeth. In some cases they are double combs having teeth on both sides, mostly different in length. Those dated belong to Naḳāda II. In *Naqada and Ballas* [7] Petrie illustrated two different types. Of one of these, with trapezoidal top and comparatively well-developed teeth, he adduces three examples from three different graves: Naḳāda, tt. 149, 1251, S.D. 40 and 1502. It is the last one which the drawing in *Naqada and Ballas* represents, and the only piece known to me from t. 1502. It is difficult to decide whether the only dated comb, from Naḳāda, t. 1251, which I can trace, is the one mentioned in the publication. It is a scratch comb with parallel sides, the short teeth all broken. The top, which is damaged, was rounded. As I can

    1 For the comb with the horns cf. *Die Altertümer*, pp. 140-1, 270. A bird-topped comb, the flints and a piece of wood at University College, London; a limestone painted disc in the Ashmolean Museum, Oxford.

    2 See below, p. 83.

    3 The comb, a decorated pot, D 43a, and possibly a bowl, B 1b, in the Ashmolean Museum, Oxford.

    4 At University College, London, from the same grave as the comb with the ostrich mentioned on p. 50.

    5 Now at University College, London.

    6 See above, p. 46; 48.

    7 *Naq. Bal.*, pl. LXIII, 52 and 54.

trace no other comb from t. 1251, I think it will be the one mentioned. Petrie does not mention it in his *Prehistoric Egypt*, though it belongs to the collection of University College, London. The comb from the third grave, Naḳāda, t. 149, is rectangular and has lost nearly all its teeth, which were thin and may not have been very long. Again it is the only comb known to me from the grave, and is now at University College, London. The three interesting amulets [1] which t. 149 contained and the brick-red polished pot, P 11M, make it fairly certain that it is of Naḳāda II date.

The other type of scratch comb which Petrie discerns is more frequent. It is the one I have called double, because it has teeth on opposite sides. The only decoration which some of these combs boast is a small incision on each side nearer the end with the shorter teeth.

Another little instrument will have to be mentioned here because Petrie counts it among the combs, a definition which I find difficult to accept. They are narrow strips of ivory or bone, much wider than they are high, sometimes the dimensions are 1 by 5. They have a notch each side just beneath the straight top, with a suspension hole in the middle between them. The bottom, often separated from the body by a straight line parallel to the top, is provided with a row of shallow incisions which in some cases are filled in with black. One, from Badāri,[2] is stained red. Petrie sees in these tools decayed hair combs "passing out of real use—".[3] For this I see no evidence. Combs, once invented, never passed out of real use, nor can I see any resemblance between them and Egyptian combs. Brunton calls them "amuletic",[4] but an amulet of a comb which does not resemble the real thing does not seem to me to be probable. The hole under the top certainly suggests that they could be tied to a string and worn, but if they were amulets they certainly were not comb-amulets, and it seems much more likely that they had some other use. The pieces in *Prehistoric Egypt* made of stone with a few large notches or a smooth bottom are without known provenance.[5] Brunton also comes to the conclusion that "it is quite uncertain what these amuletic 'combs' represent".[6] He dates them to S.D. 38 or a little later, which in itself contradicts Petrie's explanation that they are the last degradation of the combs. Brunton then points out that where the skeletons of their owners could be sexed they were female, and that in seven graves, i.e. whenever the whole contents of the graves were known, they were found together with a pair of amuletic bird palettes.

The large and sometimes elaborately decorated ivory spoons give a notion of what the Badārian ivory-worker could do. Some spoons have round, others deep rectangular bowls. One from Badāri, t. 5719, has a rectangular bowl nearly 8 cm. long,[7] more than 3 cm. deep, and about 4 cm. wide. Its strong, rounded handle has three grooves round the middle as the only decoration. Another from t. 5745, with a bowl somewhat shorter and wider, has a handle which carries on its top the stylized figure of a gazelle. A much more elaborate top of a handle from t. 5130 has lost its bowl. It is in the shape of an ibex with long horns. It stands on a small base, the opening between the legs forming a circle by which the spoon could be suspended. The most usual form of decoration is a shape rather like an anchor, with two prongs coming down from

---

[1] The comb and the pots at University College, London; the amulets, all of the cow-goddess, in the Ashmolean Museum, Oxford.

[2] *Bad. Civ.*, pl. LIII, 11.

[4] *Bad. Civ.*, pp. 58, 124.

[6] *Matmar*, p. 20.

[3] *Preh. Eg.*, p. 30.

[5] *Preh. Eg.*, pl. XXX, 15-17.

[7] *Bad. Civ.*, pls. XXII, 1, and XXVII, 6.

the top of the spoons, which end in ornaments somewhat resembling heads. Brunton thinks that these spoons may be "porridge dippers". He rejects the idea that they were for the toilet, as were those from dynastic ages,[1] and explains the remnants of malachite found in one from Mustagidda, t. 428, as the result of *secondary* use, because the spoon handle was broken. To me they seem singularly inconvenient for eating.

Besides these large spoons the Badārians also knew small ones, perhaps for dispensing salt or some powder. A tiny spoon [2] was found in Mustagidda, t. 2840. Its bowl is circular, and the end of its handle is ribbed. This, at least, Brunton thinks, must count among the toilet objects.

It may be mere chance that no spoons are known from Naḳāda I, and that they do not appear again before the middle of Naḳāda II. This was so when Petrie wrote *Prehistoric Egypt*, nor has the situation changed since his time. He wrote before the Badārian was known, and maintains that the "earliest fixed date" [3] for spoons is S.D. 46, and that they "increased in use down to the 1st dynasty". He does not say on what evidence he bases this statement, nor does he mention any spoon of that date. An ivory spoon with a deep bowl and a plain handle, its splayed end perforated, was found in Naḳāda, t. 1636, S.D. 33-48. As the grave contained the "decorated" pot, type D 16A, it will be of Naḳāda II, and may be near the date which Petrie suggests as the "earliest fixed". The width of this spoon is about 2 cm. Somewhat larger is the flat bowl (width *c.* 2·75 cm.) of a spoon from Naḳāda, t. 1848, S.D. 54. Its cylindrical handle ends in a triangular, perforated top. Side by side with these larger pieces, the "tiny" spoons were also used. Some of these were made of material more precious than bone or ivory. There is the little silver spoon [4] which was lost, and of which only a tale has come to us, or the one with a bowl made of slate, roughly oval, but with a pronounced point opposite the handle end. The handle itself was composed of a copper wire on to which black and white stone beads were threaded alternately. It was found in Naḳāda, t. 1257, S.D. 42,[5] and is therefore earlier than Petrie's fixed date. The little bone or ivory spoons are generally quite plain, a circular bowl with a thin cylindrical handle often with a splayed and perforated end. Their use for dispensing powder is confirmed by their having been found together with the remarkable horns of which one was recovered at Badāri, the other at Gerzeh. That from Badāri, t. 3804, S.D. 52-59, is of natural horn, its point carved to resemble an animal's head.[6] The contents of the horn were extracted with the little spoon through a slot near the tip of the horn which could be closed by means of a stopper. For the open base of the horn a similar closing device must have existed. A similar horn, but made of pottery, was found at Gerzeh, t. 20, S.D. 58. It still possesses the stopper for the slot.[7] Wainwright points out that such horns, also provided with small spoons, are used by the modern Basuto to carry their snuff, and is inclined to see in these horns snuff horns. Brunton thinks that there is "very strong evidence" that Wainwright's suggestion is the correct one. To me it seems rather unconvincing. A. J. Arkell lately pointed out to me verbally that these horns were most likely used for salt, which I find much more acceptable as an explanation than snuff.

But to return to our spoons. Large and decorative spoons did not return to favour before the beginning of the dynasties. Two are published in *Naqada and Ballas* (pl. III, 3 and 4).[8] The

[1] *Mostag.*, p. 54.
[3] *Preh. Eg.*, p. 31.
[5] See above, Chapter I, p. 7.
[7] *Gerzeh*, p. 23, pl. VII, 13.

[2] *Mostag.*, p. 30, pl. XIII, 17.
[4] *Naq. Bal.*, p. 46.
[6] *Bad. Civ.*, p. 60, pl. XLVIII, 2.
[8] *Naq. Bal.*, p. 46, pl. LXI, 2 and 3.

better preserved of them was found by "a woman digging for salt at Ballas", and does not come from the excavation. It is about 15 cm. long, and consists of a circular bowl, 5 cm. in diameter, part of which is missing. The handle is flat, and on it two animals are carved in the round; there may have been more. One is a dog which has a rope collar fastened by a toggle. Its muzzle touches the rim of the bowl. Behind it and attacking it is a lion. Both animals, which are well preserved, show a high degree of craftsmanship. It is interesting to note that it is the lion which is the aggressor, and that he chases the dog but is not chased himself. This is in keeping with Egyptian ideas about the nature of the lion as one of the incarnations of the king, and that therefore it is not seemly to show it in an undignified situation. The other sculptured spoon was found in a grave at Naḳāda. There is some uncertainty about the number of the grave to which it once belonged, for it is published in *Naqada and Ballas*, pl. LXI, 3, as coming from t. 1460, while on the object itself the mark is clearly 460, and this seems the correct number. T. 1460 is an unimportant grave and not sequence-dated. T. 460 is of S.D. 77, and therefore early dynastic. The spoon has a round bowl with a long and flat handle on which three pairs of animals are carved in the round, walking towards the bowl. The spoon is in rather a bad state of preservation as the ivory has flaked, which makes it difficult to identify the animals. Even when still undamaged the animals must have been less naturalistic, and with less detail, than those from the Ballas spoon. Petrie thinks they are most likely elephants. From whichever grave the spoon may have come, its style dates it to early dynastic times, or to the transition from predynastic to protodynastic times at the earliest. Of about the same date is a simple spoon from Naḳāda, t. 17, S.D. 74.[1] Its bowl is peaked towards the handle, which curves below it. T. 17 is one of the few Naḳāda tombs which were drawn and described in the publication. With its brick lining and shelf and its cylinder-shaped pots, it belongs to the early dynasties. During this period angular bowls for toilet spoons again come into fashion after having been in disfavour since Badārian times, though the shapes are not quite the same. The later ones resemble in form a truncated pyramid. The most elaborate spoon was recovered from Tarkhan, t. 1023, S.D. 78. Its bowl is covered with rows of animals in low relief, and a deer is perched on the handle near the bowl. There may have been more, but the handle is broken at that point and the remainder lost. The small spoons also receive their decoration at this time, for though the piece from Ballas, t. 224, which has a falcon perched on its top, is undated, it yet belongs to the same period.

The history of the spoons, broken by such a long lacuna from the end of Badārian to the middle of Naḳāda II, is particularly unsatisfactory. Even though one may have to reckon with more changes of fashion in toilet objects than with common household utensils, yet it seems odd that no spoons should have been used during that period. Our knowledge of Naḳāda I is very scanty, and being so closely linked with the following period of Naḳāda II, which takes over many of its material possessions, it becomes more and more difficult to disentangle it from the later culture. The problem has become still more complex since we know that even the white-cross-lined pottery overlaps into Naḳāda II. It seems therefore quite possible that spoons from undated graves belong to the "lacuna". On the other hand, large spoons were not the only receptacle in which the green paint was mixed. Throughout all periods from the Badārian onwards

---

[1] *Naq. Bal.*, p. 20, pl. LXXXII. Petrie mentions the spoon in *Preh. Eg.*, p. 32. By mistake, however, he quotes the S.D. wrongly. Instead of 74 (*Preh. Eg.*, pl. LI) he writes 47 without noticing the error, for he says that the spoon is the earliest here dated.

shells were much cheaper and more common. Remnants of fat and green colour have been found in them.[1]

The slate palettes on which the malachite was ground, and the spoons and shells in which the powder produced by the grinding was mixed with fat or resin to produce the desired cosmetic, were by no means the only utensils needed for this complicated process. There were first the little leather or cloth bags, the remnants of some of which have survived, and in which the lumps of malachite were stored before being ground on the palettes.[2] More interesting were the receptacles in which the ground powder was carried. The most usual of these were tusks, either plain or carved. They occur from the Badārian times onwards. A plain tusk containing malachite was excavated from t. 428 at Mustagidda, which is Badārian, together with other toilet articles. In t. 595 of the same place and period a pair was recovered, slightly carved, but with no remnants of former content. They also were among the toilet articles. Brunton mentions four graves of Naḳāda I at Mustagidda with tusks containing malachite.[3] One of these, t. 1825, may be from the time of transition to Naḳāda II.[4] He has no doubt that the tusks were used to store "prepared cosmetics".[5] The tusks from Mustagidda are of plain ivory, pierced by holes round their tops. Through these the leather thongs were passed which secured leather covers which closed the tusks. Similar tusks, often decorated with patterns of incised lines, were found at Naḳāda and other excavations. Even though their content may not be mentioned in the excavation reports, they will have served similar purposes. Brunton was very observant and the descriptions of his work are outstandingly good, and much of our knowledge of predynastic Egypt depends on his careful observations. Petrie describes two tusks from Naḳāda, t. 1583,[6] as containing resin, with leather tied on over the openings. Resin is in all probability an ingredient used in the making up of the green cosmetic. I find it somewhat difficult to understand why Brunton, when dealing with the close association of malachite and resin, should have rejected the view that the compound of malachite and resin was used as a cosmetic, stating that in later times it was used as a medicament. Both substances were fairly common and found together with toilet instruments. We know that the predynastic Egyptians were in the habit of painting their faces green around the eyes, while we know nothing of any medicaments that they may have used.[7]

But tusks were not the only form the containers for the green malachite were given. Since Badārian times little ivory vases had been made which served the same purpose. In Badāri, t. 5112, a grave of the Badārian period, a small ivory vase was found which contained "ground malachite in the form of a paste, and was lying with a slate palette".[8] It is of a most unusual shape for its period. From a small, flat base a full body develops with something like humps on opposite sides. The vase has a high cylindrical neck with a straight, horizontal lip. The humps to Brunton appear to be imitations of vertical loop handles. No wonder that the little vessel reminds him of Eighteenth Dynasty forms. The little thing [9] is about 6 cm. high. All the other ivory vases from the same excavation are cylindrical. As far as can be ascertained they vary considerably in shape, but have it in common that they all possess rims, a feature which the contemporaneous pottery lacks. The rim would facilitate the fastening of the leather coverings and is a much

[1] E.g. *Mostag.*, p. 57.
[2] E.g. *Mostag.*, p. 72, t. 1868.
[3] *Mostag.*, p. 88.
[4] *Mostag.*, pl. XLII, 34, S.D. 37-45.
[5] *Mostag.*, p. 88.
[6] *Naq. Bal.*, p. 29.
[7] *Matmar*, p. 22.
[8] *Bad. Civ.*, p. 28, pl. XXIII, 3.
[9] Now at University College, London.

more efficient device than the holes round the openings of the tusks, which served the same purpose. The Badārian ivory vases from Mustagidda show the same variety of design. The small pot from t. 3501, which belonged to a child, has a globular body with a funnel-shaped neck and wide horizontal rim. It contained remnants of malachite. Another vase from Mustagidda, t. 428, is nearly cylindrical but for its oval section. It is provided with two rows of horizontal knobs. By far the most outstanding example of the Badārian ivory-carver's skill is the vase in the form of a hippopotamus found in Mustagidda, t. 3522,[1] which was reconstructed from splinters. Its back is hollowed out and it carries a rim round which a cover could be fastened. It is not stated whether any traces of the contents were preserved, but as it was found in such a decomposed state, that could hardly be expected. I think we shall not go far wrong if we assume that it also served as a receptacle for the green paint.

The representation of hippopotami has been a favourite subject for the artists of most Egyptian periods, and many a museum treasures the masterpieces they have left to us. The Badārian ivory hippopotamus, the first of this long sequence, is a worthy beginning. There is nothing primitive or unsure about it. All the characteristics of the pachyderm are there, without any but the most essential details. As so often with the best of Egyptian animal sculpture, the artist understood how to create the impression of movement; the hippopotamus is treading happily along its way.

Naḳāda I carried on the tradition of carving vases out of ivory. Two cylindrical ones were found in El-Maḥāsna, t. H 29, which has given us so many precious relics. They have the narrow rim of the contemporary stone vases.[2] From the same cemetery come two hippopotamus vases, found together in grave H 45 before S.D. 41 (or S.D. 33-37, after Petrie).[3] For them the ivory-carver invented a new, and, I think, less happy solution of the problem how to combine figurine and container. He burdened the backs of the animals with tusks many times their proper size, for while the hippopotami are not much more than 2 cm. high, the tusks measure nearly 8 cm. Holes are provided round the rims for fastening the covers.

With the beginning of Naḳāda II another type of toilet vase is introduced, characterized by a distinct foot. Quite a number of these vessels are made of horn and not of ivory. Their bodies have either parallel sides or splay towards their rims. The feet may be conical or may be mere knobs. Some, at least, had small lug handles. An ivory vase with conical foot (now damaged), parallel sides and lug handles comes from El-Maḥāsna, t. 23.[4] Another from Naḳāda, t. 1412, S.D. 43-44 (Vol. I, pl. VII, 8), is provided with a rim and two holes underneath it to obtain a tight fastening for the cover. Two horn vases, one from Naḳāda, t. 1411, S.D. 42, the other from Naḳāda, t. 1759, S.D. 41, are less well preserved. They have lost their upper parts and with them any trace of how their covers could have been fixed. Cylindrical ivory vases are less well documented from Naḳāda II. A fine piece from Naḳāda, t. 128, is undated.[5] It has a cord pattern in relief round its top and underneath its rim, and therefore is probably early dynastic. No other object is known to me from that grave.

[1] Now in the British Museum, London.
[2] *Pre-dyn. Cem. at El-Mahasna*, p. 11, pl. XII, 2.
[3] *Pre-dyn. Cem. at El-Mahasna*, p. 12, pl. XIII, 2.
[4] *Pre-dyn. Cem. at El-Mahasna*, p. 21, pl. XX, 3. The excavators did not date the grave; in *Preh. Eg.*, p. 40, ascribes it to S.D. 36-43. As it contained a copper harpoon it will be of Naḳāda II.
[5] Now at University College, London.

During Naḳāda II, with the expansion of the stone vase industry, we find in some graves stone vessels, some of them quite tiny, which also seem to have been used as containers for the green cosmetic. Their content is very rarely mentioned. In a few cases known to me it was malachite.[1] An early example of small stone vases in a grave comes from Naḳāda, t. 1661. Petrie dated it to S.D. 34, but we have seen that this date is not secure, and the grave may be from the time of transition to Naḳāda II.[2] Among the stone vases it contained is a set of three cylinder-shaped alabaster pots,[3] the smallest of which is just over 3 cm. high. One would like to think that they once belonged to an elegant toilet outfit. With the increasing use of fine, hard stones for vases during Naḳāda II we find the little vases made of them also. The smallness of these vessels must have added to the difficulties of their production, but may also have added a special charm. It seems that they were preferred to those made of ivory. A black and white porphyry vase from Naḳāda, t. 399, S.D. 52-62, does not even quite reach a height of 3 cm. It is of the squat type with well-marked lip and tubular lug handles. Many more of these little vases of different shapes and materials, mostly some colourful stone, are known.

We have now discussed a considerable number of toilet utensils which all had their use in the preparation of the green paint which the predynastic Egyptians put on their faces. There is the bag of linen or leather in which the lumps of the raw material were stored. Quite often they were found still in the hands of the skeleton, and where the sheltering bag has perished the green paint still tells its tale. The lumps were ground on the slate palettes, the story of which is traced in another chapter. For the binding of the powder produced on the palettes some sort of substance was needed, evidently resin, which we find so often closely associated with the malachite in the graves. The mixing seems to have been done in shells or containers of ivory, horn or stone, or may sometimes have been done on the palettes, some of which are provided with saucer-shaped depressions. It will be shown when dealing with the green slate palettes for the green cosmetic that their prodigious development may be due to the special value thought to be vested in the green paint. The care with which the accessories needed in the production of the precious substance were treated can but confirm the idea that a beneficent quality was thought to be inherent in it, which would bring good luck or health to the user. In no instance is red colour mentioned in connexion with all these toilet tools, very rarely black galena. Malachite is by far the most common cosmetic found in predynastic Egyptian graves. Sometimes a basket or box is preserved, put within easy grasp of the body, in which all the necessities for the toilet were neatly kept together.

With the utensils for the preparation of the green paint we have approached the vast and, for predynastic Egypt, very little explored domain of the magical. To it belong many of the small objects retrieved from the graves, the meaning of most of which we cannot even guess. Trying to bring some order out of this chaos, I would like to sort them roughly under three headings: (1) those which may have been used in the performance of some magical or religious rite; (2) *ex-votos* and signs of personal piety; and (3) amulets which were thought to possess protective or healing properties, or to convey to the wearer special gifts or qualities he desired. Not that there is a hard and sharp dividing line between the three categories, but for a first attempt to study their meaning this division will have to serve.

---

[1] *Naq. Bal.*, p. 15, t. 28. *Mostag.*, t. 1860, p. 72.

[2] See Vol. I, p. 110.

[3] Now in the Ashmolean Museum, Oxford.

1. *Objects used in rites*

Among the rites known to us from other ancient or modern pagan religions which use special objects for their ceremonies, some at least must have been practised also by the predynastic Egyptians. It seems certain that they observed some fertility rites, and it is perhaps possible to find among the various objects from graves which have no possible practical use some which can be ascribed to such practices. There are first of all the heavy tusks generally found in pairs, one solid and one hollow, which I have discussed already in Vol. I.[1] Those which belong to Naḳāda II, at least, if not others, are differentiated also by their decoration. The earliest known, from Naḳāda, t. 1491,[2] is only a fragment, but those from El-Maḥāsna, t. H 29, are perfectly preserved. There were two pairs, plain but for the tips. The solid tusks, which are tall and slender, end in discs with a loop on top. The hollow ones are shorter and somewhat tubby and have mushroom-shaped tips also provided with loops. In addition, they are provided near their bases with a small hole on each side. These, the excavators think, served for pegs which would hold plugs in place to close the tusks. There is nothing so far in favour of such an assumption. The cavities are too small to have served as containers even for the malachite powder. To me it still seems most likely that they were representations of the male and female element, and I think that the engravings on some of them—the rudimentary faces and the lines which may indicate clothing or necklaces—speak in favour of my suggestion.

We must now consider whether these tusks were put into the graves of the priests or persons of similar importance who knew how to use them, or whether they were put into the graves by people, perhaps relatives of the deceased, who thought their deposition in this particular place would make them especially efficacious. The woman who was laid to rest in El-Maḥāsna, t. H 29, must have had a special position in the community to which she once belonged. Her large, square grave possessed the richest furniture of all those excavated in the cemetery. Her skeleton occupied the centre of the tomb, and there was another, smaller one, in the same grave, but the excavators only tell us that it was compressed against the west side and that at its head lay a number of vases. The main skeleton wore a large quantity of ivory bracelets, and, probably round her neck, several strings of cornelian and green-glazed steatite beads. Near them lay the two pairs of tusks together with an ivory statuette of a man (pl. IV, 1-5). As no male statue of the Badārian period has come to light so far, this is the earliest known Egyptian representation of a man. It is about 36 cm. high and very slender. The head with its square, heavy chin rests directly on the chest without showing a neck. The skull is very high and domed. The arms, which hang straight down, are separated from the body. One hand is missing, the only damage the figure has suffered. The feet, which are in one with the legs, continue in a straight line. The man is ithyphallic. This, I think, shows clearly that the whole group, tusks as well as statuette, were connected with some fertility rite. The presence of the unusual male instead of the more common woman may be because the main occupant of the grave was a woman, and perhaps the secondary skeleton also.[3] Among the pottery of the grave was the well-known white-cross-lined bowl with the four hippo-potami walking round its edge (pl. V, 6, and 7). Whether these pachyderms have anything to

---

[1] Vol. I, pp. 35-6.

[2] Now at University College, London. Not mentioned in *Naq. Bal.*, pl. LXII, where a list of these tusks is given.

[3] Photographs of the grave in *Pre-dyn. Cem. at El-Mahasna*, pl. II. Statuette and tusks now in Cairo.

do with the little animal thought by some scholars to be the first representation of the mysterious animal of Seth, which was found in the same grave,[1] cannot be decided. To answer this question it would be necessary to prove that the god Seth was already known to the people of Naḳāda I, and that the hippopotamus was associated with him at that early time. But at present our material does not allow of an answer to either of these questions. However, we have to note that the woman who was buried in the largest and most richly equipped tomb at El-Maḥāsna owned the mysterious figure as well as the two pairs of tusks, one hollow and one solid, the ivory statuette of an ithyphallic man, and the rare bowl with the four hippopotami in the round walking round its edge, besides her personal ornaments and pottery. She must have occupied a position of consequence in her community and period, and it seems to me that she was either princess or priestess, perhaps both, and that the unusual objects had some connexion with her station in life.

A similar pot with hippopotamus statuettes on the rim from Matmar, t. 2646, also belonged to a woman. She also owned an antelope-headed amulet or tag together with a plain one.[2]

Another woman who must have occupied a position in her time and community similar to that of the lady from El-Maḥāsna, t. H 29, had hippopotamus figurines in her grave. This was the owner of Diospolis, t. B 101, who in addition to several such figurines (pl. V, 5) also possessed a slate palette in the form of that animal. She lacked the two tusks among the rich equipment of her tomb, for Petrie does not mention any from his excavations in the cemeteries of Diospolis Parva. Hippopotamus statuettes in graves are sufficiently rare to call for special attention wherever they occur. The two with tusks on their backs from El-Maḥāsna, t. H 45,[3] were found together with a pair of tusks which seem to have been plain, for it is said that they are similar to those from t. H 29.[4] Grave H 45 was plundered, the upper part of the body being destroyed. It lay, contrary to the usual fashion, with its head towards the north. Its sex is unknown. The grave is rich in ivories, and its comb and pins have already been mentioned.[5] Amongst unusual objects a large corn-grinder and two cup-shaped objects of clay were found, painted red and with small holes round the top.

The pairs of tusks from graves of Naḳāda II do not differ much from those of the earlier period. A good pair is preserved from Naḳāda, t. T 4, S.D. 41. The hollow tusk is plain and ends in a disc which carried a now broken loop. The solid tusk has two discs below the loop and a face engraved on the trunk. Two eyes, one somewhat higher than the other, are shown, and, underneath, a horizontal stroke for the mouth. A pair of double lines set at an angle to each other may indicate a garment.[6] Grave T 4 is one of the rare graves which was disturbed by another of its own period which completely destroyed the lower part of the skeleton. Moreover, Petrie says that the grave had been used twice before this happened. The plan he has drawn, and the inventory he gives, concern the second interment, which he calls the main one. The grave was large and rectangular. Two sides of a wooden construction around the body were preserved. South of it and near one of the shorter walls lay the two tusks on top of an ostrich

---

[1] Cf. Vol. I, p. 34.

[2] *Matmar*, p. 13, pl. XII, 7. There are 5 hippopotami and a crocodile.

[3] See above, p. 58.

[4] *Pre.-dyn. Cem. at El-Mahasna*, pl. XIII, 4.

[5] Cf. above, p. 45.

[6] *Naq. Bal.*, pl. LXIV, 81. They and all the other objects from t. T 4 are now in the Ashmolean Museum, Oxford.

egg. Next to it and in the south-west corner lay three flat slates, rectangular and with human heads, which "were tied together by a cord through them, they lay crossing", [1] two being underneath and one on top. Petrie is of opinion that "they were intended for manipulation in some ceremonies, in the hand", and I agree. I could not trace these block figurines, and therefore do not know whether they were all alike or whether they were in any way differentiated, perhaps to show whether they were meant to be male or female. As they were put so near the two tusks, which also lay crossing the ostrich egg, it seems likely that they form one group and belonged to the professional outfit of the most important body in the grave.

Of other graves from Naḳāda II containing pairs of hollow and solid tusks too little is known to allow any inference as to their meaning. With those from Naḳāda, t. 226, S.D. 44,[2] it is the hollow tusk that is provided with the indication of a face. It has two eyes made of rings of shell, again one slightly higher than the other, and above them lines which may be meant as eyebrows. The solid tusk is plain, and has a pattern in brownish paint on it which looks as if it had been produced by a ribbon dipped in colour and then wound spirally around it (Vol. I, pl. VI, 4, 5). The grave is not published, and all I could trace from it in addition to the tusks is a rhombic slate palette [3] about 22 cm. long with damaged tips. Whether Naḳāda, t. 1539, S.D. 40-43, contained only one single, solid tusk, or whether the hollow one that should make up the pair was given to some museum with which I could not make contact, I cannot tell, for the contents of the grave are widely scattered. The tusk, a spatha shell and a small ivory vase with three incised triangles and perforations all around the top are at University College, London [4]; a black-topped and a polished-red vase together with a mushroom-shaped ivory, its long stem provided with eight pierced holes round its bottom, are in the Ashmolean Museum, Oxford [5]; a black-topped pot with a small circular hole in its bottom is in the collection of the Oriental Institute in Chicago [6]; and another one is in the Chicago Natural History Museum.[7] The grave is unpublished.

We are on somewhat safer ground with the tusk which Brunton found at Badāri in hole 3165. It is of special interest because it is the only specimen so far known which was not found in a grave, and, in type, differs appreciably from those just discussed.[8] As its body was thoroughly decomposed, it is not known whether it was once hollow or solid, but it had a groove round its bottom which none of the others possessed. The greatest difference, however, is the tip, which is the only well-preserved part. The ivory-carver transformed it into a human head. The face is indicated by two large, circular eyes, which probably were once inlaid with rings of shell, and is provided with a pointed chin, or perhaps a beard. No more details are visible. The head wears what seems to be a turban, and from it projects a short cylindrical stem with a triangular object on it. It is perforated. This remarkable object was found in a polished-red pot of Brunton's "town pottery" [9] together with a collection of singular objects. They were: eight ivory tags (a single tag, two pairs, each pair showing the same number and design of incised lines, one set of three), different from all tags so far found in graves in that they do not end in

---

[1] *Naq. Bal.*, pp. 18-19.   [2] Cf. Vol. I, pl. VI, 4 and 5.
[3] Now at University College, London.
[4] The tusk is unpublished; for the vase see Petrie, *Eg.*, pl. XXXII, 12.
[5] The vases are types B 79a and P 58b with pot-mark.   [6] Type B 25e.
[7] The vase is in a sealed case. I could not ascertain the number from the pot, but got it from the register, which, I found, is not always reliable.
[8] *Bad. Civ.*, pp. 45-6.   [9] *Bad. Civ.*, pls. XLV, 7, and XLVII, 2.

a point, but in a disc. This makes one wonder whether they were perhaps meant to signify heads, especially if we remember that the three slates from Naḳāda, t. T 4, were provided with heads, and ivory tags with heads also occur. There were in addition a rhombic slate palette, a syenite disc mace-head, two limestone spindle-whorls, a little peg of alabaster, a string of 26 natural flint pebbles, a calcite pendant, a quantity of shells pierced for stringing, 83 nummulites not pierced, three flint flakes, seven rough little pebbles, one of those little ivories usually called "amuletic combs",[1] and pieces of wood, resin, malachite and red ochre. Close to the pot and on the same level lay the slate palette, rhombic with a sort of fringed ending, which is discussed in the chapter on palettes.[2] The pot, which contained such an odd collection of objects, was found on spur 6 at Badāri. On the spur there were "remains of settlements, mostly disturbed by tombs of the Protodynastic, Old Kingdom, and First Intermediate periods". The pot stood 51 inches below the present surface, and two other large pots, T 9 and T 10, were standing "in position" near it. It is difficult to imagine how the pot came to be in that spot, unless it had originally been inside a hut, but though Brunton speaks of village remains, nothing is mentioned about huts, houses or granaries; only pottery bars from kilns for parching grain are noted. Another odd collection of objects, but without the pair of tusks, or the single tusk, and covered by a pot, was found in the neighbourhood. The only artifacts were two ivory tags "covered with leather tied on with string", and a "little double bird amulet or palette". Brunton dates the first group to S.D. 37-38, the second to S.D. 37-47. The reasons for both datings are not obvious, and I especially find it difficult to accept 37-38 for the pot which contained the tusk. None of the ivories nor the pot warrant such a definite ascription. They may just as well belong to the end of Naḳāda II.

It is difficult to deduce anything much from these two collections found so near to each other and under similar circumstances. Were these artisans' raw materials, and odds and ends, perhaps put away for some further use? Or did they belong to some priest or priestess to use for ceremonies of which all knowledge is lost? We know very little about what the Egyptians of Naḳāda II found it necessary to keep in their houses. Caton-Thompson found nothing similar in the hut foundations she excavated at Ḥammāmīya, nor do I know of any other parallel occurrence.

The tags are not uncommon in graves, being found mostly in pairs or threes, and either of ivory or of bone, though stone ones also occur. They are all provided at their tops with notches or grooves round which leather thongs or strings could be fastened, and, to judge from those found in Naḳāda, t. T 4, serve for tying them together. Some are perforated as well. They are mostly flat, though round ones also occur, especially in stone. Those of ivory and bone are incised with different linear patterns, or are notched along part or the whole of their sides. Sometimes these decorations look as if they imitated a string that had been wound round the tags spirally. None is known so far from Badārian times. Three (one of them damaged, and only the upper half preserved) were found in Naḳāda, t. 1606, S.D. 31.[3] They remain in use all through the two Naḳāda periods. Brunton found six in t. 2659 at Matmar,[4] S.D. 37-45, and three in Matmar, t. 2720, S.D. 31-61. They are found more frequently than the large pairs of hollow and solid tusks. Though none with discs instead of points has as yet been found in graves like those in the pot from Badāri, spur 6, some of the flat tags were provided with human heads or have an

[1] See above, p. 54.   [2] See below, p. 83.
[3] Now at University College, London.   [4] *Matmar*, pl. XVI, 26, 27, 28.

upper part added to them shaped like female bodies. Some have the horns of the cow-goddess or are animal-shaped. Those with human heads have been known since Petrie's excavations at Naḳāda. They are all of Naḳāda II. Like their plain counterparts many have decorations of incised lines or notches on the block which sustains the head, and notches or grooves at the bottom which indicate that they also would have been tied together with leather thongs or strings.

A remarkable pair of tags was discovered in Naḳāda, t. T 24. One has two sets of three and four lines incised, and above them three pairs of notches. The face is triangular and has the ears marked. The eyes are circles, the mouth a horizontal line, and two lines on the skull may indicate hair or a turban. Its companion, which has incised lines and no notches, shows the ears, eyes and horns of the mother-goddess at the top.[1] Nothing more about t. T 24 is known to me, and so the background against which one should see this interesting pair is lost, and nothing can be ascertained about their use and the relations in which they once stood to their owner.

Yet another important group of tags was recovered, this time at Matmar from t. 2682, S.D. 37-57. There were four of them, the lower parts grooved and with incised lines, the tops changed into narrow-waisted human figures, which were female, to judge from their waists and rounded upper parts. They have pointed chins, circular eyes inlaid with black paste, and ears far up on their skulls. Double lines below the chins may indicate garments. The meaning of three lines each side below the waists is not clear. Circles between them filled with black paste may indicate the navels. In the grooves traces of leather were preserved, an indication that these tags also were tied together. They were found in the remnants of a wooden box in the south-west corner of the well-made, rectangular grave. The three slate tags from Naḳāda, t. T 4, had been found in the same position. The owner of Matmar, t. 2682, was a man.

A set of three human-headed tags comes from Naḳāda, t. 1757 (no sequence-date). Two are of slate, the eyes inlaid with shell rings. One of them, which is narrower than the other, has a rounded base, the other a square one. The third tag is of ivory, and the figure is wearing a necklace composed of two rows of circles once inlaid with black paste; the round eyes and the eyebrows are also inlaid with black paste. The faces of all three have pointed chins, and also ears. A pair of slate tags from the same grave, though damaged, still show that they once carried the horns of the cow-goddess. The grave, which is unpublished, also contained eleven little ivory objects, between 2 and 3 cm. long and less than 1 cm. wide, grooved lengthwise on both sides. Their purpose is unknown. No pottery is recorded.[2]

Three ivory tags with the horns and eyes (or breasts) of the fertility-goddess come from the same grave, Badāri 3759, S.D. 39-44, which contained the fragment of a vase in the shape of a hippopotamus on which hunters with harpoons are painted.[3]

Yet another type of tag was found in the cemetery of Matmar, which is especially rich in these small objects. These tags end in birds, instead of in human heads. A pair made of ivory was found in t. 3123, S.D. 38-43. They are not quite alike, one being bigger than the other. The smaller one is perfect. The groove at its bottom cuts off a rounded base. Two parallel lines inlaid with black paste separate the tag from the body of the bird, which has notches front and back. The head, which is notched at the back, is set on a long neck. The other tag is

---

[1] Now in the Ashmolean Museum, Oxford.
[2] The tags, the oblong ivories and a disc-shaped cornelian bead are at University College, London.
[3] *Bad. Civ.*, pls. LIII, 49; LIV, 15.

damaged, one side with the neck and the head of the bird being broken off. Its bottom is square, and the body of the bird is taller and crossed by two diagonal lines. Brunton mentions a third bird tag of which a splinter only remained. T. 3123 is a well-constructed, rectangular grave which contained a wooden construction, either lining or coffin. Fragments of two combs were found, one with a bird top. The owner of the grave was a woman.[1]

Ivory tags with bird tops are very rare, slate being the more usual material for them. They occur at all times from Naḳāda I onwards. Two are preserved from Naḳāda, t. 1590, S.D. 33. They were not alike as far as one can still see; for one of the slates, which is severely damaged with the head only preserved, has an inlaid eye. On the perfect one the eye is not marked. The grave also contained a small fragment of an ostrich egg, a rather damaged comb, two black-topped and one white-cross-lined pot.[2] A set of three, also of slate, comes from Naḳāda, t. 1781, S.D. 47. They vary in size between 4 and 5·5 cm. In addition, two plain ivory tags were found with notches half-way up their sides.[3] Three flat ivory hippopotami marked with oblique black lines were found in the north-west corner of Badāri, t. 3823, S.D. 35-47.[4] They may have served a purpose similar to that of the tags, as they could be tied together by means of knobs on their backs.

What was the ceremony in which all these tags were once used, and in what way were they "manipulated in the hand", as Petrie puts it? There are no answers, and guesses only are possible. One thing seems to me fairly certain, namely that these tags were neither ornaments nor amulets worn round the neck or about the person. It has been pointed out that if they were worn round the neck, the heads of the tags would point downwards. If they had been meant to be worn, surely they would have had holes for suspension and not grooves, which would be a clumsy means of attachment to a necklace; leather thongs also would not be used for personal ornaments. The beads we have from predynastic Egypt have dainty perforations which would allow a thick hair or a thread to pass through, but not a leather thong. In Naḳāda, t. T 4, the tags were tied together, and that is the only purpose which the grooves and the leather thongs could have served, whatever action was performed with the objects. The position of the tags in the grave, where it has been noted, was at some distance from the skeleton in the north-west corner of the burial, or else within easy reach of the hands. I think this confirms my view that the tags were not worn on the person.

2. *Ex-votos*

It is doubtful whether the figurines of women, men and animals which were deposited in some of the graves from Badārian times onwards were used in some sort of ceremonies, or whether they were not rather deposited as *ex-votos*. This would presuppose that the grave was a specially suitable place for such offerings, and that the deity concerned was of chthonic character. The first to be thought of is the great mother-goddess, who, though she does not in Egypt represent the earth, yet had some special connexion with the dead and the grave.[5] Very likely there were other deities besides her whom we cannot identify with any of the later gods or goddesses of the

[1] *Matmar*, p 16, pl. XVI, 21-2.
[2] The slates and the comb at University College, London; two black-topped pots, B 1H and B 22d, in the Ashmolean Museum, Oxford; the white-cross-lined pot C 21E in the Berlin Museum.
[3] All at University College, London.   [4] *Bad. Civ.*, p. 51, pl. XXXIV, 4.
[5] E. J. Baumgartel, "Tomb and Fertility", *Jahrbuch für Kleinasiatische Forschung*, I, pp. 56 ff.

Egyptian pantheon. Several statuettes of women were recovered from Badārian graves, three from Badāri itself, one of ivory, one of pottery and one of unbaked clay.[1] Two were found in tombs too disturbed for the sex of their occupants to be ascertained; the third, which was the one of clay, was found in a child's grave (5769). It was put into a pot together with a small pot and some threads of cloth, which, Brunton thinks, may have belonged to a wrap for the figurine. The whole arrangement suggests to Brunton a model funeral. The figurine only very roughly resembles the human form, but is characterized as female. She is the first of a long series which has no arms. The significance of this trait is not clear. One may argue in the case of this rough sketch from Badāri that the legs are not separated either, and that the figurine is just a very rough piece of work. This does not hold good, however, for many of the figurines of Naḳāda I and II and later dates, which, though otherwise carefully and even naturalistically modelled, yet lack arms. The type is known elsewhere, e.g. in Mesopotamia, but no satisfactory explanation of it has as yet been found. Another rough statuette of a woman from the Badārian period comes from t. 494 at Mustagidda.[2] The grave was undisturbed and belonged to a female (?), richly adorned with necklaces, bracelets and anklets. "Widely scattered round the head and hands were the four pieces of a pottery female figurine, evidently broken before, or at, the burial. Opposite the knees and hands was a pet gazelle."[3] This figurine has at least stumps which indicate the arms. The legs are not separated, and they end in a straight line, not in a peg as on the figurine from Badāri. The head, like that of the Badāri doll, is a small rounded protuberance. Two other smaller figurines, also of clay, from Mustagidda, were surface finds. No male figure is known from Badārian times.

Though the first figurine with which we had to deal from Naḳāda I was that of a man,[4] it is the female figure which is predominant at that period. From Naḳāda itself we possess one clay figurine, from t. 1611, S.D. 36-38.[5] The grave is published, evidently by Quibell, and seems to have been thoroughly disturbed. The statuette lay "at mid N. side, and fragments of another in the filling". The clumsiness of the figure is enhanced by the restoration which replaces the damaged foot. The statuette has lost its head; it never had any arms. Two other figures of women were found by Quibell at Ballas in t. 394.[6] As it contained at least one white-cross-lined pot,[7] it will have been of Naḳāda I times. The figurines lay at the feet of the skeleton below what must have been a remarkable vase. Quibell describes it as "painted white, and with an incised zig-zag pattern above, and painted in red over the white on the body of the pot".[8] Unfortunately, the reference he gives to *Naqada and Ballas*, pl. XXXVI, 84, is mistaken, but later on he refers to pl. XXXV, 76, which shows a vase which is incised but does not seem to be painted. Both the figurines are armless, and only one has its head preserved. The surfaces of both are damaged and one has lost not only her head but half of the upper part of her body. In spite of this she manages to keep some of the charm she must once have possessed. She is represented sitting with her legs curved back, and, notwithstanding her enormous thighs, she is not without grace. The better-preserved figure is just a coarse piece of work. A model boat of unburned clay and some bones of a dog were found in the same grave.

[1] Vol. I, p. 23.   [2] *Mostag.*, pl. XXIV, 31.
[3] Gazelles in graves are not infrequent. Could they have been domesticated?   [4] See above, p. 60.
[5] Vol. I, pl. VI, 2-3.   [6] *Naq. Bal.*, pl. VI, 1-3. Now in the Ashmolean Museum, Oxford.
[7] *Naq. Bal.*, pp. 13, 16; cf. Vol. I, p. 99 and fig. 41, 6.
[8] Now in the University Museum, Philadelphia, Pa. There is hardly any paint left.

Clay figurines of a somewhat different type were recovered from the cemetery at El-Maḥāsna. From t. H 97 (before S.D. 41), which had been thoroughly plundered, comes the head of a very interesting piece, of the body of which only a few fragments were left.[1] The head is larger and with more details than any other we possess from predynastic Egypt. Forehead and nose form a long forward-sweeping curve. From the tip of the nose downwards another curve retreats. The nostrils are marked by small holes, the thin-lipped mouth seems slightly open, the chin recedes. The large almond-shaped eyes slant towards the nose. The back of the head would have been covered by a wig. The head was made of a fine yellow clay which was baked. The face itself is painted red with dark eyebrows and eyelids. The eyelids are outlined with a broad band of green. Whether the head once belonged to a figure of a man or a woman one cannot tell. In the debris of the same grave were found the sherds of an extraordinary vase of the white-cross-lined type. Though it is not so fine in execution as that which was found with the ivory man, yet the representations on it are of outstanding importance. The pot is a deep beaker with rounded bottom, painted inside and out. On the outside are two pairs of animals—two oxen, one behind the other, and two elephants facing each other. Separating the back of one of the oxen from the elephants is a lozenge-shaped object which, though not identical with it, yet reminds one of a similar object on a white-cross-lined vase in the Cinquantenaire Museum at Brussels, with the dancing men and women, where the object divides the women dancing round one of the men from those dancing round the other.[2] We find this still unexplained object again in the interior of the beaker from t. H 97 at El-Maḥāsna, this time between two hippopotami facing each other. Opposite this group is another formed by two crocodiles, one facing towards the rim, the other towards the bottom of the pot. Between this group and one of the hippo-potami is another object, which has been described as a plant but which does not seem to me to resemble any known variety and can just as well belong to the same class of objects as the lozenge.

A female figurine of considerable size was found in t. H 41 at El-Maḥāsna (before S.D. 56). The comparatively late date to which the excavators ascribe the grave may well be mistaken. Petrie sequence-dates it to 36-38. The grave is rectangular, and as the excavators date at least partly from the shape of the grave, assuming that a round grave must be earlier than a square one,[3] their date may well be too late. The grave had been partly plundered. In its centre lay the skeleton of a woman, in front of her in a heap the bones of a child, and behind her, also in a heap, the bones of an adult, but without the skull. The woman evidently was the main occupant. Her forearms were loaded with ivory bracelets, her necklaces were made of cornelian, shell, green-glazed, silver and gold beads. Around her neck and at her feet were large masses of resin. Among the pottery were seven pear-shaped rattles. At the extreme north-west end of the grave and on a little mound of sand a black-topped pot, a cone-shaped object of clay with holes round the lip, and a small clay gaming-board were deposited. Some small cubes of unbaked clay may have been the pieces in the game. To judge from the furniture, which contained so many out-standing objects, the woman in the tomb must have been among the great in her community. The figurine lay on the body of the skeleton. It was of clay and painted red. The excavators observe: "It lay on its side, and was of great length, the legs being drawn back into the contracted

[1] *Pre-dyn. Cem. at El-Mahasna*, pp. 12-13, 28-9, pl. XV. I could not trace the head. For the pot see *ibid.*, pl. XIV.
[2] Cf. Vol. I, p. 64, fig. 14.
[3] *Pre-dyn. Cem. at El-Mahasna*, p. 3.

position common to early burials." [1] If this is the correct explanation of the attitude of the figurine and it was indeed meant to represent a corpse, then we are confronted here with quite a new situation, the explanation of which is not obvious. Why should the image of a dead woman be laid on the corpse of a woman in her grave? Until we have more evidence I would rather assume the excavators mistaken, and that the figurine, like the one from Ballas, was meant to be sitting on her legs. The figure, which was far too long for its width, could only be saved in parts. Two photographs of it were published. One, taken as it still lay in the grave, looks rather different from the other, which was made after its removal, by which time it had lost its lower legs. It is therefore impossible to be certain about its original attitude.

Yet another grave in the cemetery of El-Maḥâsna, H 33, before S.D. 51, contained fragments of a female clay figure. Petrie dated the tomb to S.D. 43-44. As it contained a black incised pot, and another of yellowish clay incised with necklace-shaped decorations, the tomb certainly belonged to Naḳâda II. The grave, which was plundered, was large with a ledge on one side on which stood five vases. Between the ledge and the skeleton, of which too little was left to ascertain its sex, lay the legs of "a very large steatopygous clay figure painted red. Both this and the skeleton had been covered by a mat." [2]

Ayrton and Loat do not mention any clay figures of men from their excavation at El-Maḥâsna. But Garstang, who had worked there before them, found one which he published on pl. III of *Maḥâsna and Bêt Khallâf.* No description of it exists, nor is its tomb number stated.

The large tomb, Diospolis Parva, B 101, the rich content of which has taught us so much already about the possessions of a distinguished woman from the Naḳâda I period, contained two statuettes of women. One is made of pottery, the other of clay or mud.[3] They are smaller and very different from those recovered at El-Maḥâsna or at Naḳâda and Ballas. The clay statuette rather reminds one of the pottery figure of a young woman from Badâri [4] (pl. V, 3), not only because it also has lost its head, and is of a similar red colour, but also because, as on the earlier piece, the arms are free of the body, the left one being lifted, the right hanging down loosely. The chief resemblance between the two little works of art is the illusion of easy and lively movements which their creators have managed to produce with the simplest of means. The other figurine from Diospolis Parva, t. B 101, clumsy and much broken, is of the armless type.

Grave B 83 from Diospolis Parva, which contained the model of an enclosure wall with warriors behind it,[5] has preserved us some other important objects, though it was disturbed. Among them are three figures, one of a woman, the others of men, and a vase with a human head. It also contained little models of a Nile turtle and other animals in clay. The human statuettes are of pottery. The one of the woman (pl. V, 2), though not so fine as that from grave B 101, is yet a good example of the art of its time. It is of the armless type, but is otherwise realistically rendered. Its head, turned slightly to one side, is crowned with heavy hair, or, perhaps, a wig. The legs seem to be crossed, the feet are not marked. The figures of the men have lost their heads. They also are of the armless type. Grave B 83 is only vaguely sequence-dated to S.D. 33-48, but may well be of Naḳâda I date. The woman's grave, B 109, from Diospolis Parva, is of S.D. 44, and therefore of Naḳâda II. It contained a rather coarse female statuette with

---

[1] *Pre-dyn. Cem. at El-Mahasna*, pp. 29-30. I could not trace it.
[2] *Pre-dyn. Cem. at El-Mahasna*, p. 14.
[3] Now in the Ashmolean Museum, Oxford.
[4] See above, p 66.
[5] *Diosp. Pa.*, p. 32.

triangular head. The arms are mere stumps, though one of them seems to be raised. The accompanying objects are also interesting and may have been used in the profession of the owner, be it priestess or witch. There were a pair of "swimming-bird" slates carrying handles on their backs, another pair of slates, perhaps very stylized hartebeests, one of those objects which though often called combs must have had some different use, and a flint fish-tail which in shape is midway between the early and the later type.[1] From the disturbed grave, Diospolis Parva, B 119, comes the statuette of a man who was either sitting on a chair or stool which is lost, or was performing some squatting dance. The skull of a dog, an ox bone, a mace-head, a clay chisel (?) and a hoe is all that could be retrieved from the grave.[2]

Both male and female figures were found in graves in the cemetery of El-'Amrah. From the grave of a woman, El-'Amrah, a 94, S.D. 39, comes a male figure which is important because it shows clearly that the man represented wore a sheath suspended from a belt around his middle. On none of the other male figures is the belt represented, and one cannot be sure whether they wore this curious garment or not. On the statuette from El-'Amrah it is painted very carefully in black, as is also some sort of garment across the torso. The head with its curly hair, huge eyes and black beard forms rather an odd contrast with the rest of the statuette, for the body is armless and not even the legs are indicated.[3] A pair of male statues of a similar type had been put in the grave of a man, El-'Amrah, a 56, S.D. 43. Their faces resemble that of the woman from El-Maḥāsna, t. 97, in that their foreheads and noses sweep forward in the same unbroken curve, a type which we do not usually associate with Egyptian faces. Their heads are covered with curly hair. No garments are indicated on the rod-like bodies. It would have been interesting to know what the figurines of women from El-'Amrah might have looked like, but the excavators published no more about them than the fact of their existence.

There is one more type of human statuette which has to be mentioned, and that is the one which has a head roughly shaped like that of a bird. As far as I know, the only well-preserved statuettes of this type found in an excavation, those found by H. de Morgan at Mohamerieh, are of Naḳāda I times, being dated by white-cross-lined pottery (pl. V, 4).[4] The statuettes are of women wearing white dresses. They raise their arms in a dance, a pose which also occurs on the white-cross-lined pottery [5] but is more common on the later "decorated" ware. Similar figures published by Petrie in *Prehistoric Egypt*, some of them, as it seems, male, the others female, were all bought and have no provenance. One of the female figurines, which has only part of one arm left, seems to be in the same position with raised arms as those from Mohamerieh.[6] The type with birds' heads seems to be an exaggeration of the type from El-Maḥāsna, t. 97,[7] where forehead and nose form one forward-sweeping curve and the lower part of the face a retreating one. Both types exist in Mesopotamia,[8] where they were found at Al 'Ubaid and at Warka, and, though these figures are not identical with those we are speaking of, they are similar enough to them and sufficiently out of the common to make a connexion likely. Whether the bird-headed figures

---

[1] See chapter on Towns, p. 135.

[2] *Diosp. Pa.*, B 119, p. 33.

[3] Randall-MacIver, *El Amrah*, pl. IX, 11, and pl. XII, 7.

[4] Now in the Brooklyn Museum.

[5] On the vase with the dancing couple at University College, London, the man raises his arms, the woman is armless. On a vase from El-Maḥāsna a woman and a man raise their arms. *Preh. Eg.*, pls. XVIII, 74; XXIII, 1.

[6] *Preh. Eg.*, pl. IV, 4.

[7] See above, p. 57.

[8] Hall and Woolley, *Al 'Ubaid*, pl. XLVIII, T.O. 405. Jordan, *Dritter Vorl. Vorbericht . . . Uruk-Warka*, 1931, pl. 21.

from the Naḳāda vase [1] represent the same fabulous beings, I do not know. They raise their
arms like the women from Mohamerieh. Perhaps all these bird-headed persons belong to legend
rather than to myth, though in Egypt, where the combination of bird or animal heads with human
bodies is such an outstanding feature of the representation of gods, one cannot be certain. As
all the figurines in Egypt come from the excavation of graves, they will have at least some relations
with the principal gods of the time, and those who put them there will have expected some help
or beneficial influence from them either for the dead to whom they were given or, possibly, for
the givers themselves. That is why I have classified them among the *ex-votos*. It is worth
emphasizing that the combination of birds' (or animals') heads with a human body goes back to
the period of Naḳāda I, and is not a late feature of Egyptian religion.

From the material just discussed it is impossible to deduce much. Three types of human
statuettes have been discerned, one with arms, one without arms and one with birds' heads.
From the pieces studied and also from the Mesopotamian parallels it seems clear that the omission
of the arms on some of the statuettes is not a sign of clumsiness or ineptitude in their makers
nor of a general coarseness of the figures. The arms were left out because the men or women
represented were thought to be armless. It has been suggested that the female statuettes were
concubines for the dead; but they were found with women even more frequently than with men,
which seems to dispose of this suggestion. They also have been explained as servant-figures,
but servants without arms seem to defeat their own purpose. The row of vase-bearing, armless
figures from Naḳāda, t. 271,[2] have been regarded as offering-bearers, and as the forerunners of
the rows of servants carrying provisions which decorate the walls of Old Kingdom tombs. The
figurines from Naḳāda, t. 271, are quite unique, since the only comparable piece, the statuette
from Mustagidda, t. 1832, lacks the jar on the head. Coming as they do from the time of transition
from Naḳāda I to II, they must be separated by many centuries from the first offering-bearing
servants of the Old Kingdom. I therefore think we ought at least to consider whether they should
not be put into the same class as the rest of the armless figurines and regarded as *ex-votos*. There
were four of them, and we have seen that statuettes tend to be deposited in the tombs in pairs,
thus differing from the flat human-headed symbols which often appear in threes. T. 271 was a
rich and well-equipped grave which, though plundered, yet yielded a number of interesting
pieces. The vase-bearers stood upright in a bed of clean sand; which tends to strengthen the
assumption that they were more than mere servant girls. In addition, the grave contained two
mud statuettes of women formed over reeds. They have the triangular profile of the head from
El-Maḥāsna, t. 97, and are painted in red and black (pl. V, 1). Of the other furniture, a pair of
tusks survived, one solid, one hollow, which had been put in a basket, together with one flat slate
figure (evidently female),[3] a flint fish-tail, an unusual slate palette which is formed like a turtle
at one end and has two gazelles' heads at the other,[4] besides stone and pottery vases. The tomb
had been considered important enough in its time for plunderers to dig a hole down to the body,
dragging it out so that Petrie found it on a slope of earth on the west side of the pit. He does
not mention its sex.

I think that the case for the figurines with arms being *ex-votos* is somewhat stronger, especially
for the statuettes of women. Here we have parallels from later times, which indicate that they

---

[1] Vol. I, pl. X.   [2] *Naq. Bal.*, p. 21, pls. LIX, 7; LXXXIII.
[3] Cf. Vol. I, p. 35.   [4] See chapter on Palettes, p. 88.

were dedicated to the mother-goddess. From the First Intermediate Period there exists in the Berlin Museum a statuette of a woman holding a child. On it a woman has written her wish for a child.[1] No figure of a woman with child from an authenticated source is known to me from predynastic Egypt, but it seems that the child was not an indispensable part of these figures. Even in later periods they are generally naked. Nor need it in later and literate times be a figure of a woman that was used to remind the fertility-goddess of the desire of the dedicator for a child. One could send a letter. In one of the "letters to the dead" [2] a man asks his deceased father to intercede for him with "his mother" to provide him and his sister with male offspring. It is not expressly said who the mother is meant to be, but it seems most likely that the Great Mother is meant rather than the mother of the dead man. It would be the most likely explanation of these female figurines found in graves from Badārian times onward, that they were placed in the graves as *ex-votos* to the fertility-goddess to remind her of the wish for children. In some of her aspects the great goddess must have been chthonic, and hence the grave an appropriate place for the depositing of such statuettes. It would also explain why we find the figurines in graves of women as well as of men. Both were thought capable of interceding.

All this may hold good for the female figures, but how are we to explain the males? No doubt the Great Mother would have as concomitant a male god, her son and lover, called in Egypt *Ka-mwt.f*, the bull of his mother. But are we allowed to see in the male figures *ex-votos* to him? No definite answer is possible. Far more work on these figurines will have to be done, and on their connexions with the owners of the graves in which they were found, as well as with the other objects belonging to these graves. As they stand, most of the excavation reports are neither reliable nor detailed enough to be of help in such studies.

While the statuettes of humans were found in graves of many of the Upper Egyptian predynastic cemeteries, those of oxen and cows all come from the excavations at El-'Amrah and El-Maḥāsna. The predynastic cemeteries of Upper Egypt are so astoundingly uniform in their furniture that when some unusual feature is encountered it stands out as noteworthy. And yet that is precisely what one would expect. Besides the great universal gods each little township or village would be expected to have some local god or goddess to whom it was devoted. But of this we can trace amazingly little. Moreover, it seems difficult to think that the figures in the graves could be pointers in that direction, since they are the commonest domesticated animals —cows, oxen, pigs or, in one instance from El-Maḥāsna, rams, which had a cult throughout Egypt.[3] There are two other explanations which seem more likely. They may have been put in the graves for the same reason which I have inferred from the presence of the female statuettes, namely to ensure fertility, this time for the herds of cattle and not of men; or they may have been meant as food for the dead. In favour of the first explanation we have especially the evidence of the group of ox, cow and calf found in t. b 212 at El-'Amrah (S.D. 31 according to Petrie).[4] From the same cemetery come the group of four cows and some animals which are probably pigs.[5] They may be explained either way. A charming little ivory of what I think is a donkey was

---

[1] S. Schott, "Die Bitte fuer ein Kind," *JEA*, 16 (1930).

[2] Sir A. Gardiner, "A New Letter to the Dead," *JEA*, 16 (1930), pp. 19 ff.

[3] *Pre-dyn. Cem. at El-Mahasna*, pl. XXI, 8, p. 33. All we are told about them is that they were found in a late, plundered grave.

[4] Now in the Ashmolean Museum, Oxford.

[5] *El Amrah*, pl. IX. Now in the Ashmolean Museum, Oxford.

found in El-Maḥāsna, t. H 39. The excavators waver between a cow and a dog, but seem to prefer the first. But as the animal has neither horns nor udder, a cow seems unlikely. Its long head with the convex profile and long pointed ears, the straight line from neck to body, and the long tail seem to me typical of a donkey. The grave from which the little animal was taken was a disturbed one. It is dated to before S.D. 51 (S.D. 31-44 according to Petrie). Here the idea of food cannot apply, nor had the animal any resemblance to the animal of Seth.[1]

A large hippopotamus of red clay comes from Diospolis Parva, t. R 134. Petrie dates the grave to S.D. 41, but as it contained two quadruple pots, type D 91c, of a type which at Abuṣīr el-Meleḳ was found in alabaster [2] in a much later context, it is likely that it belongs to the time of transition to dynastic times. It is much larger than the little Badārian ivory hippopotamus and, perhaps, not so fine, but is in its own way a masterpiece. It is also interesting from the technical point of view. The animal is about a foot long, and being of that size might have cracked in the firing if it had been made of solid clay. The artist, therefore, did not give it a belly, but left it open and hollow. The sex of the body with which it was found is not mentioned, and it may be mere chance that the other hippopotami were found in women's graves. Yet one would like to know whether already during that early period the female hippopotamus was a goddess especially of women? [3]

3. Amulets

The hippopotamus must have been a valued animal among the earliest Egyptians, for practically all of it could be put to some use. The fertility of the pachyderm, therefore, would have been of considerable importance to them. It must also have possessed some quality which men coveted, for Brunton found amulets in the shape of hippopotami already being used in the Badārian period. One was in t. 1208 at Mustagidda.[4] It was a large grave, thoroughly ransacked. "The body was male, with light brown short wavy hair; there was also a second skull in the grave." This shows that the amulet belonged to a man. The amulet is a rather puzzling object, its resemblance to a hippopotamus not being very great. It represents the forepart of the animal only, carved out of a jasper pebble, and pierced by a large suspension hole. Two clumsy feet stick out at different angles, and the head is difficult to identify with that of any known species. What is most surprising is the little knob which grows from the neck of the figure. Similar knobs were found on the backs of the three hippopotami from Badāri, t. 3823,[5] S.D. 35-37. These had no suspension holes, and the knobs with them would have been used to tie the three pieces together so that they might serve in ceremonies similar to those in which the human- and bird-headed tags played a part. The little animal from Mustagidda was perforated and most likely was worn attached to the body for use as an amulet. It was single, and nothing indicates its possible use in ceremonies. As the grave was disturbed it is, of course, possible that there were originally more than one. We have no other indications that tags used in some magical ceremony were known to the Badārians, and yet, unless they were commonly employed in a familiar ceremony, it is difficult to explain how the hippopotamus amulet from Mustagidda came by its knob. This detail, superfluous as it is, seems explicable only when considered as a thoughtless repetition of

---

[1] *Pre-dyn. Cem. at El-Mahasna*, pl. XIX, 2.   [2] *Abusir*, p. 41, pl. 24.
[3] *Diosp. Pa.*, p. 35, pl. VI. Now in the Ashmolean Museum, Oxford.
[4] *Mostag.*, p. 51, pl. XXIX, 21.   [5] *Bad. Civ.*, p. 51, pl. LIII, 42.

a detail familiar to its maker from another context. The other hippopotamus amulet known from Badārian times lacks the knob. It was found in Badāri, t. 5740, which had belonged to a child. It is made of bone and so severely stylized that the resemblance to a hippopotamus is rather vague.[1] Its head is as indifferent as that of the piece from Mustagidda. The large suspension hole divides the front from the back legs, which are not separated from each other.

A third amulet preserved from the Badārian period differs profoundly from the two others. It is the head of a gazelle and is one of the masterpieces of Badārian bone carving. The horns and the muzzle are summarily shown. Two eyes each side of the head make it quite clear that the animal possessed two eyes even when worn hanging in profile, the position indicated by its suspension hole. In spite of its stylization and the minimum of detail given, the head has a liveliness and individuality which the hippopotami lack.[2] The gazelle's head together with some beads were found near the ankle of the man, and must once have been tied round it. Presumably this indicates the wish of the owner to be endowed with the speed of the gazelle.

It is difficult to decide whether the two red limestone hippopotami from Diospolis Parva, t. B 101, should be classified as amulets. One is 7 cm., the other $7\frac{1}{2}$ cm. long, and they are rather heavy. They carry on their backs hollowed-out knobs,[3] the larger with three, the smaller with two perforations. These are at the bottom of the knobs, which I think indicates that the objects were to be suspended by a string drawn through them. The flatness of the animals' bodies also seems to indicate that they were meant to be worn as personal adornments or amulets, for they could not stand on their feet. Though they are very similar, the two animals are not identical and may well be a male hippopotamus and its spouse. The three clay hippopotami from the same tomb are much more rounded in their bodies and could have been made to stand on their feet when they were intact (pl. V, 5). It is interesting to note that the stone animals were of red limestone, and the three clay ones had once been painted red.

The three claws (pl. III, 2), perhaps of a lion, found in Naḳāda, t. 1503, S.D. 36, are natural objects which may have been worn as amulets. It seems possible that the curious curved hooks often made of shell were imitations of these claws, which they vaguely resemble. Brunton found them in several graves at Mustagidda both with women and with men. From their position he concludes that they were worn on the forehead. He dates them all to Naḳāda I, but they were, still in fashion during Naḳāda II, and at least one from Diospolis Parva, t. U 378, S.D. 71, is early dynastic.[4]

It is difficult to make out whether the two sandals from Diospolis Parva, t. U 256, S.D. 32, should be considered as amulets. Each of them is provided with five holes through which a fastening cord could be drawn. These do not tally with the crossed stripes painted on them, and which one would like to take for the strings. The length of the sandals is 6 cm.

The most interesting amulet which first appears in Naḳāda II times is the one which has been variously called either a bull's or a ram's head. It is the combination of a conical trunk and a wide oval perched on its side on top of it. At the back of the upper part is a V-shaped perforation. The lower part of the oval is formed by a pair of horns, or perhaps of arms which sometimes, but not always, meet in the middle. Above these are two circular holes sometimes inlaid with shell or some other substance. They may be the eyes or the breasts, and the whole

---

[1] *Bad. Civ.*, pl. XXIV, 15.
[3] *Diosp. Pa.*, pl. V

[2] *Bad. Civ.*, pl. XXIV, 14.
[4] *Diosp. Pa.*, pl. X, 28.

is, I think, a symbol of the fertility-goddess. The earliest dated example so far is from Naḳāda, t. 1788 (pl. VI, 2), which Petrie ascribed to S.D. 34-46.[1] No pottery is known to me from the grave, but two plain ivory pins, the fragment of a curly wig which once must have belonged to a clay figurine, a necklace of crystal and agate beads, and a "plummet"—perhaps a bulla pendant— nearly 5 cm. long, all place the amulet securely in Naḳāda II and perhaps even later than the last of Petrie's dates. The amulet itself is a magnificent piece. It is 4·6 cm. long and made of ivory. The arms or horns—it is quite possible that like the eyes or breasts they stand for both and had a double meaning—are separated from the body. The "eyes" are small, filled in with black paste and set wide apart. The perforation at the back is set high. Others of these amulets are made of stone, and they last into the dynastic age. Some of them are very stylized and the arms or horns are no longer indicated. A little vase of green stone bought by Brunton and now in the Ashmolean Museum (pl. VI, 3) seems to me to indicate especially well the meaning of the amulet, which is carved on one of its sides. The amulet is fairly frequent, as one would expect of one symbolizing the Great Mother. It is indeed rather surprising that the amulet is not known from earlier periods, but perhaps it is only this special shape of her symbol that is new. Brunton wonders whether a pair of small slates from Mustagidda, t. 11741, S.D. 37?, may not be amulets. They have the ears and horns (now broken) of the fertility-goddess, and between the horns a large suspension hole. These, if Brunton is right, may well be an earlier form of the amulet. However, their date is uncertain, as is that of a similar but smaller pair from Ballas, t. 709. There they belonged to a necklace of various charms and were certainly amulets.[2]

Amulets in the shape of other animals are recorded from Naḳāda II, though they are rare. A crocodile in calcite was found at Ḥammāmīya, t. 1629, S.D. 44-60. It formed part of an elegant bead necklace which also had an amulet with the symbol of the fertility-goddess. The grave was that of a woman.[3] In a little piece from Matmar, t. 5108, S.D. 47-68, Brunton recognizes a hedgehog.[4] It seems to have been part of an anklet. From Mustagidda, t. 1757, S.D. 60-73, comes a pair of bone amulets in the shape of dogs. They wear collars and, like the large dogs on the smaller slate palette of Hierakonpolis to which the palette is dedicated, they have upright ears.[5] The amulets will represent the same god, and may well be of about the same date. Grave 1757 belonged to a child, and the two dogs lay on its chest. Whether the ivory figure from Badāri, t. 1716, S.D. 33-42, represents the same animal cannot be decided as only a fragment has survived. It has no collar and has a longer and more bushy tail, and may be a fox or jackal. Brunton makes no reference to the grave in the text, so nothing more is known about it.[6]

The amulet generally called a fly (or is it a bee? [7]) was found in Badāri, t. 4604, S.D. 57?, and in Mustagidda, t. 232, S.D. 48-53. In the Badāri grave, which was undisturbed and belonged to a very young person, two olivine flies were deposited in a basket close to the elbow together with a rough scrap of slate with a pebble, several beads, fragments of ostrich egg-shell and a flat unpierced pebble.[8] In Mustagidda, t. 232, there were three flies made of serpentine. Other

[1] *Naq. Bal.*, pl. LXI, 4, there shown from the wrong side with the V-shaped suspension hole. It and the necklace are now in the Ashmolean Museum, Oxford; the other pieces at University College, London.
[2] *Mostag.*, p. 86, pl. XLIII, 14. *Naq. Bal.*, pl. LVIII, Q 709.
[3] *Bad. Civ.*, pl. XLIX, 33 H 6.   [4] *Matmar*, pl. XV, 1.
[5] See below, chapter on Palettes, p. 94.   [6] *Bad. Civ.*, pl. LIII, 21.
[7] See P. Montet, "Etudes sur quelques prêtres du dieu Min", *JNES*, IX (1950), p. 23.
[8] *Bad. Civ.*, p. 52, pl. XLIX, 36 F 6.

flies were found at Naḳāda, in t. 723, S.D. 46-52, and t. 238, which is undated. Two flies of lapis lazuli are all that I can trace from this latter grave.[1]

From the end of Naḳāda II falcon amulets were recovered, one of them from the town of Nub. t.[2] Others were found in graves.[3] The most interesting is the group from Naḳāda, t. 721, S.D. 44-64, which has been mentioned before.[4] It consists of four animals, two falcons, a Seth (?) animal and, somewhat smaller than the others, a lion; three of them are made of pink breccia, the fourth of silver (pl. VI, 6-8). We cannot tell whether these were amulets or whether they belong to one of the other types, either objects used in a ceremony or *ex-votos*. The three stone animals (the second falcon of silver is too damaged to be taken into consideration) were originally fixed upon something, perhaps upon perches. The pink falcon, which is the largest, measures no more than 5·5 cm., and in size they would all be suitable for wearing as amulets. Besides the hole for the stand the falcon has three perforations. One is straight through its tail. The two others are V-shaped and run from the front of the wings to the bottom of the statuette. Two shallow holes indicate that the eyes were once inlaid. The only detail marked besides the eyes are two furrows coming from the front of the bird and continued all along its bottom to indicate the wings. What the three perforations were for I do not know. The two other animals have each a hole in their bases, the "Seth" also has holes for its upright tail and ears. One would like to identify the animals with those on the standards carried in front of the king on the Nar-Mer palette and other contemporary monuments. The two falcons and the "Seth" animal would fit, but the fourth should be the unidentified object, and not a lion. No other instance is known to me of a similar group deposited in a grave. Petrie gives a short description of the burial. The grave was 60 in. by 50 in., and 40 in. deep. Only the legs of the skeletons survived. The four animals lay in front of where the hands had been, under a "small rude oval dish of rough pottery", and behind this was "a small decorated vase (D 67c)".[5] The oval dish is not typed, and the reference after the "decorated" vase is to a squat pot with tubular lug handles painted with spirals, and with a diameter of 24 cm. without the handles. This is hardly a small vase. I could not trace any pottery from t. 721, but only the four animals and a strip of twisted copper. It is a pity that no more is known about this grave; there must have been more pottery, otherwise Petrie could hardly have sequence-dated it. The animals, and especially the little lion, are very near to those from Abydos, and it seems possible that the grave is early dynastic. Four lions similar to the one from Naḳāda, t. 721, were found by Quibell at Ballas, together with a hare, some ivory rods, plain and incised, and some small flint balls with 16 small four-sided prisms made in pairs. These objects had been buried quite by themselves and were not from a grave. They are undated. Quibell assumes that they belonged to a game. It seems very unlikely that the four animals from Naḳāda, t. 721, are gaming-pieces, though it is possible. The only dated set so far, consisting of lions, balls, prisms and rods, comes from the tombs of the courtiers of King Zer of the First Dynasty.[6]

A crescent moon, a four-pointed star and a disc bead, all of red cornelian, were recovered

---

[1] The flies from Naḳāda, t. 723, I could not trace; those from t. 238 are at University College, London.

[2] At University College, London.

[3] E.g. *Mostag.*, pl. XXXIX, 45 A 3.

[4] See p. 22 above.

[5] *Naq. Bal.*, p. 26.

[6] *Tombs of the Courtiers*, pl. VII.

from Badāri, t. 3759, S.D. 39-44.[1]   It is tempting to see in them the sun, the moon and a star, though the bead has only four rays, while the stars of dynastic times have five.   The same grave also contained the fragment of the hindquarters of a pottery hippopotamus decorated with warriors and a boat in the style of the "decorated" pottery.   Nothing more of the grave is known, and the sequence-date cannot be checked.

Several other beads are taken by Brunton for amulets, especially the imitation shells of ivory or stone.   Some of these are decorated with slanting lines inlaid with black, two from Badāri [2] being surface finds, and one being in Naḳāda, t. 1480 (see below).   An example of the little chick which decorates combs and hairpins was found, made of glazed composition, in Naḳāda, t. 1774, which is undated.[3]

4. *Personal ornaments*

Whether the ivory rings, one formed by two lions from Naḳāda, t. 1480, and the other decorated with four hawks from Diospolis Parva, t. R 159 (pl. III, 11 and 12), should be classified with the amulets or the personal ornaments is a matter of opinion.   The larger of the two is the one with the four falcons, which might have been the armlet of a child or young person.   The falcons, which are arranged so that each of two pairs look at each other, are elaborately carved.   They crouch on small bases, their tails free of the arm-ring.   Petrie dates them to S.D. 71, in the dynastic period.[4]   Nothing else is known about the grave or its contents.   The ring from Naḳāda, t. 1480, is formed by two lions joined by their legs.   The grave is not sequence-dated in *Prehistoric Egypt*, but in *Diospolis Parva*, when describing the ring with the falcons under the heading of "ivory carvings" (the only mention of this important piece in the text), Petrie says: "One ring has two lions attached to it (*Naq. Bal.*, LXIV, 78), found in a grave of between S.D. 33 and 55".[5]   On the plate in the Naḳāda publication the ring was given its grave number, which is also written on the object itself.   In the description of the grave Petrie mentions only a broken ostrich egg, a bird slate and two copper finger-rings.[6]   Besides the ring with the two lions, which may have been a finger-ring, there were eight plain ivory finger-rings, some beads and the carved shell pendant mentioned above (p. 76).   The beads are of special interest, for among them is one of glazed composition, cylindrical in shape and decorated with slanting lines, and also the only glass bead (about the colour of cornelian) which with some confidence can be ascribed to predynastic or protodynastic times.[7]   The only pot I could trace is the polished-red P 56b, to which Petrie assigns the sequence-date 35-50.[8]   The style of the ivory ring with the two lions is close to that of the two dogs from the smaller slate palette of Hierakonpolis, and in spite of Petrie's earlier date I find it difficult to dissociate it from the ring with the four falcons and the beginning of the dynasties.

[1] *Bad. Civ.*, pp. 55-6, pl. XLIX, 73 A 3 and B 3.   The grave is not published.   The three beads are at University College, London.

[2] *Bad. Civ.*, pl. XLIX, 56, H 3, K 3.

[3] *Naq. Bal.*, pl. LX, 19.

[4] *Diosp. Pa.*, p. 22, pl. IX, 23.   The grave is unpublished.

[5] *Diosp. Pa.*, p. 22.   The ring is not mentioned in the publication of the grave, *Naq. Bal.*, p. 28, but has the tomb number on pl. LXIV.   Both rings are in the Ashmolean Museum, Oxford.

[6] All in the Ashmolean Museum, Oxford.

[7] The plain finger-rings are at University College, London, the other pieces in Berlin.   The glass bead was analysed and unless it is intrusive belongs to the grave: *Die Altertümer*, II, pp. 108-9, 165.

[8] Also in Berlin.

A less fine bracelet with four birds' heads sticking out from it from Tarkhan, t. 644, S.D. 80, is also of the First Dynasty.[1]

No other ivory or bone ring with such complicated decoration is known to me from predynastic times. The Badārians sported wide armlets, some inlaid with blue-glazed steatite beads, which must have made a pleasing contrast to the white of the ivory.[2] Some were decorated with knobs, as were some finger-rings, also of ivory, though with them, as with the armlets, the plain ones predominate. The fashion of inlaying the armlets vanishes with the Badārian age, and many simple rings are now worn on one arm. Often they were made of shell, which may have been iridescent. For finger-rings the form with a knob remains, but the knob is usually smaller than those from Badārian graves.[3] Armlets made of flint, e.g. from Diospolis Parva, t. U 354, S.D. 70-80,[4] are all early dynastic. They show the art of the flint worker at its height. Few tasks can have been trickier and more difficult than to fashion a beautifully even ring out of this uncompromising material.

Whether the so-called forehead-pendants should be reckoned among the personal ornaments seems more than doubtful. All of them are of Nakāda II. Petrie's original idea that they might have served to fasten a veil cannot be substantiated. The only one provided with a hook on which a veil might be fastened [5] which was known to Petrie was from Nakāda, t. B 99, and this certainly does not follow the outline of the forehead, nor do most of the others,[6] and most of them were not found near the forehead.[7] The most likely explanation seems to be that they were used for cosmetics, perhaps for the small amount of prepared galena needed to apply around the eyes. Most of them are made of shell and are plain. One from Gerzeh, t. 33, S.D. 57-64,[8] is in the shape of a reed float, another from Nakāda, t. T 5, S.D. 50, is of grey and white marble.[9] A few are made of copper, their suspension holes being eccentric.[10]

5. *Knife handles and weapons*

The beautifully-carved ivory knife handles which are fitted to a few of the ripple-flaked flint knives have attracted attention from the time they first came into our collections. Only one of them was found in an excavation, and that not a very regular one. It comes from H. de Morgan's dig at Abu Zedan and is in the Brooklyn Museum. The handle has on one side a perforated knob by which it could be suspended from a belt or wherever it may have been worn, and is decorated on both sides with ten rows of animals carved in a low relief. There are similar knobs and decorations, though less complete, on the handles of the Pitt-Rivers knife [11] and on that once owned by Lord Carnarvon.[12] These three handles are closely connected in the motifs carved on them. The animals chosen by the carver are the same on all the three handles, though not all of them occur on all the knives. Each species occupies a row by itself into which only excep-

---

[1] *Tarkhan II*, pl. III, 10.
[2] *Bad. Civ.* pl. XXIII, 14.
[3] See *Bad. Civ.*, pl. XXIII; *Preh. Eg.*, pl. XXXI.
[4] *Diosp. Pa.*, p. 36, U 354.
[5] *Naq. Bal.*, pl. LXII, 21.
[6] *Bad. Civ.*, p. 59, pl. LIV, 3.
[7] *Gerzeh*, pp. 23-4.
[8] *Gerzeh*, pl. VIII, 26.
[9] This one and that from Gerzeh, t. 33, are now in the Ashmolean Museum, Oxford.
[10] See above, Chapter I.
[11] In the Pitt Rivers Museum, Farnham, Blandford, Dorset.
[12] Now in the Metropolitan Museum of Art, New York.

tionally an animal of a different sort intrudes. Most characteristic among these animals is the group of an elephant treading on two snakes, the meaning of which remains obscure. The handle which is the best preserved and which shows the greatest number and variety of animals is the one in Brooklyn. Two smaller handles, one at University College, London, the other in Berlin, are without the suspension knob and have only a very abbreviated version of the animals in rows on one side. On the other they have the motif of the entwined serpents with the rosettes between them.[1] The finest and most important of the ivory knife handles is the one in the Louvre called the Gebel-el-'Arak knife, for it is supposed to have been found there. In contrast to all the other knife handles so far discussed, its decoration is arranged in scenes running at right angles to the long sides of the handle, and not parallel to them. There are no long and uniform rows of animals here, but lively representations of combats between long-haired and short-haired warriors on the one side and, on the one with the boss, hunting incidents presided over by the hero taming a lion with each hand. On the obverse and underneath the two rows of fighting men there are two rows with boats, that on top showing the high-prowed "Sumerian" ships, and that below the Nile boats as known from the "decorated" pottery. Between these two, and unfortunately damaged by the largest break in the ivory, float the corpses of the slain. On the reverse and underneath the lion-tamer there are two hunting-dogs facing each other, and also two rows with various animals, among which a lion is depicted falling upon an animal the front part of which is missing; below is a huntsman belonging to the short-haired tribe who catches an animal with a lasso. He has been transferred to the obverse of the handle, filling a space which is left over by the row of "Sumerian" boats. He holds on with both hands to the lasso, the loop of which has caught an ibex around the neck. This scene, though less lively than the corresponding one on the lion-hunt palette, shows how a lasso was handled, thus contrasting with the other, where instead of being held with both hands the lasso trails into the void.[2]

An ivory handle which was acquired some time ago by the Metropolitan Museum, New York, is the latest addition to the type. Though preserved in its entirety, the surface is so badly worn that on the side with the pierced boss almost nothing is visible. On the obverse three rows of men occur parallel to the sides of the handle. The upper parts of men carrying crooks remain in the top row. The middle row is completely destroyed, and from the bottom row all that can be discerned is the lower part of squatting persons.

The question arises, what is the date and the possible use of the knives to which these handles were fitted? Where the knives or parts of them have survived they are ripple-flaked flint knives. And on these the two authors who have written careful studies about them, Georges Bénédite [3] and Helene Kantor,[4] base their date of Naḳāda II for the handles. One must take into account, however, that Naḳāda II means different things for these authors. This period extends over a larger time and, when used by Bénédite, takes in what we would now call protodynastic. While for him it still comprises what Petrie later called the Semainian, Miss Kantor, in the same article in which she deals with the knife handles, conclusively demonstrates that there is no such period and that the dynastic age develops directly from Naḳāda II. There is not much to quarrel

[1] See the gold handle in Cairo, p. 5.   [2] See chapter on Palettes, p. 98.
[3] G. Bénédite, "Le Couteau de Gebel el-Arak", *Mon. Piot*, XXII, pp. 1 ff., and "The Carnarvon Ivory", *JEA*, 5 (1918), pp. 1 ff., 225 ff.
[4] H. Kantor, "The Final Phase of Predynastic Culture", *JNES*, III, pp. 110 ff.

with a Naḳāda II date for the ripple-flaked knives. They are certainly a closely-related group, possibly the product of one workshop. But I find it difficult to accept that they all belong to S.D. fifties and stop with the beginning of the First Dynasty as Miss Kantor and Mrs. Braidwood uphold. I do not think that in their present state the sequence-dates can be used to give so precise a date. Some of the graves with ripple-flaked knives mentioned by Miss Kantor can equally well be dated to the sixties, e.g. El-'Amrah b 35, where the earlier date rests on the wavy-handled pot which belongs to a difficult group to date. All the other pots in the grave have a very large span of life.[1] The graves from Abuṣīr el-Meleḳ with ripple-flaked knives will be even later. We have now seen only too often that there is no hard and fast line dividing the end of the predynastic from the dynastic period. Therefore I think the end of Naḳāda II and perhaps the time of transition is the firmest date we can give at present for the knives. But are we sure that the handles are of the same period? These exquisite knives surely were handed down through more than one generation. Of the several dozens of them known from dated graves all have a rounded butt except those fitted with the ivory or gold handles. These are provided with a short tang to fit into the handles. Though carefully executed, the tangs are not on a par with the rest of the flint work and may very well have been made later. It is during the earliest dynasties that flint knives are provided with tangs or with handles worked in one with the blades. To decide the date of the ivory handles the style of the carvings is all we have to go upon, as the grave from Abu Zedan is too badly published to allow a precise dating and the pots can no longer be identified in the Brooklyn Museum.[2] Outside the group of ivory handles the subject of the animals in file returns on the Davis ivory comb and the lost gold handle of the mace-head from grave 1 of cemetery 137 near Seyala in Nubia.[3] The comb is without provenance, but the mace was found in an early dynastic grave. Both these pieces have the elephant treading on two snakes among the subjects represented. A third carving that might be taken into consideration is the ivory spoon from Tarkhan, t. 1023, S.D. 78. Here the elephant on snakes is missing and a base line is provided on which the procession of animals walk, a detail absent from all the other ivories and the gold handles. Bénédite is of opinion that the Brooklyn handle is the earliest, for it has the fullest repertory of animals, and that all the other handles depend on it. He puts the Carnarvon and the Gebel-el-'Arak knife latest, yet still within the Naḳāda II period. Miss Kantor does not accept this, but thinks all the handles are contemporary. To me it seems difficult to separate the three handles with the entwined snakes, one of gold, the two others of ivory, from the similar motifs on the slate palettes, and the Gebel-el-'Arak knife from the Nar-Mer palette. If anything, the Gebel-el-'Arak knife is artistically the more developed in spite of the lack of a base line. The only dated grave, that which contained the golden mace handle, agrees with the late date and so does the ivory spoon from Tarkhan. Miss Kantor thinks that the mace handle must be dated earlier than the grave in which it was found. I do not think that one can as yet come to a satisfactory conclusion whether the handles are wholly of Naḳāda II, are of the time of transition, or are early dynastic.

Bénédite has tried to assess the meaning of the rows of animals and comes to the conclusion that "the totem-animals of more or less adjacent clans, and even of internal subdivisions of the clan (family groupings), are assembled in a pictorial manner having reference to the idea of the

[1] About the dating of the wavy-handled pots see Vol. I, pp. 40 ff.
[2] This in spite of Miss Kantor's effort, which seems to me based on evidence that is too unsafe.
[3] *The Archaeological Survey of Nubia, Bulletin* 7, p. 18.

chase. . . ." [1] Bénédite takes the knives to be either sacrificial or hunting knives. I do not know about the totem animals, but the explanation of the knives as hunting knives seems to me most acceptable. What is surprising is that the grave from Abu Zedan, which in addition to the knife with the ivory handle contained two more ripple-flaked knives, is otherwise such a poor affair. A broken stone armlet is the only personal ornament, and the pots, as far as one can judge from the published drawing, are outstanding neither by their number nor by their quality. However, with one single grave one cannot draw any conclusions from this.

Of weapons made of bone or kindred material there is not much to be said. There are the harpoons, which have already been mentioned together with the copper ones,[2] and, very rarely, a bone arrow-head, such as the one from Naḳāda, t. T 57, S.D. 69. This is triangular and tanged, and was originally painted red.[3] Whether the throwing-sticks which occur in graves since Badārian times [4] were really weapons seems doubtful. Brunton thinks they may be castanets; they often occur in pairs. They certainly resemble the castanets which some of the men on the "decorated" pottery carry in one hand.[5]

[1] G. Bénédite, "The Carnarvon Ivory", *JEA*, 5 (1918), pp. 240-1.
[2] See Chapter I, p. 18.
[3] *Naq. Bal.*, pl. LXIV, 98. Now in the Ashmolean Museum, Oxford. No other piece from t. T 57 is known to me.
[4] *Bad. Civ.*, p. 32.
[5] Kantor, "The Final Phase of Predynastic Culture", *JNES*, III (1944), fig. 8, A and K.

CHAPTER IV

PALETTES

PALETTES made of a fine green slate are among the most characteristic items found in predynastic graves. They first appear with the Badārians, and they are at their most frequent and most diverse during Naḳāda II. It is at the end of this period and the beginning of the dynasties that they attain their zenith, with the carved palette of Nar-Mer and the group related to it. Yet this is a period when those in ordinary graves had already reverted to formless slabs or simple geometrical shapes, to go out of common use a short time after.

Malachite, a copper oxide of light green colour, was ground on these palettes, and the resulting powder mixed with some fat or resin to serve as a cosmetic. In a few rare instances traces of red haematite show that this substance too had been rubbed or at least mixed on slate palettes.

The earliest known palettes are either shapeless or rectangular pieces with more or less rounded sides, some having the shorter sides concave or notched. Only one from Badāri itself had some ornamentation, three round hollows at each corner which, as Brunton thought, were meant for the insertion of shell beads. A single palette which Brunton ascribes to late Badārian has the form of a pointed oval.[1] All these shapes are strictly functional, and as yet show no inkling of the variety of fancy forms which were to become so characteristic of the later predynastic periods.

At Badāri, 21 palettes were found in well over 300 graves, eight of them together with pebbles with which to grind the colour. A cake of green malachite paste was found on one palette, and traces of malachite in two more tombs. Red paint was present on one palette. At Mustagidda eleven palettes were excavated, five of them in what Brunton calls "Tasian" graves. Of these five, three were of alabaster, one of limestone and the fifth of slate.[2] Brunton is of opinion that this is a sign of age, but palettes of material other than slate occur occasionally throughout the predynastic periods.[3] In grave 2673 (of Naḳāda II?) at Matmar itself, a "grinder" was found, 27 cm. by 18 cm. and 2·6 cm. thick, of grey sandstone coloured red by the haematite or ochre for the grinding of which it had been used.[4] If, then, the occasional use of a material other than slate for palettes is no indication of period, was slate perhaps reserved for malachite only, while other materials were chosen for other cosmetics like haematite and galena?

Dr. A. J. Arkell, who has recently given some time to the study of this subject, tells me that not only in the Sudan, but certainly also during Old Kingdom and First Intermediate times in Egypt, sandstone grinders were found with red stains on them showing that haematite or ochre had been ground on them, the reason being that ochre needs a coarse material for grinding and slate is too smooth to serve.[5] With this the grinder of the predynastic grave 2673 from Matmar agrees, and strengthens Arkell's assumption that these simple objects were in use for the production of the red colouring material from very early times.

---

[1] *Bad. Civ.*, p. 31.
[3] See above, Vol. I, p. 21; *Preh. Eg.*, pp. 39 ff.
[5] A. J. Arkell, *Early Khartoum*, pp. 50-63, 108.

[2] *Mostag.*, pp. 29-30.
[4] *Matmar*, pp. 21 ff.

Thus the ancient Egyptians were in the habit of painting themselves with red and green make-up since Badārian days,[1] and the use of kohl, the black eye-paint, also goes back to that remote age, for a small bag containing galena—the chief ingredient for making up kohl—was found near the hands of a skeleton in grave 2229 at Mustagidda. Petrie says that both malachite and galena were common in the tombs at Naḳāda.[2]

But while with very few exceptions palettes or grinders not of slate were made in very simple shapes, those of slate received special attention and became objects of art, which shows that greater importance was attached to the preparation of the green cosmetic than to any of the others. Why was this? Petrie assumes that the green paint was applied around the eyes "to keep the glare off and act as germicide".[3] I do not know whether malachite can act as a disinfectant, nor whether light green colour painted at some distance around the eyes can keep off the glare. This might perhaps be said of kohl, black with a metallic sheen, which today, as of old, is painted round the eyes in Egypt. In modern times it is used only by the women, but no such distinction seems to have been made in antiquity. It makes the eyes appear larger and more lustrous, and it seems to me more probable that in ancient times also kohl was applied as an embellishment rather than for practical reasons. It may be that the green paint also was thought to improve the beauty of a face, and was used for that purpose by men, women and even children of the predynastic period.

That the green paint was indeed used round the eyes, and to colour the part of the face between the eyes and the nose, is shown by t. H 97 from El-Maḥāsna, where the large head of a female figure was found, made of fine yellow clay and baked. The face was painted dark red with almost black eyebrows. The eyelids were outlined with a broad, light green band, the space within being coloured black or very dark red.[4] This custom was still practised during the Old Kingdom. Green paint, $\int$ 𓆓 ⦂ wꜣḏw, is mentioned on offering-lists of that period, e.g. in that of Rahotep of Dynasty IV from Meydum.[5] His mummy had the eyes and eyebrows painted with green on the outer wrappings. When describing the stela of the lady Hathor-nefer-hetep from Saḳḳāra, also of the Fourth Dynasty, Margaret Murray records that "there is one very remarkable point about the personal ornamentation in vogue at the time: the face from the eye-brow to the base of the nose is painted with a wide band of green, the rest of the flesh being painted the usual yellow. The mummy of Rahotep (Petrie, *Medum*, p. 18) had green paint, a quarter of an inch wide, round the eyes; and green eye-paint was commonly used in prehistoric times."[6] Green paint is mentioned in the Pyramid Texts together with the sound eye of Horus.[7] It is, as Mercer explains,[8] a symbol of it, as is the White Crown. The green cosmetic can only have been connected with the sound eye of Horus after Horus had become an important god in Egypt, and the story of his sound and of his damaged eye generally known. We do not know exactly when this happened, but his images do not appear before the very end of Naḳāda II. At this date we also find slate palettes in the form of falcons.

If green eye-paint was symbolical of the sound eye of Horus during the Old Kingdom, it

---

[1] *Mostag.*, p. 30, who says that in grave 2840 an alabaster palette was found "stained green on one side, and red (for rouge?) on the other".

[2] *Naq. Bal.*, p. 45.   [3] *Preh. Eg.*, p. 37.

[4] *Pre-dyn. Cem. at El-Mahasna*, pp. 28-9.   [5] *Medum*, pl. XIII.

[6] Margaret Murray, *Saqqara Mastabas*, I, p. 4.   [7] Pyramid Texts, 54D, and 1681.

[8] Samuel A. B. Mercer, *The Pyramid Texts*, II, p. 35.

seems admissible to conclude that in the preceding periods it also had a symbolical meaning, which might explain the extraordinary development of the slate palettes. A short survey of the different forms of slate palettes prevalent during the predynastic ages may give an indication.

The Badārian palettes, being strictly utilitarian, as we saw, are of no help for the solution of our problem.

During Naḳāda I geometrical palettes are still prevalent, though some in animal shapes begin to appear. The most common are the rhombic palettes, much longer than wide. Quite a number of them have projections at the ends of the shorter axes. This special type tends to be made in exaggerated sizes. Pieces up to 75 cm. in length are not rare, and Brunton even describes one three feet long. They are correspondingly heavy. The ends are long and narrow, and can hardly have been of any practical use. Some, but as a rule not the largest sizes, have one to three small hollows in the middle of the palettes. They are generally explained as having been caused by the action of the pebble used for rubbing the malachite. This appears to me difficult to accept. Many palettes show striation caused by the moving pebble, but only very few have these holes, which are confined to some of the smaller rhomboid palettes or to the shapeless ones. Perhaps they were made to hold the substance which had to be mixed with the malachite powder to turn it into a cosmetic.

Just as the rhombic slates tend to grow to enormous sizes, so, at the other end of the scale, they shrink to tiny pieces, their longer axes not much more than 5 cm.[1] These small palettes can never have been used for grinding, but must have been amulets, tokens, as it were, which stood for the real thing.

Some of the rhombic palettes show decoration at one or both of their tips. One from Naḳāda, t. 1497, S.D. 33, has one tip in the form of what are probably the horns and ears of a cow. The palette is 36 cm. long and 8 cm. at its widest. The grave also contained the curious egg-shaped pot painted with chains of cross-lined diamonds in white (Vol. I, pl. VIII, 3), the sherd of a black-topped pot with a mark in the form of an elephant, an ivory comb, its top adorned with a giraffe,[2] five beads of different stones,[3] and another rhombic slate, type 92D, which is still 43·2 cm. long, though one of its tips is broken, its other tip being divided from the main body by a curved incision.[4] A palette similarly decorated with cow's ears and horns was found at Mustagidda, t. 1825.[5] A very good example of this type comes from El-ʿAmrah, t. a 97, now in the University Museum, Cambridge. It is 55 cm. long, and has the eyes marked. The grave is unpublished (pl. VI, 1). Another rhombic palette with decoration is the remarkable piece from Abadiyeh, t. B 102, already mentioned,[6] which has a harpoon near one tip and an elephant together with a Z-sign near the other. A rather unusual rhomboid palette was found by Brunton in the remains of the predynastic settlement at Badāri.[7] It is about 33 cm. long, one tip is missing, and the other, only slightly damaged, is divided from the main body of the palette by a curved row of shallow circular impressions which may have been meant for beads. It is not pointed, but cut short, and decorated by a sort of fringe made by notches carved out of the slate.[8] Brunton dated it to

[1] One was in Naḳāda, t. 1483, S.D. 35, but they occur also elsewhere, e.g. *Pre-dyn. Cem. at El-Mahasna*, t. H 17, pl. XIII, before S.D. 42.

[2] Now in the Ashmolean Museum, Oxford.   [3] *Die Altertümer*, II, pp. 108, 166, pl. 28.

[4] Now in the Museum of the Oriental Institute, Chicago.   [5] *Mostag.*, pl. XLIII, 2.

[6] See above, Vol. I, p. 12, fig. 2.   [7] *Bad. Civ.*, p. 46, 3165, pl. LIII, 11. Cf. pp. 62 f.

[8] A similar decoration occurs on a small slate (Randall-MacIver, *El Amrah*, pl. X, 7).

S.D. 37-38; the reason for this is not quite obvious. It lay close beside and on the same level as a big dark-red-polished pot of Brunton's "Town Pottery". Inside it was a large collection of what may well have been a sorcerer's outfit. There was a smaller rhomboid palette, about 22 cm. long and plain, as well as malachite, ochre and resin to make up the cosmetics. A string of pierced natural flint pebbles and pierced shells for necklaces were together with 83 nummulites and 7 rough little pebbles which were not pierced. Two limestone "spindle-whorls" may have been beads also. A little stud of alabaster was in the pot and a disc mace-head. Most interesting are eight ivory tags and an ivory tusk of which the head only could be saved. The tusk is rather elaborate, with a loop at the top for suspension. Whether the slate palette with the unusual decoration belongs to the pot is, of course, uncertain, though it seems likely. The whole collection may well belong to Naḳāda II.

The rhombic slates and those of no definite shape form the majority of these toilet implements during Naḳāda I, and they were still in use during Naḳāda II. Some palettes, however, made in the forms of animals, begin a fashion that was to become dominant later on. They are highly stylized, since the flat, utilitarian surface of the palette had to be preserved and the animals depicted had to be adapted to this. Therefore it is not always easy to decide which animal is meant. A successful piece of work is a palette in the shape of a Nile turtle, perhaps because this rather flat animal lends itself specially to representation in a flat piece of slate. It was found in Naḳāda, t. 1817, S.D. 36.[1] The feet are barely indicated, so as not to spoil the outline of the nearly circular body. The head, in contrast, sticks well out like a handle with a prominent snout and huge, circular eyes. Its longer axis, including the head, is 13·3 cm., its width 12·6 cm. Grave 1817 also contained a plain, rhombic palette and a pebble for grinding.[2] Six black-topped pots, one of which is an oval dish, a black-polished bottle and a small "rough" saucer can be traced from the pottery of this tomb.[3] Some fragments of wood may have come from a bier. Another turtle palette, not quite so fine, was excavated from t. 3823 at Badari, S.D. 35-37. It is somewhat asymmetrical, with its feet sticking out and a plain head.[4] Palettes in the shape of turtles also occur during Naḳāda II.

The representation of a hartebeest is probably intended on the slate from Naḳāda, t. 241, S.D. 31-37. The piece is rather clumsy, with its funny little legs sticking out at impossible angles at the bottom. Part of the head and the horns are broken off.[5] A palette in the shape of a moufflon or Barbary sheep is from Naḳāda, t. 1562 (pl. VI, 9). The small head with an inlaid eye and the horns curved back fits on a long neck attached to a full body. The legs are indicated only by small protuberances which follow the curves of the body. Grave 1562 is not sequence-dated, and I could not trace the pottery which once belonged to it.[6] However, a large comb of ivory with a hartebeest on the top, which was found in it, makes it likely that it is of Naḳāda I. Some

---

[1] Now in the Manchester Museum.

[2] The rhombic slate palette is in the Ashmolean Museum, Oxford, the pebble at University College, London.

[3] The pots are in the Ashmolean Museum, Oxford; in University College, London; in the British Museum (British and Mediaeval Dept.); and the Museum of the Oriental Institute, Chicago.

[4] Bad. Civ., pl. XXXIV, 3.

[5] The palette and two large sherds from a black-topped pot are at University College, London; an ivory tag in the Ashmolean Museum, Oxford; one black-topped pot each in the Chicago Natural History Museum and in the Berlin Egyptian Collection.

[6] The palette and the comb from t. 1562 are in the Ashmolean Museum, Oxford; the other pieces at University College, London.

lumps of malachite and a spatha shell in which the ground colour may have been mixed, and one of the little clay cones covered with leather, perhaps belonging to a game, are the other articles on record from it. Palettes in the form of hartebeests remained in fashion during Naḳāda II also.

Tomb B 101, S.D. 34, from Diospolis Parva, with which we have had to deal already,[1] has given us a palette in the shape of a hippopotamus. The girl for whom this, the richest grave in the cemetery, had been made must have had a special connexion with the clumsy beast, for at least seven statuettes of hippopotami were recovered from it. The palette is an artistic little piece, more carefully made and with more naturalistic details than usual. Palettes of this type are rare.

Palettes in the form of birds were to become great favourites. Petrie seems to have been in two minds whether or not to ascribe their origin to Naḳāda I. In *Prehistoric Egypt*[2] he mentions none before S.D. 46; in *Diospolis Parva* he lets them begin with S.D. 35. The piece there illustrated is from Abadiyeh, t. B 117.[3] It is a rather peculiar-looking object which is about 32 cm. long, and consists of a vaguely triangular part with a bird-like handle protruding from one of its corners. A similar palette from Matmar, t. 2631, is dated by Brunton to S.D. 41-48.[4] The bird represented has not been determined with certainty. It was popular at this period and we find it also decorating the tops of combs. It may be an ostrich, or a flamingo.

But, apart from this rather peculiar palette, there exist a few indications which show that bird-shaped slates must have begun to be used in Naḳāda I. A small fragment, 2·5 cm. wide, in the form of a bird's head, the eyes inlaid with rings of ostrich egg-shell, was among the furniture of Naḳāda, t. 1590, S.D. 33. The grave also contained a small slate palette of the type which Petrie calls "magic".[5] It is bird-shaped, and has a nearly square body with two notches at the bottom by which it could be tied to a string. From the corner of the opposite side a bird's head on a long neck protrudes, which adds about 2 cm. to the height of the object. No eye is indicated. We have seen that some rhombic slate palettes were made in miniature sizes which could have no practical use, but could only have been symbolical.[6] Tiny replicas of other types of palettes exist, but, apart from the devices which help to tie them to a string, no shapes are peculiar to "magical" slates only. This seems to indicate that the small or "magical" slates were copies in miniature of the usual types, and therefore closely linked with the real objects, and not something which existed in their own right. If, therefore, Naḳāda, t. 1590, S.D. 33, contained small palettes in the shape of birds, we shall have to assume that the real thing also was made at that time, and the broken-off head from the same grave confirms this idea. Perhaps somewhat later than this simple form of bird palette is another which is rather peculiar and demands some explanation, namely the double-bird palette. This name is somewhat misleading, for it is rather a bird with two heads on long necks that is represented, one in front and one behind. It seems to me likely that this form owes its existence to a misinterpretation. We have seen that some of the rhombic slates were decorated at one end with the ears and horns of the cow-goddess. Small replicas

---

[1] See Vol. I, p. 31, Vol. II, p. 61. The palette is now in the Ashmolean Museum, Oxford.

[2] *Preh. Eg.*, p. 37.

[3] *Diosp. Pa.*, p. 20, pls. III and XI, 12. T. 117 is not published. No other objects from it are known to me.

[4] *Matmar*, pl. XV, 29.

[5] *Preh. Eg.*, pl. XLV, 38. Now at University College, London, where are also from the same grave a comb with perhaps another bird's head, but too broken to be certain, and a fragment of ostrich egg-shell. Two black-topped vases, B 22d and B 1H, are in the Ashmolean Museum, Oxford. A white-cross-lined vase, C 21E, is in Berlin

[6] See above, p. 83.

of this type also exist. Two were found in Naḳāda, t. 1646, S.D. 33.[1] They have nearly square bodies which are notched near the bottom, and are also perforated so that they could be suspended. Their tops show the horns and ears of the cow-goddess. In this special instance the ears are treated rather fancifully, and look as if they had been tripled. This is an early example of treating ears as if they were ornaments, and something separate from the heads to which they belong, which is such a characteristic trait of later Egyptian art.

Comparing the little bird palettes from Naḳāda, t. 1590, with those with the ears and horns from Naḳāda, t. 1646, it is striking how much the silhouettes of the birds' heads and long necks and of the heavy horns of the cow resemble each other. This must have occurred to their makers some time early in Naḳāda II, if not before, and they playfully provided the outcurving parts of the horns with eyes, thus making the resemblance to birds complete, and the double-bird palette was created. They were only, or at least mainly, made in large sizes, oblong, sometimes still with the greatest width near the middle like the rhombic palettes, and the tops decorated with the double bird.[2] Petrie maintains that these palettes occur in Nubia at the end of Naḳāda I, and dates his type 65D to S.D. 37 after Reisner, *The Archaeological Survey of Nubia*. This must be a mistake, for the palette he figures comes from Cemetery 17, t. 15, dated "middle prehistoric", which means Naḳāda II. The grave contained, in addition to the palette, a wavy-handled pot, a copper bracelet, etc.,[3] which place it securely in the later period. The same type, 65D, was also found in Naḳāda, t. B 133, which Petrie sequence-dated to 46.[4] He dates somewhat earlier a type where the two heads are even nearer together (type 67T). This occurs first in Naḳāda, t. 164, S.D. 42. This palette is nearly oval, the heads being without necks and very small, so that the eyes, which perforate the stone, look enormous. It seems that the type of double-bird palette where the heads are separated from each other by a hump, sometimes deeply notched or incised, perhaps to represent feathers, developed later, for Petrie quotes as the earliest one from El-'Amrah, t. a 89, with a very modest hump between the heads, which he dates between S.D. 35-43, and the excavator dated to before S.D. 46.[5] This type survives into early dynastic times, when several variations of it are found, e.g. at Tarkhan.[6]

I do not know of any amuletic double-bird palettes of this type, for the small forms seem to remain true to the original form of horns and ears. There is, however, another form of double-bird palette of which we have pieces preserved that could not have served a practical purpose. Its origin is different from that of the palettes just described, and it must have developed from what may perhaps be called "the swimming bird". The birds represented seem to be of a different species, perhaps ducks or geese, and they are shown whole, the body as well as the heads. No piece securely dated to Naḳāda I is known to me, but one from Naḳāda, t. 1675, is of S.D. 32-48. It has a straight back and a long neck supporting a small head.[7] The eye-hole perforates the slate. This is clearly a single bird, and it has one head. Two palettes, both from Matmar, t. 2644,[8] are more bizarre in outline, for the birds carry on their backs notched and perforated excrescences by which they could be hung. Brunton dates these palettes to Naḳāda I, though

[1] The two palettes and a white-cross-lined pot, C 64u, are at University College, London.
[2] Vandier, *Manuel*, I, p. 374, calls these palettes "scutiformes", i.e. formed like shields.
[3] Reisner, *The Archaeological Survey of Nubia*, I, p. 128.
[4] The palette is at University College, London. I could trace no other object from this tomb.
[5] *El Amrah*, p. 17; i.e. Naḳāda II.　　　　　　[6] Petrie's types, 72H, 77D and T.
[7] The palette is at University College, London.　　[8] *Matmar*, pl. XV, 36.

t. 2644 contained two of the so-called amuletic "combs" which are generally attributed to Naḳāda II, and in his tomb-catalogue does not sequence-date it. These two palettes still have enough room for the grinding of malachite; the handles are comparatively small and the heads are balanced by the tails of the birds. From the same cemetery, t. 3123, S.D. 38-43,[1] comes another pair of palettes similar to those from 2644. Here the centre-pieces with perforations and notches have grown, and the bodies have shrunk correspondingly. They are no longer flanked by heads and tails of birds, but by two large heads looking either way. This type of double-bird palette often loses so much of its body that its practical use is completely lost. The result looks somewhat like a crescent with two birds' heads and a tall handle jutting out between them. Good examples of this type, which is not rare, were found in Naḳāda, t. 1419, S.D. 44, where they were with a comb, the top of which is adorned with a well-modelled bird, two ivory "horns" with incised lines and a flat tusk likewise with incised decoration.[2] It seems that these double-bird palettes were put into the graves in pairs.

Whether the type of palette which Petrie called the pelta [3] was originally evolved from the "swimming-bird" type also, is difficult to decide. The bodies are half-moon or crescent-shaped, with one straight or slightly-concave and one deeply-curved side. A small decoration is added to one corner, and in some instances another, perforated or shaped like a handle, sticks out from the middle of the straight side. The small decoration at the corner is perforated also and sometimes looks like a bird's head turned backwards. The earliest known of these, which is probably still of Naḳāda I, was found by Reisner in the Nubian Cemetery 17, t. 49. This is not really a grave, but a group of objects perhaps left behind in a heap by plunderers.[4] The slate was found together with a number of black-topped pots, which, though some of them are of types which had a long life, make the attribution to Naḳāda I acceptable. The palette is crescent-shaped, perforated at the middle of the concave side and with a small perforated protuberance at one end. Petrie thought of reed boats as the origin of this type.[5]

Some of the pelta-type palettes also have a body so narrow that it is quite impossible to grind anything on them. One from Naḳāda, t. 171,[6] is dated S.D. 34-55 in Petrie's catalogue of sequence-dated graves from Naḳāda, but dated to S.D. 52 in *Prehistoric Egypt*.[7] It is crescent-shaped, with a perforated handle in the middle of the concave side and a turned-back bird's head at one end. From there to the other end the body of the palette is covered with a row of shallow circular depressions, twelve in number, and a thirteenth below the handle (Petrie's type 31D). A similar piece, but with more excrescences and only seven depressions, Petrie's type 31J, was bought and has no provenance.

One more type of bird palette has to be mentioned, namely that of the royal falcon. It is a late development. All those known to me are early dynastic, the time during which the falcon god Horus became prominent. Two different sub-types occur at Tarkhan and elsewhere. One

1 *Matmar*, pl. XV, 35.
2 The slates are at University College, London.
3 *Preh. Eg.*, p. 37.
4 Reisner, *The Archaeological Survey of Nubia*, I, p. 118, pl. 63a, 8.
5 *Preh. Eg.*, p. 37.
6 Petrie erroneously ascribes it to Diospolis, t. 422; it is at University College, London, together with a rhomboid slate from the same tomb.
7 *Preh. Eg.*, p. 37.

is roughly triangular or shield-shaped, and a small falcon (sometimes one each side) crouches on one side of its top [1]; the other is shaped like a falcon.[2] This second type was also found at Tarkhan and in t. 3771 at Badāri.[3] All these palettes are dated to S.D. 77.

The most popular shape of palette is the fish, at least during Naḳāda II (pl. VI, 10). Petrie ascribes its origin to the later part of Naḳāda I. The two instances he quotes [4] are from unpublished graves at Diospolis Parva, from which I could not trace any other objects which would make it possible to investigate the dates. One is from Hu, t. U 214, S.D. 36. The fish is rather narrower than those commonly represented. Petrie recognizes in it an oxyrhynkhos or *nefash*. It has a pointed head, a marked eye, a protruding tail and the fins of the back incised. The other slate from Hu, t. U 252, S.D. 36,[5] is of much coarser make. It has a humped back and a small tail, otherwise no details are given. Petrie does not mention this palette in the text, and it would be difficult to fit it into his theory that the earliest palettes are more carefully made, and with more naturalistic details than the later ones. For this I see no evidence. One must not forget that quite a number of palettes were just smoothed pieces of slate, and that a casual resemblance to a fish may have provoked the maker to add a tail or an eye without bothering to convert the palette into a fish, and that that may have happened early in the period as well as late. A very elaborately detailed fish from Tarkhan is dynastic,[6] and just as characteristic for the later period as are the plainer palettes. Much more work on slate palettes will have to be done before we can venture to form an idea about their development.[7]

Fish palettes also were made in miniature. One, Petrie's type 45N from Naḳāda, t. 1577, S.D. 38-50, comes from a grave which contained two more of these little slates. None of the three is more than 5 cm. long, indeed a little rhomb is even slightly less. The third piece is a bird.[8]

Though one would think that the fish with its compact form does not lend itself to fanciful interpretations, yet we do find a few pieces where the artist has played with the simple shape. A palette from Abadiyeh, t. B 341, is provided with eyes, gills and fins. Its tail is converted into a small fish which also has eyes, gills and fins. It looks in the opposite direction to that of its parent, to which it is joined. Another double-fish palette was found in Naḳāda, t. 345.[9] The fish are of about equal size, and joined at their mouths. Two perforations may have been meant for eyes, though they are placed rather far down their backs. Otherwise the tails only are indicated.

In a few rare instances different species of animals were combined in the outline of a palette, making it appear a different species when looked at from the top and from the bottom. A piece from Naḳāda, t. 271, S.D. 38, has the head and paws of a Nile turtle at one end and the heads of two gazelles, separated by a wide hump, at the other, which is wider.[10] Another palette from Naḳāda, t. 1738, is even stranger. At one end are the head and feet of a tortoise, of which the feet

---

[1] *Tarkhan II*, pl. XXII, 10L.   [2] *Tarkhan II*, pl. XXII, 10d.

[3] *Bad. Civ.*, pl. XXXIV, 3.   [4] *Preh. Eg.*, p. 37.

[5] At least I assume that the palette comes from there, though not mentioned in the original publication. It is marked U 252 on *Corpus*, pl. LIV, 45U, and in the catalogue of sequence-dates from Hu this grave is dated 36. On p. 6 of *Preh. Eg.* Petrie says that tombs from Diospolis B, H, R, U are marked D.

[6] *Corpus*, pl. LV, type 52, *Tarkhan II*, pl. I, t. 1528.

[7] See also *El Amrah*, pp. 38-9.

[8] The three palettes are at University College, London.

[9] The palette is in the Ashmolean Museum, Oxford; a black-topped sherd with a pot-mark from t. 345 at University College, London.

[10] Both pieces in the Ashmolean Museum, Oxford.

serve at the same time as the tails of two other animals whose heads stick out at the other end. It is impossible to decide which animals are meant, as the only detail of the heads shown are the eyes. Grave 1738 is not sequence-dated, but the palette is too closely related in style to that from grave 271 to be separated from it by any length of time. Petrie dates t. 271 at the beginning of Naḳāda II, but it is difficult to ascribe the other palette to such an early date. The motif of the two animals facing each other at the sides of a palette returns on the well-known animal palette from Hierakonpolis, which is early dynastic. I do not know this motif from any other palette of early Naḳāda II. I could find only one pot which must once have belonged to these graves, and that makes their dating difficult to study. From grave 271 I could trace two ivory tags with incised diagonal lines and a necklace of red coral (*Tubepora musica*), but nothing besides the palette from t. 1738.[1]

Whether the little amulets with human heads should be mentioned here seems doubtful. It is uncertain whether they are replicas of large palettes with human heads. One such piece exists,[2] but it is a bought specimen, and I find it more and more difficult to base any conclusions on pieces which have no provenance. The little slates with human heads seem to me more closely linked with similar ones of bone or ivory than with palettes. They are the connecting link between amulets generally and those deriving from or representing palettes. The classification according to material breaks down here. They are treated under the heading of ivory and bone objects.

There exist a few other types of palettes which are not mentioned here, either because they are very rare or because their forms are so indistinct that several explanations are possible. They cannot help us in our attempt to solve the problems connected with the general story of slate palettes.

Towards the end of Naḳāda II and at the beginning of the dynastic period geometrical palettes, mostly rectangular, are again preferred. They often are decorated with a simple pattern around their edges, parallel lines being the most common. At the same time some tend to become very large. In the royal tomb of Naḳāda there were rectangular palettes with incised lines around the edges over a foot long, and Emery lists one from t. 3471 at Saḳḳāra which measures 44·2 cm.[3]

The blank surfaces of the palettes have every now and then something scratched on them. The best and most important example of early date is the rhomb which has the elephant, the Z sign and the harpoon on it.[4] That found in t. 3471 at Saḳḳāra (First Dynasty) showing a king slaying an enemy before a lion, only the forepart of which is given, is much later, as is the one from Tarkhan, t. 1579—also First Dynasty—with the little man who holds a stick in one hand and a mace-head in the other.[5]

It is only towards the end of Naḳāda II that the first examples of palettes occur with decoration in relief. The two earliest known so far were found at El-'Amrah and at Gerzeh respectively. The palette from El-'Amrah, t. 62, S.D. 56-64, is of the double-bird type, oblong or shield-shaped with a large rectangular hump between the birds' heads, which has a perforation in the middle. One of the heads is broken off; the extant one has no eye indicated. The decoration in relief is in the middle of the upper part, leaving the greater part of the surface free. It consists of the sign of the god Min and of something like a shepherd's crook, which looks as if stuck

[1] Both pieces in the Ashmolean Museum, Oxford, a black-topped from t. 271, B 76G, at the University Museum, Philadelphia, Pa.   [2] *Preh. Eg.*, pl. XLIII, 1.

[3] Emery, *Great Tombs of the First Dynasty*, p. 60, no. 562.   [4] See Vol. I, p. 12, fig. 2.

[5] Emery, *Great Tombs of the First Dynasty*, p. 60, fig. 31. *Tarkhan II*, pl. VI.

through its middle. Grave B 62 was rich, though plundered, and from the evidence of the pottery —there was only one black-topped pot—rather from the end of Naḳāda II.[1]

Gerzeh, t. 59, vaguely dated to S.D. 47-77, contained the other sculptured slate.[2] It is roughly oval in shape, and the decoration covers the whole of one side; the other, left plain, retains traces of malachite. The flat relief represents a cow's head reduced to a geometrical form with ears and large inward-curving horns. The ears, the horns and the middle of the head are adorned with stars, five in all. The shape of the horns, so different from those of the cow-goddess from Naḳāda I,[3] are similar to those of the Hathor heads of the Nar-Mer palette.[4] This is, as far as I know, the earliest example of the cow-goddess as goddess of heaven, for that is what the stars which she wears indicate. She has become connected with Horus, god of heaven,[5] and if grave and palette are really still from the end of Naḳāda II, and not of the First Dynasty, it is possibly the earliest representation of the cow-goddess as the mother of Horus. The execution of the low relief is rough and inferior to that of the Min palette, while the grave from which it came does not seem to have been otherwise in any way outstanding. Its contents were not published. The palette forms a most important link in the development of the cult of the cow-goddess from a chthonic deity, to whom dedications were deposited in the tombs, to the heavenly cow across whose belly the sun-god travels in his boat. It is also an intermediate piece in the change from the palettes with the horns and ears of the cow-goddess at their tops to the famous tablet of Nar-Mer on which the simpler forms are replaced by human heads with horns and cow's ears. These, in turn, stand between the earlier representations of the goddess which show her ears and horns only, and the classical one which is a woman's head with cow's ears, but without the horns.

In shape, the Nar-Mer palette is oblong or like a shield, as are many of the earlier slates. But its size, its rich decorations covering both sides and leaving only a small saucer-shaped depression on one side for preparing the green cosmetic, and the fact that it was a royal gift dedicated in a temple, separate it from all those with which we have had to deal so far. It was found at Hierakonpolis [6] together with a smaller palette,[7] in the great deposit of objects belonging to the temple. All the other "ceremonial" palettes which have come to light and which are decorated with more or less elaborate reliefs are not from excavations but were bought and are without known provenance. With only two well-authenticated pieces for comparison, it seems difficult to date them or to deduce a development. No critical study of these palettes has been made so far, so that we are not even sure which of them we may accept as genuine and which of them may be fakes. They are, therefore, too uncertain as documents to serve as bases for conclusions, and they will be used here with the greatest reserve.

The Nar-Mer palette is the only one of them the date of which is tolerably certain. It would

---

[1] *El Amrah*, p. 20, pl. VIII. The palette is in the British Museum.

[2] *Gerzeh*, p. 22, pl. VI, 7. The palette is in the Cairo Museum.

[3] See Vol. I, pl. II.

[4] Quibell and Green, *Hierakonpolis*, I, pl. XXIX. A. J. Arkell, "An Archaic Representation of Hathor", *JEA*, 41 (1955), pp. 125-6. The Hathor head in relief there published is reconstructed from fragments of a vase found by Quibell in the main deposit at Hierakonpolis. It has stars on the tips of the horns and ears and one on the forehead. This close parallel to the piece from Gerzeh speaks rather in favour of a First Dynasty date for the Gerzeh palette.

[5] Cf. G. A. Wainwright, *The Sky Religion in Egypt*, p. 9.

[6] Quibell and Green, *Hierakonpolis*, I, pl. XXIX.

[7] Quibell and Green, *Hierakonpolis*, II, pl. XXVIII.

be an *ex-voto* by the great king himself. Though it was found in the temple of Horus at Hierakonpolis, it is obviously not dedicated to this god, but to his mother, Hathor.[1] Her large heads
dominate the palette, and between them even the royal *sereḫ* remains without the Horus falcon
which we are accustomed to find there. Two heads are arranged on the top of each side, the
small *sereḫ* between them containing the name usually read Nar-Mer. This panel, occurring
twice, can only be meant to designate the goddess to whom the palette was dedicated, and the
name of the king who dedicated it. Underneath, on each side, the events are recorded which the
king wanted to commemorate. On the reverse, which offered more room as none had to be
reserved for the saucer on which to grind the cosmetic, the large figure of the king in the White
Crown of Upper Egypt dominates the scene. He is dressed in a tunic which leaves the right
shoulder free. Over it he wears a belt from which the bull's tail dangles behind, and fringes
topped by Hathor heads are arranged all around. This ceremonial garment, which we also know
from a fragment of a Djoser statue found in the surroundings of the Step Pyramid,[2] shows
the king as connected with the deity to whom he dedicated the palette, presumably as her son
Ka-mutef. The king is shown in the act of slaying an enemy—the first representation of this
classical pose which runs through all periods of Egyptian art. In the right hand he swings a mace
with a piriform head, with the left he grasps the enemy by the forelock. He holds the mace by
the middle of its handle, which makes the gesture appear somewhat weak. The enemy in front
of the king has utterly collapsed. He is on his knees, his arms, which hold no weapon, hang down
by his sides. Next to his head are two hieroglyphic signs which have been interpreted in many
different ways.[3] To me it seems most likely that they are either the name or the title of the fallen
enemy. Perhaps "title" is correct, since, with the exception of the king himself on the obverse,
all the other persons have only their titles given. The two signs read, I think, quite clearly a
harpoon *w'*, and underneath the pond *š*. Why the second sign is so often interpreted as "land"
I find it difficult to understand, as even the waterlines are indicated inside it, and a land sign
belonging to the group just above the enemy looks decidedly different, and similar to what is found
in later hieroglyphs. The translations of these two signs which attempt to fix the origin of the
foe have so far not been very convincing. The main sign is obviously the harpoon, since it
appears on the other side of the palette without the *š*, and therefore must be enough to identify
the vanquished. Nor does the group which is above the head of the enemy help much. Many
explanations have been brought forward for it. Its main feature is the Horus falcon, representing
the king (analogous to the picture on the obverse where he is the bull). Below him is the sign
for land out of which six stems of papyrus grow. The land sign is provided on its left end with
a bearded head, through the upper lip of which a cord is drawn which the falcon grasps with one
hand. This can only mean that the king has conquered the territory for which the sign below the
falcon stands, and subdued its ruler. Which country that may be is anyone's guess. It may well
be somewhere in Lower Egypt, though the sign of the *rekhit*, which in all probability stood for
the inhabitants of Lower Egypt on the large mace-head, is absent here. Fights with chieftains

---

[1] That the mother of Horus had a cult at Hierakonpolis is shown, apart from the many statuettes of women found
in the temple that can only have been dedicated to her, by the stela of Horemkha'uef: W. C. Hayes, "Horemkha'uef
of Nekhen", *JEA*, 33 (1947), pp. 3 ff.

[2] Firth, Quibell and Lauer, *The Step Pyramid*, II, pl. 59.

[3] H. Sottas and E. Drioton, *Introduction à l'Etude des Hieroglyphes*, pp. 23 ff.

who rebelled against or did not acknowledge the ascendancy of the Horus kings occurred, and lasted as long as the reigns of Khasekhem and even Djoser, as the engravings and reliefs on their statues show.[1] But nowhere do we ever find an enemy who is characterized as the king of Lower Egypt. The adversary in front of Nar-Mer on the slate palette was certainly a great chief. He looks in no way different from the Egyptians themselves. He is naked but for a belt from which some strips of material hang down in front, a garment which is also worn by Egyptians.[2] There is nothing to indicate his rank except the two hieroglyphs, which are as yet untranslatable.

The main scene on the reverse of the palette is completed by the small figure of the king's attendant, who carries his sandals and a water-jug. He wears a belt to which a triangular piece is fixed in front. The two long strips are either meant to be the long ends of the belt or to hang from the triangle. Fixed by a cord round his neck is a pectoral, which perhaps might be a seal-cylinder in a wooden frame. In front of him are the signs of the rosette with the hm sign which accompany also the same official on Nar-Mer's mace-head.

At the bottom and separated from the main scene by a wide line are two men who are naked and have long hair which falls over their shoulders, and the same beard as is worn by the king and his enemy. Each of them has a sign near his head, the one to the left a fortified enclosure, the one to the right what has now been convincingly explained also as a fortified enclosure in the form of a kite.[3] These two people have been explained as slain enemies on the battlefield. This is likely in view of their position at the bottom of the palette, and also because none of their feet are resting on the ground. They resemble the figure under the foot of the bull on the obverse.

On the obverse the largest panel is that which encloses the saucer for the grinding of the malachite (or perhaps for mixing the paint, as its shape seems rather inconvenient for grinding), which is enclosed between the long necks of two monsters which together with their heads form a figure of eight. The bodies belonging to them are those of large felines, and so are the heads. These animals are held in leashes by two little men who have been placed above their upcurving tails. The motif of the animals with the entwined necks which occurs more often on reliefs of this time is an importation from Sumerian art,[4] but the little men holding them are a special feature of the Nar-Mer tablet.

In the panel above, and directly below the one with the Hathor heads and the king's $\mathit{sere\underline{h}}$, is shown the most crowded scene of the palette. The main figure is again the king, who here has his name written in front of him. He wears a tunic and fringed belt, on which the Hathor heads are not discernible this time. In one hand he holds the flail, in the other the mace. The Red Crown is on his head. Behind him is the little sandal-bearer with his title, and in the space left above his head a hieroglyph set in an upright rectangle. The hieroglyph reads $db\mathit{\jmath}$, and is, according to Gardiner,[5] the reed float. Keimer, however, sees in it two feet and the rectangle as a basin, which makes it difficult to explain the line which joins the two objects.[6] In front of the king marches the $\underline{d}.t$ priest, his writing materials slung over his shoulder. He, the sandal-

[1] Quibell and Green, *Hierakonpolis*, I, pl. XL.
[2] E.g. on the Nar-Mer mace-head, where the running men wear it.
[3] Y. Yadin, *Military Contacts between Palestine and Egypt at the beginning of the Third Millennium B.C.* Paper read at the 23rd International Congress of Orientalists, Cambridge, 1954. The question still open concerns the distribution of these "kites" in the time of Nar-Mer.   [4] H. Frankfort, *Cylinder Seals*, pl. V, n.
[5] A. H. Gardiner, *Egyptian Grammar*, 2nd ed., p. 514, T 25.   [6] Vandier, *Manuel*, I, p. 598.

bearer and one of the four little men carrying the king's standards are without beards. Whether this designates them as priests I do not know. The standards are the same as those on the mace-head of Nar-Mer, the two falcons, the jackal of Asyūt and the unidentified object. This solemn procession marches towards a gruesome scene. Ten enemies disposed in two rows with their heads neatly placed between their feet lie on their sides. Above them is a door with the hieroglyph meaning great behind it, a boat, and above this the king as a falcon on a harpoon. The explanation of these signs is again doubtful. If we may draw an analogy from the sign of Horus on the *Nbty*, the falcon on the harpoon would mean that Horus (the king) has vanquished the man described by the harpoon, and he is the enemy whom we saw at the king's feet on the other side of the palette. What the boat means we can only guess. We have to remember that boats were the only means of transport at the time. The great door is thought to be a place-name. Vandier suggests Buto, the Great Door of Horus.[1] Whether the whole represents a battlefield or a human sacrifice of prisoners in the temple of Hierakonpolis is one more unsolved problem.

The bottom panel of the obverse is filled by the picture of the king, this time in the shape of a bull, treading upon his prostrate enemy, and, with his horns, demolishing the hostile city, the name of which is written with a two-handled bag. This makes it doubtful whether the Great Door can have been the name of a city also, since then one would expect to find the same name here. It may be the country of which the harpoon man was the chief. However, that is just another guess.

That both sides of the palette refer to the same event seems to me almost certain. They commemorate the victory of King Nar-Mer over an important enemy whose title or name was written with the sign of the harpoon. The chieftain was slain, and, if we interpret the land sign with the six stalks of papyrus correctly, his country added to the dominions of Nar-Mer. Where this country lay cannot be determined with certainty. To identify it with Lower Egypt, and to call the palette a memorial of the first unification of Upper and Lower Egypt, is certainly going too far. Nowhere is there the sign of the papyrus and the lotus entwined around the hieroglyph, which symbolizes the unification of the two countries; nowhere is the enemy characterized as the king of Lower Egypt. On the contrary, if the Red Crown, as in later days, is the sign of the Lower Egyptian Kingship, then Nar-Mer is already King of Lower Egypt, and nothing shows that this is a new acquisition of his. The enemy may well have been one of the grandees of Lower Egypt, considering the papyri with which his country is characterized. But then fights with rebellious chieftains from there must have occurred all through the First and Second Dynasties, and perhaps even later,[2] which gives point to the assumption that the unification was a long-drawn-out process and not the feat of a single mythical king, Menes, whom much later tradition called the first king of the First Dynasty. Be that as it may, King Nar-Mer and the harpoon occur on both sides. By far his largest representations show him as king of Upper Egypt, wearing the White Crown, and this is, therefore, his most important kingship. On the same side he is also represented as the living Horus, the falcon who is the patron god of Upper Egypt. On the other side with the Red Crown he is shown as the king of Lower Egypt. Here he is the "strong bull", that is the god who represents Lower Egypt. The Nar-Mer palette shows, I think conclusively, that Horus and the bull-god are the patron gods of Upper and Lower Egypt at the

---

[1] Vandier, *Manuel*, I, p. 598.

[2] Cf. the statues of Khasekhem with the vanquished people of Lower Egypt at the base, Quibell and Green, *Hierakonpolis* I, pls. XXXIX and XLI, and also the base of the Djoser statue, Vol. I, p. 45.

time of Nar-Mer. The bull is most probably Min, for no other god is so closely connected with the kingship. Seth does not occur at all. That there was a fight, in which Horus was the victor and Min the vanquished, is shown by the statuettes of the Horus falcon crouching on the Min sign which were excavated from First Dynasty tombs at Helwan.[1] One would like to see in them rewards for those who helped in the fight against Lower Egypt.

The tablet of Nar-Mer (pl. VII, 1) has often been hailed as the beginning of the classical Egyptian style. Not only was the scene of the king slaying his enemy accepted henceforward as the representation of the victorious pharaoh, the whole arrangement with its division into registers became the preferred arrangement for the officials and representative art of Egypt. It has the dignity and quietude which was thought appropriate to a king of Egypt, qualities which on the other hand made the official art lose much strength and vividness of expression.

The other slate palette which was found together with that of Nar-Mer is called the small palette of Hierakonpolis, though, compared with the ordinary palettes, it is still large enough.[2] It is often thought to be earlier than the Nar-Mer palette because it is of a very different style. Two large animals frame its upper part. Their heads, one of which is missing,[3] face each other, their front legs touch. They seem to clutch the palette between them, for they appear on each side of the slate, one half on the obverse and one half on the reverse, their backs and tails following its outlines closely. They are by far the largest and most important animals represented, and, just like the Hathor heads on the Nar-Mer palette, must be the divinity to whom the palette was dedicated. They have often been called dogs, though they are different from some dogs which are seen on the obverse chasing antelopes. These have flap ears, long thin tails and wear collars, while the large animals framing the palette have upright ears and bushy tails. They also appear several times on the faces of the palette, where these peculiarities are clearly shown. It therefore seems more likely that they are jackals, foxes or even wolves. They must have had a chapel in the temple of Hierakonpolis in which this palette would have been dedicated. As there were different gods, or perhaps one god under different names, in the shape of jackals, foxes or wolves, we cannot state with certainty which of them may be meant here. As the Wepwawet of Asyūt is on one of the standards carried in front of the king on the large palette and also on the Nar-Mer mace-head, it seems most likely that he was the one to whom a chapel in the sanctuary of the new royal god Horus was devoted. It may be that to him also belong the statuettes of dogs in ivory which were found among the great treasure of ivories in the temple. He must have been a god of the hunt, for hunting scenes are sculptured on both sides of the palette. On the obverse with the saucer are the two snake-necked lions we met already on Nar-Mer's palette. But here their necks are not entwined, but waved in corresponding movements around the saucer. Between their heads is a bird with opened wings and raised tail, and below it an antelope already broken down or dead which the two snake-lions lick (or devour?) with their long tongues. This scene is completed by three images of the "lord of the palette", one in the middle underneath the saucer, and one each side near the top. Below this fairly symmetrically arranged group is another, an antelope hunt. It is displayed in two rows one above the other, but without dividing lines either between the rows themselves or to separate them from the scene above. Three different species of antelope run before a dog which has just reached the last of them. Below, two dogs

---

[1] Z. Saad, *Ann. Serv.*, Cahier 3, p. 165, fig. 15.   [2] Height 43 cm.
[3] It must have been repaired in antiquity, as the bore-holes show.

attack a large hartebeest which turns its head towards the one pursuing whilst another dog springs at its throat. While the obverse of the palette shows some success in the endeavour of the artist to arrange his figures in a system and to keep the two scenes clearly separate, on the reverse his efforts have more or less broken down. Again there are two scenes. The upper one has single fights between different animals. Directly below the legs of the framing animals are two antelopes each attacked by two lions in antithetical groups. The fighting creatures face each other, as do those of the next pair, the snake-lion and another antelope. Beneath them a leopard has just reached the antelope he is pursuing, which turns its head towards her attacker. So far a certain order in the arrangement of the groups can be observed. This is destroyed by the figure of the divine animal interposed on one side which causes the next group to be on the slant. It does not take part in the fights, but turns its head towards them as if watching them. The pair below consists of a winged griffon biting into the foreleg of a hartebeest, which turns its head away from it. The griffon, being a good deal below the hartebeest, intrudes into the second scene below, which seems to be of a peaceful nature. On the left is a man with an animal head and tail playing the flute. It is difficult to say which animal may be meant, but it is just possible that the head belongs to the divine creature. The ears, though different from those of the other representations, are upright and the tail is bushy. Three animals seem to dance in a sort of circle before him, a giraffe, a bull and a billy goat. None of them occurs in any of the other scenes, and they must be friendly to the god of the palette for they are not involved in any fighting. As there are no human beings on either side, perhaps with the exception of the flute-player, it seems likely that the reliefs refer to incidents in the myth of the god and not to events in the life of the dedicator. Since we are not sure who the god is to whom the palette was dedicated, and we do not know any myth to which the palette might allude, we are left very much in the dark.

It is the rather untidy and cramped arrangement of the scenes on the small Hierakonpolis palette which has led to the assumption that it must be older than the Nar-Mer palette. That is not necessarily so. Throughout Egyptian art, and with very few exceptions, reliefs and pictures involving the king are more formal in style than those with animal, and especially hunting, scenes. It does not follow, even if the new style had been found for the pharaoh, that it had already spread to all schools of artists, or that the older and less rigid way of design was no longer practised. It does not seem likely to me that the palettes should be divided by any length of time. The snake-lion occurs on both, and while on the Nar-Mer palette the necks of the animals are entwined in Sumerian fashion, on the small palette the Egyptian artist made free with the motif and neatly separated the necks. This, if we have to assume a difference in time at all, rather indicates a later state of development than that of the Nar-Mer palette. To me both tablets and the mace-heads seem to form a closely-connected group, and with our scanty knowledge of the art of the time it seems impossible to ascribe them to different stages in their period, especially if it means apportioning one to predynastic and the other to protodynastic times. They both follow in general shape and arrangement the earlier and more utilitarian palettes. In the small one, one may still see a rhomb, its widest part being in the middle. The god or goddess is placed at the top end, and in consequence all the scenes had to be arranged along the shorter axis of the palette. But this, however, had the advantage that on the Nar-Mer palette the king could be shown in overpowering size. On the other hand, the scenes involving a number of persons appear rather crowded.

The Sumerian influences manifest in the two tablets have often been pointed out. The arrangement in registers, the details of the serpent-necked felines and also of the winged griffon are older in Sumerian art than they are in Egyptian. Of these ideas, the arrangement in orderly array was never abandoned by the Egyptians. But again, as with the vase painters, the Egyptian sculptor did not imitate, but assimilated, the patterns coming to him from abroad. The spirit of the palettes is wholly his own. A look at the stela of King Eannatum of Lagash (pl. VII, 2), with which the Nar-Mer palette (pl. VII, 1) has often been compared, will show what I mean. King Eannatum marches in front of the phalanx of his knights under whose feet the slain enemies lie. He is not bigger than any of them; he is *primus inter pares*. Nar-Mer tackles and subdues his enemy single-handed, those pictured with him are not his equals but his servants, whose help he does not need. Nar-Mer is a god, Horus and Ka-mutef, son and husband of the great goddess to whom the palette is dedicated, Eannatum is the First Servant of his god and the leader of his people.

If we now return to our question whether the green paint, and the slate palette which was used in its manufacture, had a meaning for the ancient Egyptians unconnected with its practical use, I think the answer must be in the affirmative. From the moment in the period of Naḳāda I when the rhombic slates began to grow to unwieldy sizes on the one hand, and to tiny ones which are unusable on the other, they must have acquired some potency beyond that of a toilet utensil. The green paint must have been thought to impart some form of luck which set it apart and above the other cosmetics. At about the same time or a little later the green paint and the palettes were brought into connexion with certain gods, and this tendency is most marked during Naḳāda II. During this period it is especially the fish which lends its form to the palettes, and it therefore must be assumed to have something to do with the green colour. We know very little about the fish-gods, though they must have been of special importance during the periods with which we are concerned. The great king himself called himself after the Nar-fish. There was a fish cult at Lepidotonpolis, which is in the Thinite county, and the kings of the First Dynasty are said to have originated from Thinis. But the Lepidotos is not the Nar, and how far this has any bearing on the question of palettes I do not know. Of course, the thought of green as the colour of the vegetation and the life-giving water comes to mind, but this is too vague to be of much help. That the Great Mother should be associated with the green paint is perhaps easier to understand, but she was only one among many we find on the palettes. To me it seems that the green colour would have been a colour of lucky augury independent of any special god, and could be connected with all. A less general answer to the questions involved can only be given when we know more about Egyptian religious beliefs and the myths which were told about their numerous gods.

Of the four most important palettes which are without known provenance and which show reliefs all over one or both sides, three have lost their upper parts, where, by analogy with the two dated pieces, we should expect to find the gods to whom they were dedicated. Only one of the four, the fragment in Cairo with the destruction of the towns on the one side and the "Libyan country" on the other, has hieroglyphic signs on it. The palette which is fairly complete is the "Lion Hunt" palette, of which two fragments are in the British Museum and one is in the Louvre. A smaller piece out of one side is missing. The pieces in the British Museum were acquired in 1890, eight years before Quibell excavated the two Hierakonpolis palettes. They were bought from an Egyptian dealer who alleged that the fragments came from Abydos. Maspero, who had seen the fragment in Paris and those now in the British Museum in the hands of a dealer before they left Egypt, says they came either from Abydos or from Saḳḳāra. Budge published all the three pieces as belonging to one and the same relief,[1] and says that the pieces in the British Museum were acquired together with the fragment of the "battlefield palette". This is interesting as it makes it likely that they came from one and the same source, though this might have been neither Abydos nor Saḳḳāra. The lion-hunt attracted the greater attention, and was thought to be made in Egypt by foreigners; Syrians were preferred, but Libyans also were mentioned. Much later, Ranke [2] claimed the palette to be earlier than those from Hierakonpolis, and in accordance with the Delta hypothesis thinks it was made in the Delta and sees Libyan influences in it. Budge, who wrote before the Hierakonpolis palettes were excavated, ascribes the palette to the time of Amenophis III.

The palette which gave rise to such diverse commentaries indeed differs in so many ways from the authenticated slates of Hierakonpolis that its position in Egyptian art and its date are even now by no means clear. Its shape is an elongated triangle, one side of which is covered with scenes in low relief. Though the reverse is left plain and would allow ample space on which to rub the green paint, yet the obverse is provided with a circular saucer—a duplication which none of the other palettes provide. It is the only palette on which the scenes are arranged sideways along the longer edges; all the others have them arranged across the faces. No single group or figure is in any way outstanding either by its place in the picture or by its size—again a unique characteristic of the palette. In consequence, it is impossible to know to which god the palette was dedicated.

The main subject represented is a lion-hunt. Two large male lions, one at the top, the other at the bottom, are both pierced by many arrows. The one at the bottom of the palette may perhaps be meant to have been killed. His back is turned towards the other figures, he seems to walk out of the picture. The other, on the contrary, is still very much alive. He is at the top right-hand side of the palette, and though he has two arrows sticking in his head, ferociously attacks a heavily-armed hunter who runs away from him, while another is aiming an arrow with a chisel-head at him. The rather clumsy way in which the bowman is represented has often been pointed out.[3] Behind the attacking lion is a much smaller one, usually thought to be a cub. As it seems rather odd that the cub should follow the he-lion, some authors speak of it as the lioness. The smallness of the beast and its inactivity speak rather against this.

Above these two lions, squeezed right into the corner, are two signs which have been explained in different ways. They are a house with a domed roof, such as is known from early representations of sanctuaries,[4] and next to it two foreparts of bulls joined together in the middle, a sign known from the Pyramid Texts, where it has the meaning of double door (ḥns).[5] Two different interpretations of these signs exist. One says the double bull is a god and the house is his temple. Against this the god in the shape of two bull protomai is not known from early Egypt, and the signs are in an inconspicuous place and are rather smaller than the other figures. In all the other

[1] E. A. Wallis Budge, "Sculptural Slabs from Mesopotamia", *Classical Review* (1890), pp. 322 ff.

[2] The early literature about the palette is put together in H. Ranke, "Alter und Herkunft der aegyptischen 'Löwenjagd-Palette'", *Sitzungsber. d. Heidelberger Ak. d. Wissenschaften* (1925).

[3] Vandier, *Manuel*, I, pp. 574 ff.

[4] E.g. *Royal Tombs*, II, pl. X, 2.

[5] Sethe, *Pyramidentexte*, 416.

palettes where the upper part is preserved, the gods to whom they are dedicated are prominent both in size and in position. The other interpretation sees in the group hieroglyphic signs indicating the place where the hunt took place or the temple in which the palette was dedicated. The position of the signs, their size and the use of the double-bull hieroglyph in the Pyramid Texts would well agree with the second explanation. Vandier [1] even tries an identification of the place, and suggests it might be a canal in Lower Egypt mentioned in late texts as belonging to the 3rd nome, for to him, as to Ranke, the palette is of Lower Egyptian origin. The reason for this is supplied by the ensigns which the hunters carry, but before we try to analyse them it seems better to finish the discussion of the hunting scene.

Underneath the bowman and along one edge of the palette marches a single file of heavily, though somewhat incongruously, armed men. The first carries the falcon ensign with the feather which sometimes stands for the West. He grasps it with his left hand and brandishes a piriform mace in his right. He is followed by three men who each carry two different weapons, piriform maces, a spear, a bow and throwing-sticks. These throwing-sticks are different from any known from early periods in that they end in a peculiar pointed top wider than the stick. After these comes another ensign-bearer with the sign for East on a stick. Behind him are five more men, the first of whom carries a bow and three chisel-headed arrows, the only one of the bowmen to be provided with what would seem an indispensable accessory. The next is throwing a lasso, the noose of which he holds in his right hand while the end trails into the void; for, though his left hand is lost in the crack which here splits the palette, the lasso can be followed for all its length, and nothing on it shows that it was held in a hand or fastened in any way. The spears which two of the figures carry have attracted attention because they are nearer in type to those which are known from the Twelfth Dynasty than to any other, being provided with hafting sockets which develop into midribs. One man carries what we must identify as a double mace, for with its rounded outline it is hardly a double axe, as has been suggested. No such weapon is known from early Egypt. On the other edge of the palette the row of huntsmen is again led by a standard-bearer carrying the same emblem of the falcon as the leader on the opposite side. The man behind him is running and leaning forward, grasping the line of a lasso which has caught an antelope by the horns. The rope passes behind him and is then lost in the break, which is the only serious injury to the scenes. Only three huntsmen survive behind this break; the first of them is damaged, so that one cannot be sure what he had in his right hand—it may have been the shaft of a spear, or, as seems more likely, the end of the stick which supported the emblem of the East. The two others are armed with bow, spear and maces. In addition to these weapons the three last huntsmen carry on their backs objects which Keimer has explained as shields made of carapaces of large tortoises.[2]

The space between the two files of men is filled with the representation of a hunt in the desert. Dogs chase antelopes, a stag, an ostrich, and a hare which is divided from the rest of the animals by the saucer, as is the antelope caught with a lasso, which nevertheless belongs to the hunting scene, just as do the two lions. Similar hunts are represented on the walls of Old Kingdom tombs. The stag, the gazelles, the hare and even the lions are there, but there is one significant difference. While the lions on the palette are hit by arrows, none of the archaic, Old or even

[1] Vandier, *Manuel*, I, p. 578.
[2] L. Keimer, *Bulletin de l'Institut d'Égypte*, 32 (1950), pp. 76 ff.

Middle Kingdom representations of hunting scenes show the lion other than completely untouched by the turmoil around him. The hunters do not take any notice of him other than threatening him with an outstretched finger, a gesture similar to that used in modern times to avert the evil eye.[1] This is not surprising, since the lion is one of the animals by which the kings are represented, and the early artists took care not to show him in an undignified position. The different attitude which the artist of the lion-hunt palette adopts is even stranger if we remember that it turned up together with the battlefield palette, which makes it likely that they have the same provenance. On the battlefield palette the king, represented as a lion, dominates the scene of the slaughter.

The men on the hunt palette are dressed in short folded skirts which are fastened by a wide belt, a costume otherwise unknown in archaic times. To the back of the belt the tail of an animal is attached, perhaps that of a fox, also a unique feature. The hunters wear long hair or wigs into which one or two feathers are stuck. This suggests to Budge Egyptian soldiers,[2] to Ranke a Libyan tribe, especially as the men have pointed beards, which at once suggests to Ranke the Delta, and this, he feels, is supported by the standards of West and East because they can only mean the 3rd and 14th nome of Lower Egypt. Furthermore, he asserts that the distribution of the pictures all over the face of the palette, the archaic and at the same time free representation of the human form and the lack of distinction between the main and the secondary figures are all signs that the palette is the oldest of all known ceremonial palettes. As no feature of the palette in Ranke's opinion is in any way Upper Egyptian, it must be a product of a vastly superior Lower Egyptian civilization, much older than Menes, which knew how to write in hieroglyphs long before this art was known in Upper Egypt. This seems somewhat arbitrary, as the only authenticated ceremonial palettes were found at Hierakonpolis in Upper Egypt. To distinguish a figure by making it bigger than the less essential personages is a primitive feature which occurs on the "decorated" pottery,[3] and even if the hunters were Libyans, which is doubtful, that would not point to the Delta, for Libyans lived all along the Egyptian western frontier.

The representation of the fleeing huntsman and of the man grasping the lasso with which the antelope is caught is indeed much more realistic and based more on direct observation of life than anything that is known from archaic art. With this the lame attitude of the man shooting the lion and the conventionally-drawn hunters are oddly contrasted. Yet another problem is that the hunters are so heavily armed that they look much more like soldiers than like hunters going out to the chase.

Very far-reaching and eccentric explanations have been brought forward and seriously discussed about the meaning of the lion-hunt palette. One originated by Sethe and elaborated by Ranke finds the whole early history of the Delta embedded in it. The Delta, they say, was originally divided into a western and an eastern kingdom, hence the two standards of the west and the east. At the time when the palette was made, they were already united into one kingdom. For the purpose of a lion-hunt volunteers were called for from both halves, because it was too dangerous an undertaking to be performed by one-half only. It all sounds a little like the

---

[1] W. Wreszinski, *Löwenjagd in Alten Aegypten*, Morgenland 23, p. 5. Whether the animals on the Hierakonpolis fresco are lions seems doubtful, nor are they hit by arrows.

[2] Wallis Budge, "Sculptural Slabs from Mesopotamia", *Classical Review* (1890), pp. 322 ff.

[3] Vandier, *Manuel*, I, , p. 353, fig. 238, showing "decorated" vases where the women, being of greater importance, are much bigger than the men.

"translations" of hieroglyphic texts in the years before Champollion,[1] and a new attempt at an interpretation will not be out of place. It is elaborated in the following pages.

In trying to find a solution to the many and contradictory problems of the lion-hunt palette it is first necessary to reconsider the question of its date. Ranke's suggestion that it is before Menes, i.e. predynastic, has been accepted without questioning, and it seems time to go into this more deeply.

Of the various palettes with scenes in relief, only the Nar-Mer palette has a reliable date; there is no reason to doubt that it was made during the reign of this great king. But, unfortunately, with the animal palette found together with it under the temple at Hierakonpolis uncertainty already begins. It is generally believed to be earlier than the Nar-Mer palette, but the stylistic reasons for this are by no means indisputable. Especially is this so since we know that in later times at any rate the more formal style was reserved for the king. Hence it may be that the more lively and less severe style of the animal palette may not mean a difference in period but only in social standing.

All the other palettes, or more precisely fragments of palettes, for none of the others is complete, were bought. Of these the lion-hunt and the battlefield palette were, as far as I know, the earliest to come into the market, years before the Nar-Mer palette was found, and before it was known what these "sculptured slabs" were meant to be. This makes it fairly certain that they are authentic, but does not give any help as to their date. Since the grinding of malachite on palettes had already gone out of fashion in the early Old Kingdom, all the ceremonial palettes were lumped together and dated either archaic or late predynastic, and it did not occur to anybody to look for analogies of style other than to pieces of the time of Nar-Mer. And yet we know that objects, once they had been included in the furniture of gods and of tombs, were made long after they had gone out of fashion in everyday life. Thus, we find bad imitations of black-topped vases among the grave outfits of early dynastic tombs at Abydos,[2] and imitations of the rectangular flint "razors" made of limestone and completely useless were dedicated in Tut-Ankh-Amun's tomb by people who evidently had long since forgotten their original use. Therefore, it seems possible that slate palettes, once they had been taken into the traditional outfit necessary for the toilet of the gods, were kept, or perhaps even renewed if necessary, in times when their original use had long since been forgotten. Such a possibility means that each of the palettes which has no known origin will have to be studied on its merits, and the question about date and origin seems more difficult than ever.

It is perhaps easiest to begin with the study of the battlefield palette (pl. VII, 4) which made its appearance together with the lion-hunt, because the figures on its obverse are drawn in such an extravagant style. The main figure on the remaining fragment is a large lion mauling a fallen man. Though the animal with its large mane is not unlike those hunted on the other palette, what a difference there is in attitude ! The lordly beast dominates the battlefield in spite of the tail, which, oddly enough, it has drawn between its legs. The man it has thrown seems to be constructed out of the most astounding curves and angles. His body is strained upwards, one of his legs is curved backwards between his two arms, which are bent at different angles, and on one of which his head rests. The other slain soldiers on the battlefield are also given most extraordinary attitudes, part of their bodies being twisted into the oddest shapes. I know of only one

---

[1] Vandier, *Manuel*, I, pp. 578 ff.   [2] Petrie, *Abydos*, I, pl. VI, 9 and 10.

instance of Egyptian art on which slain enemies are shown in similar extravagant poses, and that is on the bases of the Khasekhem statues from Hierakonpolis [1] (pl. VII, 3). The figures there are in very flat relief, and their attitudes are, if possible, even more exaggerated than those of the battlefield palette, but the style is the same. Here also parts of the bodies are contorted in most extravagant curves, and even the flexed-back leg between the two arms occurs again with one of the slain on one of the Khasekhem bases. As I know of no other monument which can be compared in style to the battlefield palette, and the resemblances between it and the bases are so very close, I feel that the palette should be dated to the same period, i.e. to the time of Khasekhem.

This does help us for the dating of the lion-hunt palette, but only in so far as it throws doubt on the generally-held assumption that all the ceremonial palettes, simply because they are ceremonial palettes, were made during the same epoch. I think we know far too little about the furnishings of an Egyptian temple to be so positive about this. In fact, there exists in the Cairo Museum the fragment of a palette (pl. VIII, 1), which shows that the palettes were still known during the New Kingdom. The fragment, which was bought in 1917,[2] is 15 cm. high and 11·5 cm. wide. On the obverse are the remains of three rows of figures all marching towards the right. They are not actually divided from each other by dividing lines, but the arrangement of the feet and the undercutting of the stone give the impression of a clear separation of the rows. Only in the middle register are there three figures which are fairly intact. They wear long hair or wigs down to their shoulders, and a belt with a bow in front. They have long pointed beards. Their arms are folded in front of their breasts. But, funnily enough, another arm hangs behind their shoulders, and a line at the back of their heads may very well indicate a second head behind the first. If so, we should have to assume a second warrior marching behind the one in front, to whom the spare arm would belong. In the row above, the feet and the lower parts of long kilts are all that is left of the figures, but even in their broken state they convey the clumsiness and the shuffling gait of the persons represented. Of the lowest panel, only the upper parts of two offering-bearers are preserved. One carries an animal on his shoulder which looks rather like a cross between a baby crocodile and a dachshund. He also has the pointed beard. The other man is too damaged to distinguish what he once carried. Only the wig is well preserved, so that one can see that neither on his head nor on that of the man behind is there the incision which indicated in the row above the possible presence of a second figure.

The style of the relief, with its deep undercutting of the stone and its summary and rather untidy rendering of the figures, shows a knowledge of the technique of relief-working far beyond that available to any archaic artist. It separates this palette from the two Hierakonpolis pieces as well as from the battlefield palette. And, as if to emphasize the differences, we find on the reverse of the Cairo palette the remains of the cartouche of Queen Tiyi, and she herself seems to have been represented underneath. Two high feathers, the vulture head of her crown, and the flail is all that is left of her. Was the palette dedicated or rededicated to her? The engraving of cartouche and picture is clumsily done in deep grooves at a time when the palette was either still intact or, at least, much bigger than it is now. Von Bissing, who published the palette,[3]

---

[1] Quibell and Green, *Hierakonpolis*, I, pl. XL; see especially the first on the left of the third row with its legs between its arms.

[2] *Cairo E.J.*, 46148, 1917.   [3] F. von Bissing, *Archiv für Orientforschung*, VI, pls. 1 and 2; pp. 1-2.

assumes that it was used as a trial piece by a much later artist who availed himself of the empty back for his own purposes. This assumption seems rather unlikely, for we know from the Hierakonpolis palettes that objects dedicated to a god in his temple retained their sanctity even when no longer used, and were carefully buried. To use such an object as a trial piece seems somewhat sacrilegious. However, it can just as little be proved that the engraving on the reverse is contemporaneous with the relief on the obverse, though what is left of it suggests either the copy of an archaic work by an artist of much later period and tradition, or an archaistic work which, even if not a direct copy of an existing archaic prototype, yet represents the effort of an artist to work in that long-forgotten style. He may have been asked to decorate this palette, which, though still necessary for the service of a god in his temple, had otherwise long since been out of fashion. Even its original use may have been forgotten. This last is hypothetical. All we can be sure of is that ceremonial palettes still existed at the time of Queen Tiyi. Moreover, we can see that the style and execution of the Cairo fragment make it unlikely that it could be of the archaic period, quite apart from the question whether or not the obverse and the reverse may be contemporaneous. To go into this last question more deeply would take us too far from our main subject. All that is intended is to demonstrate that the ceremonial palettes do not form a closely-connected group, and that the variations in their dates may be considerable.

If, with this in mind, we return to the lion-hunt palette, it seems to me that its many discrepancies, the wrong orientation of the reliefs, the absence of the god to whom it was dedicated, the peculiar equipment of the hunters, the style of the figures, and last but not least the subject of the lion-hunt itself, are best explained if we see in it not an archaic but an archaistic piece. Again, it would take us too far afield to go further into this. The question when the Egyptians began to copy their own ancient art has not been sufficiently studied. There are more indications than the slate palettes that the brilliant days of the early dynasties and of the Pyramid Age served as examples for later generations.

There is one more fragment of a palette now in Cairo that deserves consideration here, though in its broken state it denies us just the answers to those questions which, we think, it would have been able to clarify for us. I mean the palette with the destruction of the towns. This much published piece agrees in style with what we should expect of a work of the early period. Only the lower part has survived, but this is fairly intact. It is now 19 cm. high, and 21·5 cm. wide.[1] On one side four panels are left, divided from each other by straight lines. The top one is damaged by the break, and some of the right-hand side is splintered off. Three rows of animals fill the three upper panels—bulls, donkeys and rams. On the lowest panel two groups of olive (?) trees,[2] one above the other, are preceded by the sign of a throwing-stick on a land sign, the hieroglyph for Libya. The other side is far more damaged. Of the upper panel three human feet only are preserved, walking towards the right. Below in a large panel seven towns are shown, four above and three beneath. Each of them is being destroyed, for on each, as far as can still be seen, stands a victor who hacks into the city walls with a large hoe. The first victor in the top row is a large falcon, presented in the archaic way with huge beak and horizontal tail. Those on the three following towns are missing, but they have survived on the three towns below. There

---

[1] Its number is Cairo 14238 red, J.E. 27434. It was bought.
[2] Against the explanation of olive trees see Keimer, *Ann. Serv.*, 38 (1938), p. 299. He does not suggest any other identification.

they are the lion with the heavy mane we have met on the battlefield palette, the scorpion which we shall find on one of the mace-heads,[1] and two falcons on perches. All the towns are surrounded by roughly rectangular city walls. They have bastions, but the entrance gates are not indicated. The signs inside these enclosures represent in all probability the names of the conquered cities. The space left vacant by them is filled with small squares which may indicate houses. The signs in the upper row are an owl, a heron, two men facing each other, perhaps wrestling, and a toad or frog. In the lower row are the raised arms of the kȝ, a hut and a plant, perhaps the sw.t. None of the signs can be identified with the names of Egyptian towns.

The name of Libya in front of the trees no doubt indicates the place where the action represented on that side of the palette took place. The rows of animals in the upper panels are generally explained as being booty or tribute from a victorious campaign against the Libyans, which is quite possible. Whether the towns on the other side should also be imagined as being in Libya seems doubtful, though many authors favour this explanation.[2] It is just as likely that some other campaign of the king was commemorated on that side. It is interesting to note that all the towns are shown as if they were square, and the houses, if houses they are, rectangular. On the Nar-Mer palette the city which is destroyed by the royal bull is oval. The animals with the hoes have been explained in different ways. Sethe,[3] I think, was the first to identify them with the king. They are the different gods of whom the king is the manifestation on earth. He is Horus, the falcon, he is the lion-god, whatever his name may have been, and he is the two lords. This leads to the conclusion that he is also the scorpion who is one of the victors, as it seems impossible to read this sign differently from the rest of them, and to take it as a personal name. And yet, on the strength of the sign in front of the king on the large mace-head from Hierakonpolis,[4] this has been done. It seems to me a clear indication that the sign on the mace-head is a title, and that the belief in a king with the personal name "Scorpion" has to be abandoned. The scorpion is prominent among the animals represented on the "decorated" pottery, any number were found among the ex-votos found in the large deposit at Hierakonpolis. Surely all this goes far to show that the scorpion must have been a great god or goddess during the time of Naḳāda II and the beginning of the dynasties. That we do not know about him or her in later times, unless she be Selkis, may be due to a change in the Egyptian religion which brought other gods into favour, or to our own ignorance. It is a great pity that the victors of the other cities are lost, for it might have given us a full list of the gods with whom the oldest Egyptian kings identified themselves. We miss the bull which represents Nar-Mer as the conqueror of a city on his great palette, but it is futile to speculate as to whom the missing gods might have been. It is fitting that in a polytheistic religion the king should be identified with different gods, as, in fact, he was during historical times.

There is nothing left on the palette to indicate to which god or goddess it was dedicated, nor to assess its date. From the style, the division in horizontal panels separated from each other by straight lines, and the archaic forms of the falcon and of the hieroglyphs, one is inclined to ascribe it to the beginning of the First Dynasty, not much later than the Nar-Mer palette to which it is inferior in workmanship. Vandier [5] wants to assign it to the period preceding Nar-Mer,

[1] See below, pp. 116 f.
[2] For instance, Vandier, *Manuel*, I, pp. 591-2.
[3] *Ä.Z.*, 52, 52 (1915), pp. 55 ff.
[4] See below, p. 116.
[5] Vandier, *Manuel*, I, p. 591.

for he takes the scorpion as the personal name of a King Scorpion whom he places before Nar-Mer. I have said above why I cannot follow him in this.

More fragments of ceremonial palettes exist in the different museums. Some have on one of their sides an antithetical group of two giraffes with a palm tree between them, the shoots of which they nibble. We do not know the significance of the group, but it seems influenced by Sumerian art, which likes antithetical groups, whilst they are rare in Egypt. It shows how widespread Sumerian influence was during this period that it should have been adopted for such a peculiarly Egyptian object as a palette.

For there can be little doubt that the green slate palette for the preparation of the green cosmetic is intimately bound up with the predynastic Egyptian civilizations. Already present during Badārian times as utilitarian objects, the palettes, and with them the green cosmetic, begin to acquire some special beneficial meaning and some connexion with certain gods during the period of Naḳāda I. From simple toilet objects they develop partly into unwieldy, large palettes up to three feet long, or they take the shape of the gods under whose special protection they were put. They are most common and most diversified during Naḳāda II. At the end of this period they return to simple shapes, mostly either rectangular or shield-shaped, but tend to be very large. They also were made in diminutive forms for use as amulets, perhaps already during Naḳāda I, certainly during Naḳāda II. This emphasizes their magical value as well as that of the green paint, from which it is quite possible that they derived their importance. As late as the Old Kingdom green paint is still found round the eyes of mummies. Dr. Murray takes this to be a fashion in vogue for the living also during the Fourth Dynasty.[1] It seems more likely to me that it survived for the dead as a protection at a time when the living had long since given up its use, for, though mentioned in the offering-lists in the graves and painted on some mummies, it is never found on statues which represent the living. I do not know at what time the palettes ceased to be placed in the tombs. The large rectangular ones are common in the graves of the First Dynasty. During this period they acquire a new and important significance in the temples, where they form part of the outfit used for the toilet of the gods. At least from the time of Nar-Mer they were dedicated to special gods by the king or perhaps other important persons, and decorated with scenes in relief which commemorated important events or, as seems likely in the case of the smaller palette from Hierakonpolis, mythical scenes connected with the god to whom they were dedicated. Again, we do not know how long this custom survived. The only two palettes which were found in an excavation are the two from Hierakonpolis, and already with the smaller of them the difficulties of dating begin. From the battlefield palette it seems safe to assume that they were still in fashion at the time of King Khasekhem. On the other hand, the lion-hunt and the Cairo palette with the name of Queen Tiyi make it at least possible that some palettes were still made long after archaic times, because they had become a necessary, even though obsolete, item in the proper outfit of a god in his temple. Why it was that the green cosmetic, but neither the red nor the black, acquired this special virtue, I am at a loss to tell. The fact remains that neither the grinders for the red nor for the black paint ever had an importance in any way comparable with that of the green.

That objects which had acquired such prominence in Egypt during Naḳāda II and the beginning of the dynasties should also be found in countries outside Egypt is only to be expected,

[1] See above, p. 82.

but no special research has so far been done in the subject. Therefore, only chance remarks can be collected, or objects seen in museums. Slate palettes for common use and without special form have been found in Algiers,[1] in some dolmens excavated by Siret, and now in the Museum of Toulouse. From the East, I only know that one was found by Sir Leonard Woolley at Alalakh.[2] Whether these pieces are contemporaneous with the Egyptian palettes or whether they are late survivors it is impossible to say without a thorough study of the question. Some slate palettes decorated with geometrical engravings and with a human head on top resembling the Egyptian type with the pointed chin were found among the material from El Argar in Spain. It seems likely that in the last resort they also derive from the Egyptian examples. But without further research in the subject no conclusions other than ones of a very general nature can be drawn from this.

[1] Baumgartel, *Tunis*, in Ebert, *Reallexicon der Vorgeschichte*.
[2] Sir Leonard Woolley, *A Forgotten Kingdom*, p. 45.

CHAPTER V

MACE-HEADS

THE accepted division of the Egyptian mace-heads into disc-shaped and pear-shaped ones has been followed here. This does not mean that it is a very good one, for it does not cover all the known types, nor are all the objects mentioned under these headings necessarily mace-heads. However, it seems simpler to retain the accustomed nomenclature and state the objections than to invent a new one and cause confusion.

Spindle-whorls, in particular, seem very difficult to sort out from among the mace-heads. Whether a given piece is a large whorl or a small mace-head, it is sometimes impossible to decide, nor are the whorls always to be distinguished from large beads. It seemed, therefore, advisable to add a paragraph on spindle-whorls to this chapter.

I will also include here the so-called double-pointed mace-heads, sometimes described as battle-axes. This seems appropriate, for they are weapons of similar use and also are made of stone.

THE DISC-SHAPED MACE-HEADS

The name was ill-chosen from the beginning. By a disc we understand a flat circular object which is symmetrical in every respect. No such mace-heads exist in Egypt. They were, however, used by some primitive tribes in New Guinea, and a comparison will show the difference. The weapons from New Guinea are made of slate, mostly circular (though some oval ones exist), and are flat on both surfaces. Their average diameter is about 14 cm., their thickness 2 to 3 cm. The perforations in the middle are about 2·5 cm. wide, and, though bored from both sides, have straight walls. A heavy wooden handle up to 1 m. long is pushed through these holes, and sticks out at least 10 cm. through the top. It is fixed in the hole by a wedge driven into a cleft in its upper end. The handle where it is driven through the hole is encased in a piece of matting to prevent its slipping.

How different from these true weapons are the Egyptian disc mace-heads. Some are made of a soft limestone (and these are among the earliest) and either have a flat or slightly concave top with a domed back, or they are cone-shaped.[1] Others are of a lively-coloured black and white porphyry, or of veined marble. The limestone maces are decorated with patterns in black, outstanding among which is a Maltese cross covering the whole of the top, the spaces left vacant being filled with dots. Others are painted with small dots all over, or have a curved line cutting off a sector. White stripes cross the tops of some, and on these the background is coloured a dark grey (Vol. I, pl. VII, 1-3). The effect sought for is a sharp contrast of black and white, produced either by painting limestone or by the choice of the mottled and veined stones. It seems impossible to decide whether the more precious stones were chosen because they resembled the painted patterns or whether the painted patterns are imitations of the stones. The cross, however,

[1] *Naq. Bal.*, pl. XVII, 1 and 4.

can hardly be said to be an imitation of any stone. Quite often these objects are painted on both sides.

The average diameter of the disc-maces is 8 cm. The holes, which are rarely exactly in the centre, are bored either from one or from both sides, and the hole is always much smaller at the top than at the bottom. At its widest it is rarely more than 10 mm., at its narrowest often not more than 6 mm. Where it is bored from both sides it often dwindles in the middle to a very small opening so that no stick or handle could be thrust through it.

If these pieces with the domed backs show some resemblance to real discs, this can hardly be said of those which look like flat cones with concave sides. They are mostly made of one of the mottled stones, though painted limestone ones also exist.

The earliest disc-shaped mace-heads so far known are two from Naḳāda, t. 1443, S.D. 31. One is of a fine-grained white limestone, originally painted black or dark grey on both sides, and with only two white stripes left. It is shaped as a low cone with concave sides, the top being slightly concave also. The other, of a coarser limestone, was also painted grey or black, with two white stripes of thick paint laid over it. It also is roughly cone-shaped, with a concave top. Three fragments of sticks with leather bindings were found in the same grave and may be fragments of the handles, or at least of their lower parts, for their diameters would be too great for the openings of the discs. Two similar discs were recovered from Naḳāda, t. 1418, which is undated. They are somewhat shallower than those from t. 1443, have level tops and are made of the same soft white limestone as the first mentioned from that grave. One, which has been split in two and glued together in modern times, has a pattern which leaves only two white stripes across each side; the other was painted black or dark grey all over and then decorated with white spots, and has a white line cutting off a sector. The only other object I could trace from t. 1418 is a "fancy" pot, Corpus type F 12, dated S.D. 36-44.[1] Another broken and recently-mended limestone disc from Naḳāda, t. 1416, has only faded traces of the painting left; it is dated S.D. 36-38. The only other object known to me from this grave is a polished-red pot, type P 4, with an engraving of a lion in the style of the white-cross-lined pottery. As the grave is sequence-dated, there must have been more pottery in it, but up to now I have been unable to trace it.[2]

Two discs were found in El-'Amrah, t. a 90, which dates before S.D. 41 according to MacIver, S.D. 34 according to Petrie.[3] One is of soft white limestone, with concave top and domed back, and is painted with black dots; the other, says the excavator (who refers us to pl. X, 6, of *El Amrah and Abydos*), is of diorite. But the diorite mace-head there is from t. a 102[4]; next to it is the little spotted one just described; and a third, clearly marked a 90 on the plate, looks much more like limestone than like diorite. Three white-cross-lined pots were found in this tomb. The most interesting disc mace-head from El-'Amrah comes from t. a 23, which dates before S.D. 41 according to MacIver, S.D. 32 according to Petrie. MacIver describes it as follows: "Baton of clay painted

---

[1] The two mace-heads from t. 1443 (dimensions 8·1 cm. and 7·9 cm. respectively) and from t. 1418 (dimensions 10 cm. and 8·5 cm.) are in the Ashmolean Museum, Oxford, where there is also a white-cross-lined pot, type C 43H from t. 1443. The fragments of the sticks, together with a black-topped sherd with a pot-mark and a bifacial flint knife from t. 1443, are at University College, London. The "fancy" pot from t. 1418 is in the Ashmolean.

[2] Both objects at University College, London.

[3] Petrie sequence-dated the tombs from El-'Amrah in *Preh. Eg.*, pl. LI. The limestone mace-head with the dots is in the Ashmolean Museum, Oxford.

[4] See *El Amrah*, pp. 16 and 23.

in red stripes with imitation mace-head of clay." The line drawing on pl. XII, 1, shows a mace-head with a Maltese cross (in black?) on top and four (?) stripes at the back. It is cone-shaped. From the reproduction it seems as if the "baton" and the head were made in one, the whole being about 15 cm. long, though from the drawing of t. a 23, where the object can be seen lying in front of the skeleton (*El Amrah and Abydos*, pl. V, 1), it seems much larger. The slanting red stripes of the handle imitate a leather binding, and sticks bound with leather were found in t. 1443 mentioned above together with two disc mace-heads. The leather seems to reinforce the handle and not to bind the top to it. Unfortunately the publication of this "clay" mace-head and handle from El-'Amrah is so bad that details of the construction cannot be made out from it, nor are the colours of the painting mentioned. Where this important piece is kept now, I do not know.[1]

Clay and pottery mace-heads are known from other excavations also. A cone-shaped one was found in Hu, t. B 56, S.D. 34, together with another broken one,[2] probably of stone, though it is difficult to be sure from the publication. The clay mace-head is of grey, smooth clay. Whether it was painted originally cannot now be ascertained (diameter 6·3 cm.). It is doubtful whether the pottery disc from Naḳāda, t. 202, belongs to the same type of objects. It might be a lid in spite of the hole, which is slightly eccentric. Its diameter is 20·2 cm., and it is 2·5 cm. thick. No other objects from this tomb could be traced. A smaller disc of pottery from Naḳāda, t. B 124, is made from the bottom and part of the adjoining wall of a vase so that on one side it is about 2·5 cm. high and on the other barely 1 cm. The perforation, with a diameter of nearly 2 cm. and nearer to the low edge, is bored from both sides. It is difficult to guess what purpose such an asymetrical object might have served, unless it was a lid.[3]

Another disc mace-head of white limestone, also broken and mended, and painted with a black Maltese cross and dots, comes from Naḳāda, t. 234, S.D. 63 (Naḳāda II). It is the nearest approximation to a true disc yet mentioned, having a back which is only slightly domed. It would be interesting to know whether there was another mace-head in this grave, for in all the instances so far met they were deposited in pairs. The same question can be asked about Naḳāda, t. 824, from which a heavy cone-shaped limestone mace is preserved, also decorated with the Maltese cross and dots. The perforation was made from both sides, and the two holes do not perfectly meet, so that the opening becomes oval in the middle and does not measure more than about 6 mm. at its narrowest. The grave is undated. A rough bowl, a black-topped one and a single disc-shaped cornelian bead are the only other objects known to me from t. 824, hence it is not impossible that it is of Naḳāda II date. The little disc mace-head from Naḳāda, t. 1417, cone-shaped and only 5·9 cm. wide at the top, is painted with the dot pattern through which a single black stripe is drawn. At the back, part of this stripe is all that survives of the painting. This mace-head has a trace of red colour on the top, near the hole, which may be the remnant of a circle which once surrounded it. T. 1417 is sequence-dated to 35-41, but belongs probably to Naḳāda II, on account of three rough flint flakes, one of them twisted, which were found in it. Two combs were also recovered from it.[4]

---

[1] The distribution list says the piece is in the British Museum. This seems to be a mistake.
[2] *Diosp. Pa.*, pl. V, bottom left.
[3] The clay mace-head and both the pottery ones are in the Ashmolean Museum, Oxford.
[4] The mace-head is in the Ashmolean Museum, Oxford. The flakes, a comb with bird head and a piece of wood are at University College, London; the other comb with a Hathor head is in Berlin.

A pottery object from Naḳāda, t. 1437, S.D. 32, may possibly be a mace-head of this type, though its perforation does not go through the top, which has a diameter of 7·6 cm. It is mentioned here because pieces of a stick were also found in the tomb, two of which were bound with leather, while four pieces (of the same stick?) are coloured red. A quantity of leather thongs twisted or rolled were also recovered.

What emerges from the discussion of some examples of disc mace-heads made of soft limestone and painted is that only three patterns were used for their decoration. The first pattern consists of white stripes against a black or dark grey background, which are parallel to each other on each side of the central hole, and are continued on the backs of the maces. The second is made up of dots which, in all but the piece from El-'Amrah, have a line drawn across, dividing off one sector of the surface. In the third we have the Maltese cross also continued on the back with larger dots in the openings. It seems unlikely that the restriction to these three patterns is mere chance, though I do not see what can have decided the choice in each case.

The disc-shaped mace-heads made of a stone other than limestone are either of a spotted diorite or breccia or of a dark marble with one or two white stripes right across the top. As with the limestone disc mace-heads, they either have a domed back or are cone-shaped. The tendency is to draw out the hole to a sort of collar, or even to a short tube. At the same time the top becomes concave. This is difficult to explain in a weapon which uses its edge for battering, as it weakens it. I know of no piece with an intact edge.

If we can trust the sequence-dating, the disc mace-heads of coloured stones begin somewhat later than those of limestone. The earliest so far seems to be one from Naḳāda, t. 1654, S.D. 34, a tomb that also contained the fine pin with the snake top (Vol. I, pl. IX, 1). It is of dark grey marble with white stripes or veins.[1] The most important find of disc mace-heads of striped marble was made at Abadiyeh, t. B 86, S.D. 35-40. Two of them were found together with their handles, one of horn the other of ivory.[2] T. B 86 was a large grave and contained three bodies, seemingly undisturbed. It yielded a third disc mace-head but without a handle, and nine flint fish-tails. Petrie does not mention any of the pottery which must have been in the grave, nor whether there was any other furniture which might have thrown some light on the character of the persons interred. The horn handle, which is 31 cm. long and 2 cm. at its widest, fits loosely into the hole of the mace. How it was made to stay in the mace-head is not evident, since there are no traces of leather or binding. Petrie, who of course saw that neither the ivory nor the horn handle could have served for a weapon, assumes that the discs were ceremonial, just as he calls the soft limestone cones substitutes for those of a more lively coloured rock. This does not seem obvious.

A disc mace-head with domed back and a pear-shaped one were found together in Naḳāda, t. 1488. The grave is undated, and the only other object I could trace from it is a plain hollowed-out ivory tusk.[3]

From the main deposit of Hierakonpolis large quantities of mace-heads were discovered Among them were disc-shaped ones of various forms and material. Some look like saucers, others have domed backs, and still others have developed long handle sockets. Some have plain

[1] *Die Altertümer*, I, pl. 8, 143.
[2] *Diosp. Pa.*, p. 33, pl. V, top right. Now in the Ashmolean Museum, Oxford, but without the ivory handle.
[3] The mace-heads in the Ashmolean Museum, Oxford, the tusk at University College, London.

tops, others concave ones.[1]   The largest, of black and white diorite, has a diameter of 26 cm., fit only for the hand of a god.   The top in its thickest part measures not more than 1·3 cm. and thins out to about 0·5 cm. towards the edges.   It has a tubular socket for the handle.   There are smaller ones of 15 cm. diameter.   The tops of all the outsize pieces are concave.   Their date is not certain; they are most likely early dynastic.

The claim for the disc maces being weapons rests very largely on their occurrence among the objects painted on some coffins of the late Old Kingdom and the Middle Kingdom.   There, next to the pear-shaped maces, we sometimes find another form resembling but not quite identical with the discs.   It is a slender cone with a flat top such as would be accepted easily as a mace-head.   In a coffin now in the Cairo Museum, however, there is one which with its curved outlines recalls some of the more extravagant pieces from the main deposit at Hierakonpolis.[2]   Next to it is clearly written the word "*mnw*", which means mace.

The few disc mace-heads found in settlements make it certain that they were more than mere votive objects dedicated in tombs and temples.   From the debris of the village at El-Maḥāsna both the cone-shaped and the domed-back types were recovered.[3]   In Kom W, Desert Fayum,[4] a cone-shaped one of hard limestone was found.   It is unpainted and measures 7 cm. across the top, while its perforation, which was bored from both sides, measures 1·3 cm. at its narrowest. The closest parallel to this, cone-shaped and bevel-edged, but with a smaller perforation, belongs to the temple deposit at Hierakonpolis.[5]   One excavated by Brunton at Badāri, t. 130, S.D. 34 (?), is of similar type.   The sequence-date is questionable, as the grave contained only one pot, which cannot be accurately dated; nor was there any other object to confirm the early date.[6]   Brunton describes the mace as "almost intermediate between the disc and the pear forms".   Another piece which does not seem to fit into either category is a model complete with handle found by Reisner at Naga-ed-Der and now in Cairo.[7]   It is not dated, nor does it seem to be published. The head, made of clay, is conical with a slightly-domed top.   It was painted red and black in geometrical patterns inlaid with narrow strips of straw.   The handle, also of clay over a reed, is broken at the end.   It is painted in three horizontal stripes of red and black divided from each other by rings of straw.   The little weapon is 17·5 cm. long, the head 4·2 cm. wide.

The Pear-shaped Mace-heads

The type called "pear-shaped" covers a variety of forms, pear-shaped, globular (called by some apple-shaped), biconical, barrel-shaped, and many more.   All varieties have this in common, that they seem much more appropriate as weapons than the disc-shaped mace-heads could ever be.   The stones of which they are made are hard and heavy.   They are the classical weapon of early Egypt, and remain so far into dynastic times.   The pharaoh on the Nar-Mer tablet swings one to slay his vanquished enemy, as do many pharaohs after him on countless reliefs.   As the

[1] Quibell and Green, *Hierakonpolis*, ii, p. 41, pl. XXVII, 1-14.
[2] P. Lacau, *Sarcophages antérieurs au Nouvel Empire*, i, p. 106, 66; fig. 276, *Cairo Catalogue*.
[3] *Maḥâsna*, pl. V, top right.
[4] Caton-Thompson, *The Desert Fayum*, p. 33, pl. XXX, 2.
[5] Now in the Ashmolean Museum, Oxford.
[6] *Bad. Civ.*, p. 58.
[7] *Cairo E.J.*, 37757.

pear-shaped mace was used in Mesopotamia and Persia long before it was known in Egypt, it will have been an importation of the Naḳāda II people.[1]

The handles were fixed with leather strips which were first fastened round the tip of the handle, which protruded beyond the head, and then, crossing the head, were wound round the lower part of the handle, as can be seen on reliefs of the Old Kingdom.[2] In some cases the leather bindings extended all over the handle, in others they were short, only covering the part nearest the head, while another near the bottom prevented the weapon from slipping, and would give a better grip for the hand.

The earliest pear-shaped mace-head mentioned by Petrie [3] is the one from Naḳāda, t. 1401, S.D. 42.[4] It is of alabaster, 5·4 cm. high, 5·4 cm. at its widest, and narrowing towards the base. The same grave contained two magnificent disc mace-heads, one of black and white speckled porphyry, the other of pink and white breccia, with a small collar to serve as socket at the back. Petrie does not mention the clay object from El-Maḥāsna, t. H 29, the grave in which was also found the strange little carving so often hailed as the first representation of the Seth animal.[5] The excavator calls it a mace-head, and the reproduction shows a roughly pear-shaped object with no discernible perforation. It seems somewhat dangerous to see in it the picture of a pear-shaped mace-head as long as no real pear-shaped mace-head has come to light from Naḳāda I. It may have been a clay cone like those found in El-'Amrah, t. 163 (S.D. 36-38 according to Petrie). A similar object but with a clay handle was found in a woman's grave, Mustagidda, t. 1727 S.D. 40-57.[6]

Another mace-head also dated to S.D. 42 comes from Naḳāda, t. 1257. It is rather squat and approaches in shape the disc from the Desert Fayum. It is 4·6 cm. high and 5·7 cm. at its widest [7] but is more rounded than the piece from the Desert Fayum or that from Hierakonpolis. The socket is so narrow—not more than 4 mm. where the perforations meet—that once more we wonder what sort of a handle could have been inserted. Yet the piece cannot be dismissed as "model made for the grave", for it shows distinct traces of battering. T. 1257 is a rich grave, and has already been mentioned (p. 7) on account of the silver beads and tray recovered from it. Another dated specimen comes from Naḳāda, t. 369, S.D. 55-74. It is of black and white porphyry about 6 cm. high and of about the same width across the high shoulders, but narrowing appreciably towards the base. The piece feels beautifully balanced, and yet again we must ask whether it could ever have been used, because the perforations from both sides do not exactly meet and the opening left in the middle is barely 5 mm. wide. A similar mace, but a little smaller, was found in Hu, t. U 198, S.D. 51.[8] It is of a hard white limestone, has a much larger hole carefully smoothed, which measures 1·7 cm. in diameter at the bottom and 1·6 cm. at the top. There can be no doubt that this mace would fit well on a handle.

[1] Ghirshman, *Sialk*, pp. 21-2, from Period I. H. de Genouillac, *Fouilles de Telloh*, I, p. 55, pl. 8, "époque de Warka".

[2] E. G. L. Borchardt, *Das Grabdenkmal des Koenigs Sahu-Re*, II, *Die Wandbilder*, pl. 18.

[3] *Preh. Eg.*, p. 22.

[4] The three mace-heads are at University College, London, a black-topped pot in the Oriental Institute, Chicago and the red-incised pot (see Vol. I, p. 100) in the Ashmolean Museum, Oxford.

[5] See p. 49; Vol. I, p. 34.

[6] Brunton, *Mostag.*, p. 89, pl. XL, 13.

[7] Now in the Ashmolean Museum, Oxford.

[8] *Diosp. Pa.*, pl. XXVIII, top left. Now in the Ashmolean Museum, Oxford.

A perfectly-globular mace-head comes from Naḳāda, t. 483. The grave is not sequence-dated, and the only vase I could trace from it was a polished-red bowl, loosely polished on the outside with a few strokes, which points to a date towards the end of Naḳāda II. A barrel-shaped mace-head with a small collar at the top is of brownish limestone and was found in Naḳāda, t. 690, S.D. 52.[1] Another in the form of a double cone with flat top and bottom and marks of battering around the middle where the bases of the two cones meet comes from Naḳāda, t. 309.[2] It is made of black haematite. Yet another type of mace-head, nearly cylindrical in shape with a convex top and a large perforation, might be the handle of a stick, and is made of white alabaster with a greyish vein.[3] The grave, Naḳāda 1840, is undated. A black-topped pot, B 27a, also belonged to it.

With the material at our disposal it does not yet seem possible to bring order into the typology of the pear-shaped mace-heads. Even Petrie seems to have given up the attempt. This is partly due to the lack of accuracy of our publications, which either state "pear mace-head" without any more detailed description or merely show a reproduction from a photograph which, especially when taken from above, makes it impossible to form an idea of the shape of the original. No development of shape can be traced, nor can the different shapes be ascribed to different periods or uses, be it for hunt or war, for ceremonies or as badges of office.

The greatest deposit of mace-heads of all types ever found was in the main deposit of the temple of Hierakonpolis.[4] They will have been *ex-votos* to the warrior-god Horus, who is represented on the *sereḥ* of King Ḥor-Aḥa carrying a mace in one of his claws. Some of the pear-shaped mace-heads from this deposit assume enormous sizes, as did the disc-shaped ones. A mace of white quartz is 10·5 cm. high, and 10·5 cm. across the shoulder. The diameter of its perforation is 5·5 cm. at the base and 5 cm. at the top. There is another, slightly smaller and not completely perforated, but with a small boring at the top and a larger one at the base, which is divided vertically into seven sectors by shallow furrows which would facilitate binding it to a handle. These two large mace-heads cannot be dated. No attempt has as yet been made to find out the differences between the mace-heads of the predynastic period and those of later times. One would like, however, to be able to associate them with the protodynastic period, for it seems that a predilection for over-life-size votive offerings then existed, as is shown by the sculptured mace-heads of a king of the early First Dynasty found also at Hierakonpolis.[5]

Pear-shaped mace-heads were found in most of the settlements so far excavated. A good piece, of fine hard limestone, comes from the North Town of Naḳāda,[6] others were excavated by Caton-Thompson at Ḥammāmīya in Naḳāda II surroundings,[7] by Garstang at El-Maḥāsna,[8] and at Merimda.

DOUBLE-POINTED MACE-HEADS OR BATTLE-AXES

Most of these are shaped like cigars, but with both ends pointed; some have a convex bottom. Rarely, the points remain blunt, and then they recall the double axes. They are pierced in the

---

[1] Now at University College, London. Two pots are known to me from this grave: the decorated one, D 50, in Oxford, and the smooth brown one, L 17f, in the Chicago Oriental Institute.

[2] Now in the Ashmolean Museum, Oxford.   [3] Now in the Ashmolean Museum, Oxford.

[4] Quibell and Green, *Hierakonpolis*, ii, pl. XXVII.

[5] The slate palettes of protodynastic times show a similar tendency.   [6] Now at University College, London.

[7] *Bad. Civ.*, pl. LXX, 40.   [8] *Maḥâsna*, pl. V, top right.

middle, generally from one side only. The perforation is large at the base, but cone-shaped so that it becomes much smaller at the top. Mace-heads of this type found in Nubia have a groove round the middle and are not perforated.[1]

I do not know why Petrie dates these mace-heads to Naḳāda I.[2] The earliest he quotes is from Abadiyeh, t. B 102, S.D. 33-41. There were five bodies in the grave, and from Petrie's description one gains the impression that they were not interred at the same time, but that some of the skeletons were pushed together to make room for the new burial.[3] The tomb furniture is very rich. Unfortunately Petrie does not mention any pottery, but only reproduces some objects without describing them, so that it is not clear whether they were all that were found. Two disc mace-heads are among the furniture illustrated. The grave may belong to the time of transition from Naḳāda I to Naḳāda II.

The double-pointed mace-head is of white alabaster, about 125 mm. long and 45 mm. high. Its upper side is concave, the lower conical. The perforation measures 2 cm. at the bottom, narrowing to 9 mm. at the top. Both points show signs of battering.

Three similar mace-heads were excavated from t. H 23 at El-Maḥāsna.[4] They are of "finely polished pink stone", and, as shown by the illustration, of different sizes and shapes. Two of them, together with a disc-shaped and a pear-shaped mace-head, lay in front of the head of the skeleton. They had wooden handles. The grave, which was lined with wood, also contained a footed ivory vase which is said to have had two loop (?) handles originally, a clay mace-head and a copper harpoon. The excavators did not sequence-date it, but Petrie [5] assigns it to S.D. 36-43. Such a date appears to be doubtful, for the pottery—only three vases seem contemporaneous— is of a wide range, and the grave may well be later.

More securely dated to Naḳāda II is the double-pointed piece from Naḳāda, t. 1475, S.D. 45. It is of hard brown limestone, with one end damaged, and is 13 cm. long and 3 cm. high.[6] A similar piece, also of brown limestone and with one point broken, comes from Naḳāda, t. B 110, which is undated.[7] Eight shallow holes are drilled more or less symmetrically over its upper surface. Whether they once held shell inlays is difficult to decide, as no traces remain.

Perhaps the most interesting piece was found by Brunton in the undisturbed grave Badāri, t. 4601.[8] The weapon is shorter and thicker than the usual double-pointed mace-head and has no points. It resembles a double axe. Brunton describes it as "oval".

A mace-head of pink, hard limestone, now in the Cairo Museum, is rather an oddity.[9] It was found at Sahil-el-Baghlieh (Gebel Tarif), the source of much interesting predynastic and protodynastic material in the Cairo Museum. It has four points, and looks like two double-pointed mace-heads joined together along their longer axis. The cone-shaped perforation is bored from below, 2·3 cm. wide at the bottom, 0·8 cm. at the top. The piece is 10·9 cm. long. One of its points is broken.

---

1 *Archaeological Survey of Nubia*, I, pl. 62c, 7 and 8, from Cemetery 17, Bahan.
2 *Preh. Eg.*, p. 23.   3 *Diosp Pa.*, p. 33, pls. V, IX, XII.
4 *Pre-dyn. Cem. at El-Mahasna*, pp. 21 and 32, pls. VIII, 39 and 40; XX, 3.
5 *Preh. Eg.*, pl. LII, Maḥasna No. 23.   6 *Die Altertümer*, I, p. 83, pl. 7.
7 *Naq. Bal.*, pl. XVII, 23. Now in the Ashmolean Museum, Oxford. Nothing else of the contents of tt. 1475 and B 110 is known to me.
8 *Bad. Civ.*, p. 52, pls. XXXIV, 5; LIII, 10.
9 Quibell, *Cat. Gén., Cairo E.J.*, 14421, 31444.

Where the dates of the double-pointed mace-heads could be ascertained they either belong to the transition from Naḳāda I to Naḳāda II, or to Naḳāda II proper, during the whole of which period they occur occasionally. They are never very common, and only a small number of them have survived. Whether they were still in use in dynastic times remains an open question. I could not trace a piece later than Naḳāda II. There was none in the great deposit of the temple of Hierakonpolis with its dozens of disc- and pear-shaped maces. No double-pointed mace-head has been excavated so far anywhere north of Asyūt.

MACE-HEADS OF DIFFERENT SHAPES WITH DECORATIONS, MOSTLY IN RELIEF

In the main deposit of the temple at Hierakonpolis three very large pear-shaped mace-heads were found covered with scenes of a religious and historical nature in shallow relief. Two of them are now in the Ashmolean Museum, Oxford, the third at University College, London. The smallest (c. 20 cm. high) has the *sereḥ* of King Nar-Mer on it. From their style, the two others cannot be much different in age. These three mace-heads are unique. We know too little about the ceremonial and religion of this early period to decide with certainty what the scenes represent which are sculptured on them. Only on the smallest mace-head have we got the full design, as it is the only one which is complete, but its surface is not well preserved (pls. VIII, IX and X).

The main event figured on the small mace-head is a meeting between King Nar-Mer and a person in a palanquin followed by three running men. The king is seated on his throne under a pavilion approached by nine steps (pls. VIII, 4, IX, 1). He wears the Red Crown and is dressed in a coat which is too damaged to assess its length. In his hand he holds the flail. The person in the palanquin and the three men following are on the same level as the king and of about the same size. The closed palanquin stands just opposite him. The person inside it is the most important figure after the king and seems to be a woman (pls. VIII, 5, IX, 2). She has no beard such as her three followers have, and her hair falls over her shoulders. The three men are enclosed between sets of three lunulae on each side, which also separate them from the palanquin (pl. VIII, 2 and 3). If the figure in it is indeed a woman, she can only be the queen, and that is made likely by the picture immediately above her, which represents a cow and her calf inside an enclosure. That they and the figure in the palanquin belong together seems clear, for the basal line which separates the four standard-bearers from the running men below stops short before reaching the enclosure with the cow, so that the palanquin and the enclosure are united into one scene. Since we know [1] that the mother of Horus had a cult in the temple of Hierakonpolis, it would be she who is depicted here, above as a cow and below in her human representation, the mother or wife of the king. Opposite the enclosure, and hovering above the pavilion which it protects with its wings, is a large bird. This is the largest and in consequence the most important figure on the mace-head. As the mace was dedicated in the temple of Horus, this can only be the Horus falcon protecting the living Horus, the king. The motif of Horus spreading protecting wings around the king occurs on the Djoser reliefs from the Step Pyramid [2] and, most impressively, on the statue of King Khefren in Cairo. The bird on the mace is very summarily drawn, without

---

[1] W. C. Hayes, "Horemkhaʿuef of Nekhen", *JEA*, 33 (1947), pp. 3 ff.
[2] Firth, Quibell and Lauer, *The Step Pyramid*, II, pls. 40, 41, 42.

much detail, and has an exaggeratedly curved beak, as has the falcon on the *sereḥ* with the king's name, which lies some little way behind the main group and above the two panels with the king's retinue (pl. X, 1). In the retinue there are three men in the upper row. The man next to the pavilion is probably a priest, for he wears a large wig and the panther's skin, and the two behind with long sticks will be soldiers. Above the priest a *d* is sculptured, perhaps with another hiero-glyph (a *t*?), now lost, below. In the panel below, an official carrying the king's sandals and a ewer marches first. In front of him are two signs, one a seven-leaved rosette, the other difficult to discern.[1] He wears an elaborate kilt, with a tail at the back. Two fan-bearers stand next to the throne. The three men behind the palanquin are bearded and wear wigs (pl. VIII, 2-3; pl. X, 2). They hold their hands in front of their chests in what may be an attitude of dance or worship. They run or dance between objects which are the same as those between which the king performs his ritual runs, originals of which still stand in the courtyard of Djoser's Step Pyramid. One looks like one, the other like two lunulae. Behind them, but on a base by itself, and somewhat lower, is a fourth figure, kneeling and with his arms behind his back. Of his head hardly anything is preserved, and to him belong some numerals, 102000, which are written underneath. In front of him, but somewhat lower and in a panel by themselves, are a bull and a goat, again accompanied by numerals (pl. X, 5), 400000 for the bull and 1422220 for the goat. If this represents the number of animals given to the temple by the king on the occasion immortal-ized by the mace-head, the 102000 behind the kneeling men may mean a large number of slaves handed over on the same occasion.[2] In the top panel above the running men, and marching towards the king, are his four standard-bearers (pl. X, 2). They carry the Wepwawet of Assiut, the fetish of Abydos, and two falcons on their long poles. Separated from this large scene by vertical lines is another. It is smaller and less important than the first, and it is not obvious what it has to do with it. Above is a chapel (?) inside an enclosure, and on top of the little edifice stands a long-legged bird (pl. X, 3) which Quibell[3] thinks may be an ibis, which he connects with Thoth. In front of it is a pole with a forked top and a vase in a stand. Whether the bird is an ibis, a heron or another water-bird it is impossible to decide, as is the connexion in which it may stand to the picture underneath it, which shows three gazelles (hartebeests?) in an oval enclosure (pl. X, 4). No human being is represented on this smaller part of the mace, nor is there any hint as to why it is put there. The main scene has been taken to be the first representation of the *heb sed* festival; Petrie calls it a marriage.[4] Both these explanations may be correct. That the most important festival which a king celebrated should be commemorated in what was probably the most important temple of the First Dynasty seems appropriate, and it is equally appropriate that at this early period the sacred marriage should have been its most important incident. The running between the two sets of three lunulae is known from later *heb sed* representations, but on the mace-head it is not the king who is running, but three bearded men. The dedication of large amounts of cattle is a feature of later *heb sed* festivals also. Perhaps the smaller scene with the heron or ibis and the three gazelles simply indicates that these gods were present at the festival.

[1] It is probably a ∩-sign upside down, as can be seen from the Nar-Mer palette, where a man with the same title occurs.

[2] The numbers must not be taken at their face value, but rather as symbols, meaning a great many.

[3] Quibell and Green, *Hierakonpolis*, I, p. 9.

[4] Petrie, *The Making of Egypt*, pp. 78-9.

The largest of the Hierakonpolis mace-heads is about 32 cm. high. Only about a third of it is preserved, but what there is is better and artistically finer than either of the other mace-heads. The most important figure extant is a king wearing a short tunic which leaves one shoulder free. To his belt the bull's tail is attached. On his head he has the White Crown of Upper Egypt. With both his hands he grasps a large hoe. What is most unusual for an Egyptian king performing a public function is that the king does not wear a beard. However, on the *heb sed* reliefs from the Sun Temple of King Ne-Woser-Re [1] the king in the White Crown also lacks this part of his insignia, though it is worn by King Djoser on the reliefs underneath the Step Pyramid.[2] The king on the large mace-head, in contrast to King Nar-Mer on the smaller, is by far the largest person represented. In front of him are two signs, a rosette with seven petals above and a scorpion below. The scorpion has a rectangular piece attached to it similar to those attached to the scorpions on the reliefs under the Step Pyramid. The group is commonly read King Scorpion, the rosette being taken as an otherwise unknown sign for king. This seems open to doubt. The rosette, which was found on the smaller mace-head together with what is most likely the *ḥm* sign, appears in contemporary settings where it cannot possibly mean king, for example between the entwined snakes of the gold handle of the Cairo flint knife [3] and on the ivory handle at University College, London. These pieces are strongly influenced by Sumerian ideas. The two snakes in Mesopotamia were a symbol of the blessings of fertility,[4] and the rosette a symbol of Ishtar.[5] I think we must keep this in mind, especially as the remainder of the relief on the large mace-head is decorated with more signs which belong to the cycle of fertility symbols. The signs behind the man who follows the king, and who appears in a similar context on the Nar-Mer palette, might rather be a priestly title which would correspond to the $ḏ.(t)$ priest with whom he appears. It is unfortunate for these researches that the fragment of a second rosette from the large mace-head was found on a splinter which cannot be fitted into any of the scenes preserved, but must have belonged to the lost part. If the rosette should be a symbol of the fertility-goddess, how then is the scorpion to be explained? In the decoration on the painted pots the scorpion is not rare. In the main deposit of Hierakonpolis, from which the mace-heads come, statuettes of scorpions were found by the dozen. On the reliefs of the Djoser Pyramid and on those of the Sun Temple of Ne-Woser-Re the creature is sculptured with the same unidentified object attached to it as on the mace-head. The only Egyptian divinity in the form of a scorpion known to me is Selket, the one who causes the throats to breathe. She must have been closely connected with Hathor, or perhaps was originally an animal of Hathor's, otherwise she could not have been so popular at Hierakonpolis. But she is undoubtedly a woman, and it seems unusual that a king should take the name of a goddess. In spite of his title of the Two Ladies, I do not know of an Egyptian king who called himself by the name of a goddess. That the scorpion was an animal of the fertility-goddess in Mesopotamia is well known. On an early dynastic Mesopotamian seal-cylinder with the sacred marriage on it the scorpion is shown under the marriage couch.[6] Like

---

[1] F. W. von Bissing and H. Kees, *Das Re-Heiligtum des Königs Ne-Woser-Re*, II, pls. 4, 9, etc.

[2] Firth, Quibell and Lauer, *The Step Pyramid*, II, pl. 44.

[3] See above, p. 5.

[4] See below, p. 117, note 1.

[5] E. Douglas Van Buren, "Symbol of the Gods", *Analecta Orientalia*, 23, p. 40, and "The Rosette in Mesopotamian Art", *Zeitschrift für Assyriologie*, 45 (1939), pp. 99 ff.

[6] Frankfort, *Cylinder Seals*, p. 75, pl. XV, l.

the rosette it is a symbol of Ishtar.[1] All this seems to speak strongly against the reading of King
Scorpion for the two signs in front of the king.[2]

What the scene on the large mace-head is meant to commemorate poses a problem as difficult
as that of the two symbols in front of the king. Quibell thought that it was a record of public
works performed by the king, especially of irrigation works that he is inaugurating. Laudable
as such actions may be, they do not seem ever to have been the subject for an official representation
of an Egyptian king. All the reliefs known on which the king is shown with a hoe in his hands
are connected with the foundation of sanctuaries,[3] and in spite of some unusual features, such a
scene seems to be represented on the large mace-head. The king has excavated the foundation-
trench with a hoe, and an attendant brings the clean sand which has to be spread in it. Both
these ceremonies occur in other foundation-scenes.[4] The two symbols in front of the king, and
the man with a bunch of ears of corn, are unusual. This bunch of ears we know from much later
times to belong to the festival of the procession of Min, and on the mace they may be a symbol
of Horus, who, as was thought likely before, has here taken the place of Min. The signs before
the king and those carried by the attendant might represent the gods to whom the temple was
dedicated, namely Horus and his mother, and the mace may have been made in commemoration
of the foundation of the very temple at Hierakonpolis in which the mace-head was found. Above
the man with the basket was the procession of the king's standard-bearers, of whom fragments
of the last two are all that is left. Behind him are his two fans, and five flowering plants which
might be the *šwt* plants, symbols of Upper Egypt, arranged in two registers. They divide the
foundation-scene from the end of a procession, the beginning of which is lost and which must
have been the subject on the other side of the mace. There were two rows of figures, one above
the other, which are not separated by a line like the plants. This indicates that they belong
together. In the upper row a person in a palanquin, this time an open one, and the fragment of
another, can be seen, and behind them a man with a stick. From analogies with similar scenes
the figures in the palanquins can only be the royal children.[5] Underneath them, probably to
be imagined as at their side, are the remnants of three, possibly four, dancing girls with long
hair falling down their backs. They are clapping their hands. Above these scenes and in a panel
by themselves around the upper opening of the mace are standards of gods, probably those
supposed to be present at the solemn acts shown below, unless they represent the king in his
different aspects. Most of them are lost, but a jackal, the Seth animal, the sign of Min, a second
Seth animal and the sign of the mountains are left. Of a sixth standard, only the lower part
is preserved. Suspended by the neck from the top of these standards are *rekhit* birds, which
represent Lower Egypt.[6] On a fragment from another part of the mace the remnants of three
more standards are preserved, but only on one has the symbol remained intact—the falcon on

[1] C. Frank, *Studien zur Babylonischen Religion*, p. 248.

[2] On the fragment of a slate palette (see above, p. 103) showing the destruction of enemy cities a scorpion is one of
the animals destroying a town with a hoe. This has been taken to be a male scorpion-god. For this there is no proof,
It may, however, be a personification of the king, like the Two Ladies, and may indicate that the scorpion, like Ishtar,
was also a war-goddess.

[3] *Das Re-Heiligtum*, II, sheet 2.

[4] *Das Re-Heiligtum*, III, text. Kees, *Die Grosse Festdarstellung*, pp. 4-5.

[5] *Das Re-Heiligtum*, III, sheet 14.

[6] See Vol. I, p. 45.

the crescent moon. Suspended from these standards, as far as one can make out, are bows, which represent the foreign enemies of Egypt. The falcon looks in the opposite direction from that of the other symbols on the standards.

Below the main picture with the king and the hoe remain fragments of another, too broken to allow of an explanation but obviously of great interest. There seems to be plenty of water, a main river running round the mace and another one flowing into it at right angles and then curving away to the right. A short distance below their junction are two men in identical attitudes, one on each side of it. Of the left one, the upper part only is preserved. What they are doing is not clear. They stretch their arms forward as if to wash them. Behind the man on the right is another who holds a hoe, not as if he were using it, like the king, but rather as if he were carrying it by the top. Where the river curls away to the right the fragment of the forepart of a boat remains, which floats on the river. On the small piece of land on the other side of the river, and at the very bottom of the mace, can be seen a building with a domed roof and elevated sides such as are known from other early representations. In the plot, which is enclosed by the rivers on three sides and in which the two little men are at work, stands a tree inside a fence. It seems to be the same tree, with its hanging branches and flower at the top, as is found so often painted on the decorated vases of Naḳāda II. From its position one will have to assume that it is a sacred tree. It must have been the rivers on this lower part of the mace which gave Quibell the idea that irrigation work was commemorated on the mace-head. To me it seems that the scene with the king and the hoe has to be separated from the scene below, the significance of which escapes us because the fragments left are too incomplete.

The third of the three great mace-heads of Hierakonpolis is the most fragmentary of all, and its surface is badly damaged. What is left seems to indicate that it belongs to the same cycle of *heb sed* and foundation ceremonies as the two other pieces. A king wearing the Red Crown stands in a pavilion. As far as can be made out he also has no beard. Inside a panel on another part of the mace there are to be seen three pigtailed men who are dancing. Two are more or less wholly preserved, of the third only the pigtail is left. The one in the middle, who is bearded, carries a vase with two small knob-handles in one hand and lifts up the other arm. The man behind him, who is also bearded, lifts one foot in the air. He holds in one hand an object which may be a bull's tail or a piece of cloth and which hangs down past the lifted foot. Of the panel above, the feet and legs of three persons are all that is left. Of the first, a leg is visible from above the knee downwards; of the two following ones, parts of kilts reaching well down the calves are preserved. The few traces of other parts of the relief are too insignificant to allow of any deductions concerning the pictures to which they might have belonged. No signs or hieroglyphs are left, but from the style of the fragments one would think this mace to be more closely related to the mace with the *heb sed* festival than to that of the foundation-ceremony. The reliefs are flatter, and less attention is paid to details; the subdivision of the pictures is less strict, and the execution and drawing seem less assured than those on the other large fragment. Nevertheless, the three mace-heads form a closely-connected group, and cannot be separated either in time or in subject from each other. Though the two last described have not a royal name on them, it seems to me difficult to separate them from other works with the name of King Nar-Mer. It is possible that the royal name was on one of the parts which are lost to us. As we saw on the Nar-Mer mace-head, it need not have been close to the representation of the king.

The subjects depicted on the three mace-heads all seem to belong to the cycle of the *heb sed* festival, which, as we know from the sun temple of Ne-Woser-Re, included scenes with the king on the throne, foundation of temples, and processions. All these are present on the mace-heads. (Those on the third are too damaged for us to be sure, but what is left does not make it impossible for it to have represented part of the *heb sed* ceremonies.) Whether the three men running between the threefold lunates have anything to do with the running of the king which occurs on a contemporary label from Abydos [1] remains an open question.

If we accept the thesis that the three mace-heads are representations of the *heb sed* festival, then they are the earliest testimonials of the existence of this important ceremony. Their having been discovered in the ruins of the temple of Hierakonpolis gives them a special importance. This was a temple for the new god of the king, Horus, and for his mother, the old fertility-goddess, with the cow horns. As nothing dating before the beginning of the First Dynasty was found in it, it was very likely a foundation of that age. As we have seen in the chapter on palettes, there were probably other gods of minor importance who were venerated in the temple. Some of the furniture belonging to the earliest sanctuary was recovered by the excavators, who unfortunately were neither careful nor thorough enough to reap the full benefits of their extraordinary discoveries, nor did they publish more than a very cursory report. The three sculptured mace-heads make it likely that Nar-Mer himself was the founder of the Hierakonpolis temple, the more so as all the important First Dynasty pieces which were recovered are his, unless one insists on introducing a King Scorpion who, with the exception of one doubtful cartouche in ink,[2] is otherwise unknown. The mace-heads for the first time show the Egyptian king in his ceremonial attire on his throne and wearing the White Crown of Upper Egypt.[3] The solemn festival which is commemorated illustrates a period when the people of Lower Egypt, symbolized by the *rekhit* birds, were still looked upon as subjugated adversaries who, like the bows, the foreigners from outside Egypt, were suspended by their necks from the standards of the winning side. Nothing is there to suggest that the ceremonies represented do not belong to Hierakonpolis and Upper Egypt. If the temples of Nub.t and Koptos had been excavated, we could probably speak with more certainty still, but nothing here indicates an ultimate Lower Egyptian origin for the ideas underlying Egyptian kingship or the ceremonies connected with it. In fact, the pictures of the king on the different mace-heads are the earliest known of a pharaoh performing these sacred functions in the principal sanctuary of Upper Egypt. There would have to be very special reasons to deny that they belong to the *nswt*, who, as the *rekhit* birds suspended from the standards on the largest mace-head show, still counted Lower Egypt among his enemies.

Whether more than these three mace-heads decorated with reliefs ever existed, or whether if we were to excavate another early temple more would be discovered, it is impossible to decide. But, while we possess only the two excavated palettes from Hierakonpolis against the three mace-heads, and quite a number of decorated slate palettes, no decorated mace-heads have come to light elsewhere in Egypt. Outside Egypt, in Mesopotamia, decorated mace-heads are more frequent, and they also belong to the equipment of temples dedicated to warrior-gods.[4] Many of

[1] The king who runs is King Djet, perhaps the successor of King Aḥa: *Royal Tombs*, I, pls. XI, 14; XV, 16.

[2] H. Junker, *Bericht über die Grabung auf dem Friedhof in Turah*, pp. 6 ff., fig. 4.

[3] The Red Crown appears for the first time on a black-topped sherd from Naḳāda; see Vol. I, p. 33.

[4] H. Frankfort, "Early Dynastic Sculptured Mace Heads", *Miscellanea Orientalia. Analecta Orientalia*, 12 (1935), pp. 106 ff.

them have inscriptions like the one now in the British Museum, which bears a dedication from Eannatum of Lagash to the god Ningirsu of Eninnu. The inscription is arranged round the top of the mace. Underneath in the centre of the picture is the lion-headed eagle grasping two animals by their hindquarters. The king followed by two attendants not much smaller than himself marches in an attitude of devotion towards the god. Nothing could show more clearly the differences between the Egyptian and the Sumerian ideas of kingship: in Egypt the god incarnate, in Sumer the first servant of the god.

The little "mace-head" found at Hierakonpolis which Quibell calls a "sceptre head" should be mentioned here, though its actual use is doubtful. It is of green serpentine, roughly conical and about 3 cm. high, about 4·5 cm. wide at the top and 3 cm. at the bottom (pl. VI, 4 and 5). On a narrow circle with a herring-bone pattern another circle is displayed formed by dogs biting lions and lions biting dogs in a closely-interlocked chain. This is a Mesopotamian method of decoration,[1] and one wonders whether on top of the little object which is now broken there were once the two lions so characteristic of Mesopotamian sculptured mace-heads. In the middle of the top there is now an irregular hole through which a small copper rod was once fitted.[2] The remnant of this still sticks inside a cylindrical piece of stone, which fits into the hole of the mace-head (?), but rather loosely. It was held in place by another copper rod, now broken, which fitted into a small hole perforating the wall of the head. It has a smoothed top and rough base, and though it moves inside the hollow of the head, its supports being now broken, it does not fall out. The purpose of this inner stone rod is not obvious. It may once have been longer and been the top of a handle, but why was it then fixed to the head in such an ingenious fashion and not made in one with it?

The frieze of the lions and the dogs is worked in a much deeper relief than is ordinarily found in archaic times in Egypt, the heads of the animals being nearly fully in the round. The lions have huge manes which extend over a good part of their backs and underneath their bellies. They are represented rather as if they were composed of scales similar to the manes of the two little ivory lions which Petrie found in one of the tombs of the courtiers of Djer.[3] One of the lions on the mace-head, of whose back more can be seen than those of the others, has its tail curved back, nearly reaching the beginnings of the mane. The dogs, with long tails hanging, stretch out one paw towards the lions. They wear collars.

SPINDLE-WHORLS

Spindle-whorls had been known since Badārian times. Brunton [4] found pierced pottery discs in his Badārian village sites, though he is somewhat doubtful about their use as whorls, saying: "they are scarcely heavy enough for spindle whorls, yet from their round shape it may be inferred that they were meant to rotate". However, I think that they can hardly have had any other use. Similar discs were found in other village sites [5] of later date. What seems the

---

[1] Frankfort, "Early Dynastic Sculptured Mace Heads", *Miscellanea Orientalia. Analecta Orientalia*, 12 (1935), p. 110.
[2] Quibell and Green, *Hierakonpolis*, I, pl. XIX, 6; II, pl. XXIII.
[3] *Royal Tombs*, II, pl. VI, 3, 4.
[4] *Bad. Civ.*, pp. 34, 71.
[5] Most are mentioned in *Bad. Civ.*, pp. 34, 71.

main reason for Brunton's objection, apart from their lightness, is that the spindle-whorls from the town of Naḳāda are mostly either dome-shaped or barrel-shaped, and made of limestone. These limestone ones are certainly heavier; but one or two [1] are made of bone, and can hardly weigh more than the pottery discs. Nor does it seem necessary for a whorl to be very heavy in order to serve its purpose. The kindly guard at Saḳḳārah, who tried to teach me how to spin wool, used a light rectangular plate of bone which rotated very well, at least with him. If found in an excavation, nobody would have dared to call such an object a spindle-whorl. Since the majority of those found from Badārian times onwards come from village and town sites, I cannot imagine any other use for rotating discs. As many of the dome-shaped whorls differ from the mace-heads only in size, one wonders whether those disc-shaped objects of pottery or soft lime-stone with painted patterns were not also meant to rotate. It is not unlikely that what we lump together as disc-shaped mace-heads covers in reality objects of different uses.

Like all tools, spindle-whorls are rare in graves. Brunton found one in t. 5152 at Badāri,[2] made of breccia. One was in Naḳāda, t. 177, S.D. 46-61.[3] While the Badārian piece is rather like the pottery ones, though a little more rounded, the one from Naḳāda is conical. Two from Naḳāda, t. 267, one of white the other of pink marble, are dome-shaped. The grave is not sequence-dated, but a pottery dish, black inside, red outside and polished only with a few strokes, dates it to Naḳāda II.

[1] One in the Ashmolean Museum, Oxford.
[2] *Bad Civ.*, p. 34.
[3] Now at University College, London; a pot from the same grave is in the Chicago Oriental Institute.

CHAPTER VI

GRAVES, CEMETERIES, BUILDINGS AND SETTLEMENTS

IN predynastic as in later periods graves and cemeteries are our main source of knowledge about ancient Egyptian civilizations. As far back as Badārian times, i.e. as far as we can yet reach to the beginnings of uninterrupted settlement in the Nile Valley, cemeteries were lavishly equipped with the best that the people could produce; and this custom grew stronger and more extravagant with the increasing riches of the country. These very riches have attracted first the tomb-robbers and later on archaeologists, who found it easier and more rewarding to unearth row after row of tombs than to dig in the ruins of towns. For excavation of settlements needs much more care and labour, and the results, though of great value for the history of ancient Egypt, may not be spectacular. Nonetheless, some of the more outstanding finds have been made in the few excavations undertaken on dwelling-sites, including, for example, the Nar-Mer palette, the copper statues of Pepi and his son and the golden hawk at Hierakonpolis, and the bust of Nofretete and many other splendid, though not so popular, pieces of sculpture in the ruins of Akhenaton's city at Amarna.

GRAVES AND CEMETERIES

The only coherent attempt to trace the development of the Egyptian tomb during the earlier periods was made by Reisner.[1] He devotes some space to the predynastic graves, but only as an introduction to what existed in the Old Kingdom. For more detailed descriptions we have to rely on the different excavation reports, and especially on those of Brunton.[2] Nobody before or after him—for unfortunately nobody succeeded him and continued his work—has left us such full details about all aspects of the graves he excavated. I am relying especially on Brunton's reports for the following observations.

Most of the Badārian graves are roughly oval. A few circular ones occur. The better graves are rectangular, often with rounded corners. Brunton states [3] that "a well squared grave" was generally aimed at. But as the nature of the soil into which these graves were dug was sandy gravel, this cannot have been an easy task to accomplish. The tools used in the process may have added to the difficulties. It seems that potsherds were used, for in some of the cemeteries [4] they have been found, scoop-shaped and with edges smoothed through use. That would explain why so many of the graves have rounded corners. A well-cut, rectangular grave would have required more labour and trouble, and therefore might not have been obtainable by everybody.

It is not sure that either in Badārian or in Naḳāda I times attempts were made to strengthen the sides of the graves to prevent them from crumbling and help them to retain their shapes. But fragments of twigs and matting indicate that at least some were roofed. Nor was any super-

---

[1] G. A. Reisner, *The Development of the Egyptian Tomb down to the Accession of Cheops*, 1936.
[2] *Bad. Civ., Mostag.* and *Matmar.*
[3] *Mostag.*, p. 43.
[4] E.g. Möller, *Abusir*, pp. 9-10; *Matmar*, p. 24, t. 102, last lines; *Mostag.*, p. 38, t. 1219 Badārian.

structure ever discovered which would have marked the place of the graves. Yet each must have been marked by some sign, for hardly ever have graves been found which cut into each other. Reisner thought they were marked by tiny heaps of sand, or by a few small pebbles arranged in a circle above them, just as the poorer graves in modern Arabic cemeteries. This would explain why no superstructures of predynastic graves are now visible. And, indeed, if one travels along the edge of the cultivation in Upper Egypt and sees the modest cemeteries of the villagers, one can hardly escape the impression that they faithfully repeat a pattern used since the beginning of time.

Brunton remarks that there is a difference in the size of the graves according to sex, and that during the earlier Badārian period the larger graves are those of women, while during the later part those of the men are largest. All the big graves tend to be rectangular. This leads to the question whether we know enough of the period to distinguish early from late Badārian. In Matmar, Brunton attempts to establish dates within the Badārian period.[1] He bases his suggestions on three groups of Badārian graves (his nos. 2000, 2500 and 3000-3100) and deals first with those he thinks intermediate in age, neither early nor late (2000). He finds that that group is characterized by the form of its slate palettes, and by the equal number of black-topped brown and black-topped red pots. There was only one example of an "angled bowl", and none of a bowl with an everted rim. The female graves were larger than the male. The cemetery which Brunton labels as "distinctly late" (3000-3100) had no black-topped brown pottery, but it contained one pot with an everted rim, a quite unique painted pot (MS 18) from grave 3104. The grave was denuded, and the ground had been re-used in predynastic and later times.[2] It may, therefore, be that the pot was intrusive. Certainly no far-reaching conclusions should be based on it. In this cemetery the male graves were larger than the female. The group of graves which Brunton thinks to be "perhaps the earliest of all" (2500) had only one example of a black-topped red pot, "but the pottery is so poor and so scanty that it is difficult to make deductions from it". The presence of shell fish-hooks and the beak of a spoon-bill in one of the graves[3] also suggests to Brunton an early position within the Badārian period. The female graves are larger than the male. "On the other hand," Brunton adds, "the presence of a few cornelian beads is not what would be expected." I have dwelt at some length on this one attempt at classifying the Badārian material, because we so sadly lack a new chronological system to bring some order into the material of the different predynastic periods. It has to be given due consideration because of Brunton's unrivalled knowledge of Badārian material. As it stands, I am afraid it is founded on too little material to be treated as anything more than a pioneer effort, especially as it is based only on the finds from Matmar, and leaves out those from Mustagidda and Badāri itself. As for the comparative sizes of the female and male graves, I think that the chronological differentiation is at least not proven. The small group of graves (3000-3100) comes from a much-used plot of ground, and it does not even seem safe to accept as Badārian all the graves which Brunton ascribes to that period. With that in mind we have at least to consider whether there are not other explanations

[1] *Matmar*, p. 11.

[2] *Matmar*, p. 9, 3104.

[3] A similar beak was found in a woman's grave at Mustagidda, which Brunton says in *Matmar*, p. 11, "may even be Tasian". On pl. XXII, 2e, in *Mostag.* it is called Tasian. It seems doubtful whether a natural object occurring twice can be used for dating. The difference in ascription to Badārian or Tasian shows how uncertain Brunton was in distinguishing between these "periods". See Vol. I, p. 20.

which would account for the differentiation in size between the female and the male graves (see below, p. 125). The lengths of the Badārian graves vary from not much more than a metre to well over two metres; their average depth is about one metre. In them the dead were laid to rest in a loosely-contracted position, "naturally", as Brunton puts it, "as if they were asleep". This seems to me the correct explanation of their attitude, at least for Egypt. In the streets of Cairo or any other Egyptian town at noon or towards evening one can see people asleep on the pavement in just such attitudes, their hands on or under their faces. The idea sometimes advanced that the dead were put to their last rest in the position they had held as an embryo seems to me rather far-fetched, and not in accordance with Egyptian beliefs of the continuance of life after death. Already during this early time, just as during the later part of the dynastic period, most of the bodies were laid on their left sides, the heads towards the south facing the setting sun.

Some provision was made to shelter the bodies from the earth with which the graves were filled in. They were wholly enveloped in mats or, sometimes, in hides. A pillow filled with chaff was sometimes slipped under the head. Coffins, at least of wood, seem to have been still unknown. Constructions of sticks and twigs existed which were probably hampers, but may sometimes have been attempts at lining the pit [1] (pl. XI, 1). The furniture was mostly deposited outside these mats or hampers, and occasionally small niches scooped out in one of the walls served as receptacles for pots.

The graves were grouped in cemeteries; the one at Badāri, which is still the biggest of those excavated, containing several hundred burials. They were dug near to each other, but were grouped in dense clusters with emptier spaces in between. We do not know whether a part of the cemetery was reserved for the more important graves.

The cemeteries of Naḳāda I date do not seem to differ in essentials from those of the Badārians. MacIver and Mace at El-'Amrah,[2] and after them Ayrton and Loat at El-Maḥāsna,[3] tried to date the graves they excavated according to their different shapes. They presumed that the circular graves were the earliest, and that the oval, the straight-sided with rounded corners, and the rectangular graves developed from them. As we have seen, all these forms existed side by side in Badārian times and the differences seem to indicate social differences rather than chronological order. It is certainly not possible to use shape as a means of dating. Only the furniture the graves contain can be a help for that. Apart from the known differences in the types of pottery, ivories and so on, there seems to be a custom which comes in with Naḳāda I that was unknown to the Badārians. The finely-made flint knives which are an invention of Naḳāda I were nearly always broken before they were put into the graves. Brunton states more than once [4] that he could not find all the splinters of such a knife in an undisturbed grave, and there is hardly an unbroken specimen in any of our museums.

Brunton is inclined to ascribe the majority of the rectangular graves of Naḳāda I to men, in accordance with his theory that only during the earlier part of the Badārian period were the larger graves prevalently female. This seemed doubtfully true even for the Badārian. For Naḳāda I we have even less to rely upon, for many of the excavations were made by excavators much less conscientious in their recording of finds than Brunton was. The largest and most

[1] E.g. *Mostag.*, pl. VI, 8.
[2] *El Amrah*, pp. 7 ff.
[3] *Pre-dyn. Cem. at El-Mahasna*, pp. 3 ff.
[4] E.g. *Mostag.*, p. 72, grave 1854.

lavishly equipped grave from Diospolis Parva, Abadiyeh B 101,[1] belonged to a girl. It is of S.D. 34, according to Petrie.

In most of the excavations so far made the Badārian cemeteries were by themselves, and where a later grave overlay a Badārian one it seems that it was dug in ignorance of the earlier burial. In contrast to this, the periods of Nakāda I and II use the same cemeteries. This may be a reason for our scanty knowledge of everything which belongs exclusively to Nakāda I, and may explain why we cannot discern any development in the character of the graves during this earlier period. In graves which do not contain painted pottery, and that is the majority of them, ascription is very difficult. This can be seen, e.g., in the grave catalogues which Brunton publishes for Mustagidda and Matmar. He sequence-dates the graves as far as possible. Few have sequence-dates that belong exclusively to Nakāda I, many more are dated over a period beginning well within Nakāda I and extending deeply into Nakāda II. Brunton calls the majority of the pre-dynastic graves in Mustagidda simply "Amratian" (Nakāda I). This shows that he could not find enough data for a more precise attribution, and, especially when the grave contained few pots, his ascription is sometimes based on a general feeling which may not always be correct. Taking all this into consideration, it seems quite possible that some of the new features which we shall describe as a development of Nakāda II may well have started during the preceding period.

The new features of the Nakāda II graves are mainly better methods of construction. The effort to create rectangular pits is now rewarded with more success. The walls of the graves are strengthened by wooden linings, at least in the better tombs. Two different types occur. Sticks and matting or a wicker framework are fastened against the walls (pl. XI,), the sticks having perhaps also supported a roof; alternatively, constructions of wooden planks are erected around the corpse.[2] These had neither top nor bottom, and therefore cannot rightly be termed coffins, though they may be the beginning of them. On the other hand, they are the beginning of the development of the wood-panelled central chambers which were found in some of the Royal Tombs at Abydos [3] and in the great mastabas excavated by Emery at Sakkāra. The roofings of these predynastic graves were of sticks or matting, occasionally plastered over with mud.[4] Heavier roofs made of planks also occur, though rarely.[5] It seems that sometimes the walls were plastered with mud, but no brick-lined graves are as yet known from predynastic times.

As the lining of the walls prevented the scooping out of niches or the construction of ledges to accommodate the grave furniture, which became more and more numerous, other means of storing it had to be sought. The simplest was to enlarge the pit and put the pots and other objects in the same room as the dead. Sometimes the lining seems to have been very low, and a niche or a ledge could be constructed above it; or again planks used to stiffen the sides of the graves were erected at some distance from the walls, and the furniture was placed in the space between walls and planks. This made the constructions lose the character of a lining, and Brunton, indeed, refers to them as "coffins",[6] though they generally have no floors and may be covered with sticks in the ordinary way. They certainly seem half-way to real wooden coffins. In due time the process is, so to speak, reversed, and instead of building a special niche for the furniture a sort of *loculus*

---

[1] *Diosp. Pa.*, p. 33.   [2] *Pre-dyn. Cem. at El-Mahasna*, pp. 6-7.
[3] *Royal Tombs*, I, pl. LXV.   Emery, "The Tomb of Wadji", *Illustrated London News*.
[4] *Mostag.*, p. 82.   [5] *Bad. Civ.*, p. 53, t. 3740, S.D. 38-44.
[6] *Mostag.*, p. 82.

is scooped out for the body. This takes place only towards the end of the predynastic period, or perhaps rather during the time of transition, when it is difficult if not impossible in the present state of our knowledge to be sure whether a grave is predynastic or protodynastic. In contrast to the niches for the pots, those for the bodies are now at a lower level than the floor of the graves. In the predynastic cemetery at Matmar the walls of their pits were lined with planks and mud plaster, or, as Brunton says, "possibly sometimes with bricks; but the 'bricks' may be merely a very thick coating of mud".[1]

If the facts stated above are correct, and Brunton and his predecessors have not misrepresented their finds or overlooked the more striking constructions, and this can hardly be considered, then the well-known tomb of Hierakonpolis with the painted walls can scarcely be of Naḳāda II, if indeed it was a tomb at all. The Hierakonpolis building was a rectangular construction made of bricks. It was divided into two chambers of roughly equal size by a brick wall, and its walls were plastered and covered with frescoes in the style of the decorated pottery. Among the subjects represented is the hero between two lions. The exact position of the grave in the ruins of Hiera-konpolis was lost after the excavators had found and copied it,[2] and the few fragments of the fresco in the Cairo Museum are so black that one can hardly discern any painting at all. Our considera-tion of the subject must therefore be based on the copies, scarcely a very safe ground on which to base conclusions. Brunton wondered whether the building was not perhaps a house or temple rather than a grave. On visiting the site he found no other predynastic graves in the area where the tomb is presumed to be, but only protodynastic ones. To me this seems to be one more reason for dating the structure to protodynastic times rather than for questioning its use as a grave. Also, it was several feet below ground, and had no apparent entrance. What, I think, settles the question is that more than a dozen vases all complete and unbroken were found in the structure. The field of ruins which marks the ancient site of Hierakonpolis, and at the edge of which the excavators say it was situated, is covered several feet deep with potsherds, five to six feet in some places. Among these millions of fragments it is hard to find a single complete vessel, not to speak of over a dozen well-preserved specimens, such as were found in the structure. Miss H. Kantor, who has recently made a study of the grave and its contents,[3] fails to reach a decision whether it be a grave or a house. Following Brunton, she dates the building to Naḳāda II, though she has to agree that at least one of the vases from it is not otherwise known earlier than the protodynastic period. The rest, though they occur at the end of Naḳāda II, are still in use in the succeeding period. Her main argument in favour of the earlier date is based on the picture on the fresco of the hero between the two lions, whom she compares to the person between two lions on the handle of the Gebel-el-'Arak knife. The knife she dates from the fluted flint blade to which the ivory handle belongs. To me it is not at all certain that the handle is contemporary with the fluted flint knife to which it is fixed, and not rather a somewhat later addition.[4] Myself, I would prefer to date the Gebel-el-'Arak knife from the Hierakonpolis tomb instead of vice versa. But, though I disagree with Miss Kantor on this point, I think that even this difference of opinion helps to emphasize her main argument, namely that the end of Naḳāda II and the beginning of

[1] *Matmar*, p. 17.
[2] Quibell and Green, *Hierakonpolis*, II, pls. LXXV ff.
[3] Kantor, "The Final Phase of Predynastic Culture, Gerzean or Semainean", *JNES*, III (1944), pp. 110 ff., fig. 2.
[4] See chapter on Ivories, pp. 77 ff.

the Dynasties are so closely linked and merge so imperceptibly into each other that no hard and fast dividing line can be drawn between the two periods.

The cemeteries of the Naḳāda periods are just as crowded as were those of the Badārians, though now, e.g. at Naḳāda itself, the graves count in thousands and not, as at Badāri, in hundreds. Once again graves very rarely cut into each other, yet no superstructures have been detected, and it is to be hoped that one day an excavation in a predynastic cemetery will be attempted which has at its disposal the most modern techniques so that a solution can be found to the problem of how these graves were marked above ground. Though the graves cluster together more tightly in some parts of the cemeteries than in others, nothing in the plans or the descriptions published allows us to decide whether special parts were reserved for the more prominent people of the communities, for their chieftains or for their kings.

Brunton has not extended to the Naḳāda periods his investigations on the relations between the size of the graves and the sex of those buried in them. In Matmar [1] he tries to correlate the rectangular graves with the sexes of the owners, and finds that "they are rather more frequent for males than for females". The number of the graves examined seems, however, rather too small to warrant any generalization. From a survey of his grave lists, and from what can be gathered from other excavations, I find it difficult to come to a definite result, especially as in the earlier publications the sex of the skeletons discovered in the graves is very often not mentioned. At El-Maḥāsna as well as at Diospolis Parva the largest and most important graves of Naḳāda I belonged to women. They contained furniture of outstanding interest, including many unique objects. The grave at El-Maḥāsna, H 29, before S.D. 41, is called "square" by its excavator.[2] In it were the ivory figurine of a man and the white-cross-lined pot with the hippopotami set on its edge as well as the famous Seth (?) animal, to mention only a few of its more spectacular contents. At El-Maḥāsna the most important Naḳāda II grave of all also belonged to a woman.[3]

Animal cemeteries are not known so far from these early periods, but animal burials were found among the graves of the people. As Caton-Thompson has already pointed out,[4] two different aspects of these burials occur, those where the animals were deposited in human graves and those where they were granted separate burial. As far as I can see, there are mainly three different zoological species which occur: bovines, canines (either dogs or jackals) and gazelles, or goats or perhaps sheep.

In the original Badārian cemetery at Badāri animal burials were excavated.[5] Some were of "bovine animals". Professor D. M. S. Watson states of one that it is a cow, perhaps a buffalo, as it had remarkably big horns. Some were of sheep or goats, for one which Professor Watson examined was "probably a sheep". In the Badārian cemetery at Mustagidda animals occur only in human graves, and were restricted, as it seems, to one species only, which Brunton calls "gazelle (?)". This predilection continues at Mustagidda into Naḳāda times, at least as far as their species could be identified at all. In the Badārian cemetery at Badāri a grave of a dog or jackal was also found. All these animals were wrapped in mats, just as were the human beings, and their graves were in no way different. A dog in its own wooden "coffin" of stout wood [6] was excavated in the grave of a man at Matmar, t. 3128, S.D. 52. Pots were placed over it. If these

---

[1] *Matmar*, p. 17.
[2] *Pre-dyn. Cem. at El-Mahasna*, p. 11.
[3] *Pre-dyn. Cem. at El-Mahasna*, pp. 13 and 16, t. H 41.
[4] *Bad. Civ.*, pp. 91-3.
[5] *Bad. Civ.*, p. 42.
[6] *Matmar*, p. 17.

pots belonged to the dog, then the burial differs from all those mentioned so far, for none of them had any furniture at all.

In a pit in Cemetery T at Naḳāda the bones of about twenty dogs were found, apparently unaccompanied by furniture. Petrie mentions this find only on the occasion of a dog's skull being found in t. 286,[1] but gives no details. In his conclusions [2] he says that "the dog must have been valued or sacred, by the burial of dogs in the graves, and by a grave full of dogs in the cemetery". A similar dog burial was discovered by Caton-Thompson at Ḥammāmīya. Bones of at least fifteen animals were massed beneath three large blocks of limestone, without furniture. Caton-Thompson dates the grave to a period extending "from Middle Predynastic, contemporary with the layer in which it occurred, to Old Kingdom, when its position would be intrusive".[3] I do not think that the dog burial in Cemetery T at Naḳāda can be dated any more precisely. Cemetery T is of the latest phase of Naḳāda II, possibly overlapping into protodynastic times. There were, however, later graves also, for Petrie mentions one with a vaulted brick chamber and a well for access.[4]

BUILDINGS AND SETTLEMENTS

If we consider how uncertain our conclusions are about the types and development of predynastic Egyptian graves and cemeteries, in spite of the comparatively rich and well-published material, we must be prepared for much poorer results where houses and settlements are concerned, of which so few have been excavated and studied. Where there is so little to go on, theories have been developed and accepted which do not even take into consideration the few established facts. If we are convinced that two strictly separate civilizations developed in predynastic Egypt, one in Upper Egypt and one in the Delta, and that the Delta civilization is by far superior, then we have to find the differences, be the material evidence ever so scanty.

It is a widely-accepted hypothesis that the predynastic Egyptian houses were the prototypes of their graves, and that we can therefore deduce the form of the houses in which the people lived from the shape of the graves. Brunton has already pointed out the fallacy of such [5] an assumption, especially in discussing whether the earliest house form in Egypt was circular or rectangular. In the present state of our knowledge we have no answer to this. To Brunton it seems likely that both types existed side by side. As with the oval and rectangular graves, the shape may rather be an outward sign of social standing—whether the owner was rich or poor, a city dweller or a peasant—so that it has little to do with the dating.

No certain facts are available concerning Badārian houses. Numerous sites were recognized by Brunton as being the remnants of Badārian settlements on the spurs of the desert from Qau to Der Tasa. Sometimes he speaks of granaries lined with basket-work or matting, which reminded Brunton of the Fayum granaries, which were lined with basket-work. It seems likely, however, that living-quarters were similarly furnished. In one of the rare instances at Matmar,[6] area 2000, where Brunton mentions measurements, the foundations were 270 cm. wide and 300 cm. deep. In it were found some Badārian sherds, part of a large limestone millstone and

[1] *Naq. Bal.*, p. 26, t. 286.   [2] *Naq. Bal.*, p. 62.
[3] *Bad. Civ.*, p. 94.   [4] *Naq. Bal.*, p. 24, t. T 15.
[5] *Bad. Civ.*, p. 48.   [6] *Matmar*, pp. 4 ff.

fragments of charcoal. All of this seems to indicate living-quarters rather than a granary. Other holes in the ground were much smaller and may have been granaries. The techniques in which they were built is not stated.

The only well-dated huts of the two Nakāda periods are those excavated by Caton-Thompson at Ḥammāmīya. Erected between S.D. 35-45,[1] they had fallen into disuse by S.D. 50. They were circular, as were some excavated by Brunton near Badāri. Two which were partly covered by the later temple he calls "early".[2] From the list of objects found in the rubbish of the adjacent village they may begin contemporaneously with those from Ḥammāmīya. A little statuette of a Horus falcon indicates that the huts at Badāri lasted until the end of Nakāda II (pl. XI, 2).

Not all of the nine hut-circles investigated by Caton-Thompson at Ḥammāmīya were living-quarters. Some, perhaps most, were store-rooms. One of the smaller ones (no. 112) was used as a fuel-store, for it was found still filled with desiccated sheep or goat dung to within a foot of its rim. One of the larger hut-circles (no. 248), with an internal diameter of 6 feet, had indications of a hearth on its north-west side. All the huts were sunk into the ground, and were one to three feet beneath the original surface. They were built on circular foundations of mud mixed with limestone chips and a few blocks of limestone of considerable size. On them the superstructures, some pieces of which were preserved, were of reeds and plastered. No openings for the entrances were left in the foundations.

The foundations which Brunton excavated were either circular or oval with mud floors. One possessed an opening for a door, and it was also distinguished by a wall "which acted as a sort of revetment"[3] (pl. XI, 4, 5, 6, 8) built of small rough stones, mud-plastered. This is of special interest, for as far as I know this is the earliest yet known occurrence of stone used as building material in Egypt. Another had a wainscot of two courses of bricks.

It is most distressing that Brunton gives no description of the rectangular brick house he found underneath the temple at Badāri, and that he could not make up his mind as to its date (fig. 15). On the plan of the temple[4] he labels it "predynastic (?)". In the text he says that the walls ran down to rather below the level of the predynastic mud floors, and may have been contemporary with them; and in the same context, for reasons which do not seem very convincing even to Brunton himself, he ascribes the house somewhat doubtfully to the early dynastic age. The house resembles in plan and size those excavated by Garstang at Hierakonpolis, which he dates to the Third Dynasty. These small rectangular houses are divided into a larger room, about 2 m. square, which Garstang thought was roofed, and a smaller one which may have been an open courtyard (pl. XI, 7).[5] The Badāri house also is a rectangular building divided into a larger room about 2 m. square and a smaller one. Brunton excavated more village remains at Mustagidda as well as at Matmar.[6]

In his article on the predynastic town-site at Hierakonpolis Brunton mentions again the use of rough stones in the construction of predynastic houses.[7] He found a considerable quantity of stones at one point of the ruins which reminded him of the huts he excavated at Badāri, and of the stone wall found there. He does not doubt that the ruins of Hierakonpolis are of the same

[1] *Bad. Civ.*, pp. 82-8.
[2] *Bad. Civ.*, p. 48.
[3] *Bad. Civ.*, p. 44.
[4] Brunton, *Qau and Badari*, I, pp. 18-19, pl. XXIII.
[5] See below, p. 130.
[6] *Mostag.*, pp. 75 ff.; *Matmar*, pp. 4 ff.
[7] "The Predynastic Town-site at Hierakonpolis", *Studies presented to F. Ll. Griffith*, pp. 272 ff.

date, for he is of opinion that the town is early predynastic.[1] Garstang, who excavated several
houses near what he calls the fortress, dated them from the sherds and the stone vases (not
published) to the Third Dynasty.[2] In at least one of the houses, which were rectangular with a
walled-in courtyard in front, rough stones were used for the foundations. The houses abutted
on a street 3 ft. wide. Garstang is of opinion that "the township seems to have been in full vigour
during the 1st, 2nd, and 3rd Dynasties", and that agrees with my own impression when walking
over the field of ruins. That the beginnings of Hierakonpolis reached back at least into Naḳāda I

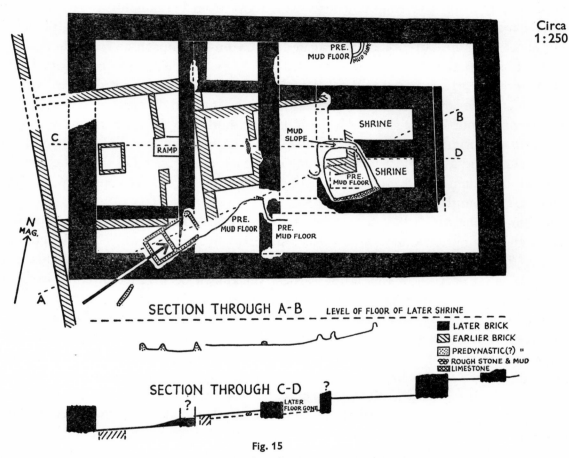

Fig. 15

Rectangular house after Brunton, *Qau and Badari*, I, pl. XXIII. (Arrow indicates brick house.)

is, however, likely from the white-cross-lined sherds which Brunton collected on the spot, and
from the graves which Garstang excavated under the fortress. This, with its buttressed façade,
is early dynastic, perhaps rather a palace than a fortress, though it may have been both. The
low wall which surrounds it seems too low and too near the main building to afford much protection. On the other hand, the entrance to the building is behind a curtain wall, which suggests
that security was aimed at.

Brunton did not ascribe any great importance to his discovery of rough stones as building
material in predynastic Egypt, and yet we may here have the beginning of stone building in that
country. Up to now the pavement made of large slabs of granite in King Den's tomb at Abydos

---

[1] *Bad. Civ.*, p. 48.
[2] Garstang, "Excavations at Hierakonpolis, at Esna, and in Nubia", in *Ann. Serv.*, VIII (1907), pp. 132 ff.

has been considered as the earliest use of stone as material for building. The suddenness of the appearance of stone building in Egypt has always been commented on. In the use of rough stone for the construction of houses we may perhaps have an indication of where to look for its beginnings. In this connexion it may be worth remembering that Petrie discovered several structures of rough stones in the cemeteries of Naḳāda. The most important of them was a step pyramid, 60 ft. 4 in. square at the base [1] (fig. 16). Under it was a pit which passed through a "coat of gravel into the sand beneath". The construction, to judge from Petrie's drawing, is similar to Djoser's pyramid, with the significant differences that it is square and all the stones used bore no sign of dressing, even the surface blocks being "brought to a fair surface by the careful selection of the blocks". The pit had been searched and probably robbed before Petrie's excavation, and nothing was found to indicate a date. Petrie thought that it was probably "the oldest work that he examined". In considering this statement one must keep in mind that at the time of his publication of Naḳāda

1:500

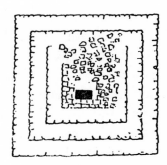

Fig. 16 Pyramid, Nub. t.

(After Petrie and Quibell, *Naqada and Ballas*, pl. LXXXV.)

and Ballas he had erroneously placed the predynastic civilization, which he had discovered, after the Old Kingdom. Therefore his "oldest work" will have to be taken to mean before the Fourth Dynasty. Petrie may, of course, be mistaken in his relative dating, but one should remember that his intuitions very often came near the mark. Two tumuli of rough stones, standing in a prominent place near the cemetery to which Petrie gave the letter T, were also excavated by him. There was no indication why they were erected, as no sign of a pit or other construction which would mark them as burials could be found. They both measured about 60 ft. across at the bottom and still stood to a height of about 10 ft. Petrie reckons that their original height must have been about 14 or 15 ft., and that about 1,000 tons of stone must have been used in each of them. As for their date, all that Petrie could say is that they were pre-Roman, "the ground around them being thick with late burials, extended full length with iron objects, while not a single such burial lay in the ground which we searched within the tumuli".

The only well-authenticated instance of a grave with a superstructure of rough stones comes from the early dynastic middle-class cemetery at Saḳḳāra, which Macramallah excavated.[2] Similar stone heaps covered graves recently found near Maʿadi, which, as far as I could see, date also from the beginning of the dynasties. The large cemetery at Helwan, excavated by Zaki Saad,[3] also provides some examples of the use of rough or roughly-dressed stones, some of huge dimensions. All these examples of building in rough stones have so far received little attention. Yet it seems to me that without a closer study of them, and either accepting or discarding them as a phase in the development of Egyptian stone architecture, we shall not be able to form an idea about its beginnings.

[1] *Naq. Bal.*, pp. 65-6, pl. LXXXV.

[2] Rizkallah Macramallah, *Une Cimetière archaïque de la classe moyenne du peuple à Saqqarah*, p. 8.

[3] Zaki Saad, *Royal Excavations at Helwan, 1945-1947: Suppl. aux Ann. du Service des Antiquités de l'Egypte*, Cahier no. 14, p. 3.

In a country such as Egypt which possesses stone in abundance, and which in the Nile mud has a good material for mortar, it seems reasonable to suppose that both were used for the construction of houses, together with the homely reed or papyrus and such pieces of wood as the indigenous trees would furnish. Indeed, for circular huts these seem the most suited components. That wattle-and-daub was also used in the construction of rectangular houses has been assumed from the unique model house found in t. a 4 at El-'Amrah, S.D. 44-64 [1] (pl. XII, 3). It is 45 cm. long, 27·5 cm. wide and 20 cm. high. Its walls are sloping and have somewhat higher corners. In one of the shorter walls is a door topped by a large beam which extends each side for nearly a third of its length. At a distance below this and within the door frame is what may either be a stick which divides the higher part of the doorway from the lower or else a rolled-up mat with which to close it. The doorway, which has sloping sides, is not in the centre of the wall but nearer its right-hand corner. In the opposite wall of the house are two small windows, high up, near its top. The beams above and below them are much wider than the small openings of the actual windows. Five perforations, two on each side in the upper half and one towards the bottom left-hand corner, as well as four similar ones along the bottom of one of the long sides, have no obvious use, unless the house was originally meant as a coffin for a small child. It is not certain whether the house had a lid or roof. A slab of clay which is preserved with the house, and must have been found with it, seems to contradict the assertion of the excavators that there was no roof.[2] On the other hand, the slab, which seems perfect but for small damage at one corner, does not seem to fit the house and certainly would not cover more than half of the top opening. One of its ends shows the slightly-vaulted profile which we know from representations of early buildings, e.g. those of the store-houses in the blue-tiled rooms under the Step Pyramid [3] and the large mastaba within its precincts, while the other end is smoothly finished. It is possible that the door was meant to lead into an open courtyard, such as Garstang found at Hierakonpolis,[4] and that only the back with the windows was roofed. But there is nothing inside the model to indicate that such a partition existed. If this reconstruction of the model is correct, and the house under the Badāri temple was a courtyard house, as were those at Hierakonpolis, then there is some reason to assume that this type, which has survived until today, is the original Egyptian house. All presently-known rectangular houses of the predynastic and protodynastic periods can be so explained, including the one found at Ma'adi.[5] But only more excavations can show whether or not it is possible to maintain this assumption that the one-cell house with a walled-in courtyard was the earliest rectangular Egyptian house.

The model house from El-'Amrah has a red stripe painted all round the lower parts of its walls. This calls to mind the painted red stripe, 4 in. wide at a height of 22 in. above the ground round the walls of the Middle Fort at Abydos.[6] An attempt has been made to estimate the size of a real house from the height of the door of the model, which is 10 cm., and this has produced an approximate length of 8 m. and a width of 5·70 m. Such dimensions are considerably larger than those of the houses at Badāri and Hierakonpolis. Caton-Thompson, as well as Vandier,[7] has taken the size and the rectangular shape of the house as indications that it is of later date than

---

[1] *El Amrah*, pp. 22, 42.
[2] *El Amrah*, p. 42.
[3] Firth and Quibell, *The Step Pyramid*, I, pp. 21-2; II, pl. 38.
[4] See above, p. 130.
[5] A Badawy, *A History of Egyptian Architecture*, p. 17, fig. 6.
[6] Ayrton, Curelly and Weigall, *Abydos*, III, p. 3.
[7] *Bad. Civ.*, p. 82. Vandier, *Manuel*, I, p. 499.

the circular huts. The sequence-date 44-64 of the grave from which the model comes puts it firmly into the Naḳāda II period, so that it may have been built when the village at Ḥammāmīya was still flourishing. I would like to suggest that the rectangular house is a town house similar to those indicated on the slate palettes [1] and thus different from the Ḥammāmīya huts and those at Merimda, which are peasant dwellings. That the Egypt of this period possessed towns is known, for we can locate at least two, one at Hierakonpolis and one at Naḳāda, as well as an early dynastic

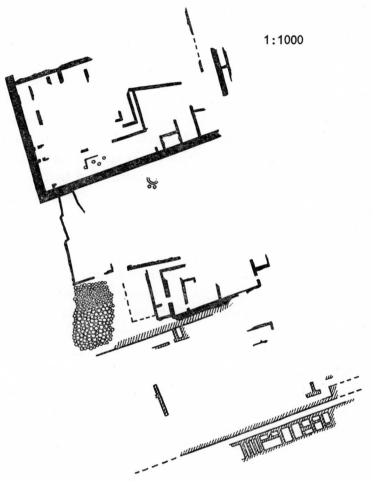

1:1000

Fig. 17 Town south of Temple of Nub. t.
(After Petrie and Quibell, *Naqada and Ballas*, pl. LXXXV)

one at Maʿadi. Hierakonpolis is still awaiting excavation, and we do not know whether the houses of an earlier date were of the same type as those excavated by Garstang. At Naḳāda Petrie found rectangular houses, though they showed "carelessness about squareness and angles".[2]

The map and the description given by Petrie of the town of Naḳāda (fig. 17) are so poor that all one can be sure of is that the houses were indeed rectangular, and that their builders, the old inhabitants of Nub. t, used bricks in their construction as did the builders of the houses at Badāri. Perhaps the house model from El-ʿAmrah also represents a brick building plastered with mud, but this cannot be proved. As we cannot be sure of its material, we depend on the

[1] See chapter on Palettes.　　　　　　　　　　　　[2] *Naq. Bal.*, p. 54.

houses from Naḳāda and Badāri for an answer to the question whether the pre-dynastic Egyptians used mud bricks or not. There can be no doubt that Nub. t had existed since the time of Naḳāda I. The sherds which Petrie collected confirm his statement, for among them are white-cross-lined specimens, and some of the flints also indicate the Naḳāda I period. But were the houses as early as Naḳāda I or II? Petrie thought that they were, but since his time we have come to know that some of the graves from the Naḳāda cemeteries are of the early dynastic period, as is shown by the plate [1] with the wavy-handled pottery in his publication of Naḳāda. The cylindrical pots in the bottom row, nos. 71a to 90, clearly demonstrate it, and those in the row above are of the same date. On the other hand, Petrie mentions pits in the ground which, as we know from Brunton, are characteristic of predynastic settlements, and Petrie was far too experienced an excavator to have overlooked circular hut foundations underneath the rectangular ones if there had been any. In the ruins of the North Town,[2] which Quibell excavated near Ballas, it is explicitly stated that he found "no bricks, to indicate the material of the dwellings; it is therefore possible that they were of wattle and daub".[3] Peet, who excavated a predynastic settlement at Abydos, is also doubtful whether the predynastic Egyptians used bricks for the building of their houses.[4] He reminds us, however, that bricks were used in the construction of the grain kilns, which are such a characteristic feature of predynastic Egyptian towns. As remnants of them were found by Quibell in the North Town of Naḳāda, it seems possible that the clay dust he mentions came, at least in parts, from bricks and not exclusively from wattle-and-daub huts. As the layer of the ruins seems to have reached the surface, and was only something between half an inch and two feet thick, it must have been greatly denuded, and it is quite possible that mud bricks would have completely disintegrated. The archaeological layer of the South Town, Nub. t, was considerably deeper. Petrie describes the bricks as "11 in.× 4½ in.× 3 in. in size and poorly made". I think, weighing up the arguments, that it seems likely that the brick houses were of the predynastic date which Petrie ascribes to them, especially as otherwise the grain kilns could scarcely be dated to that period.

These grain kilns, which have just been mentioned, are of the greatest interest for the knowledge of the habits of the early Egyptians. Long trenches lined with bricks were built, and inside them stands made out of special fire-bricks were lined with clay to receive large pots, about 50 cm. in height. Peet mentions 23 in one of the trenches.[5] The pots contained smaller dishes to prevent the grain from falling right to the bottom. Charcoal, sometimes mixed with sheep dung, was the material used as fuel.[6] These constructions are far too large to have served the needs of a single individual and must have been constructed for the benefit of the whole of the settlement to which they were attached. This shows that a common administration must have existed to organize the use of these grain parchers. Their date is difficult to assess precisely. The settlement at Abydos is dated by Peet as "late", which from the evidence of the published pottery means of late Naḳāda II. The other places range over a much longer period of time, and it is difficult, if not impossible, to decide whether some can be dated back to Naḳāda I. Garstang dates the cemetery he excavated at El-Maḥāsna to S.D. 32-56, but it is not certain that it belonged to the settlement he found there, for Ayrton and Loat claim that the cemetery which they found may

[1] *Naq. Bal.*, p. 1, pl. XXXII.   [2] *Naq. Bal.*, p. 2.
[3] *Naq. Bal.*, p. 2.   [4] T. E. Peet, *The Cemeteries of Abydos*, II, p. 10.
[5] Peet, *The Cemeteries of Abydos*, pp. 7 ff.   [6] *Naq. Bal.*, p. 2.

have belonged to that settlement.[1] Neither the North Town of Naḳāda nor spur 6 of area 3002 at Badāri,[2] where traces of such kilns were found, allows for a closer dating.

Another feature of the predynastic settlements are the wind-screens, which, open at two sides, only provide shelter against the north wind which prevails in Egypt. They are made of uprights, the holes for which were found in the ground at El-Maḥāsna and also at Ḥammāmīya, and between which reeds or straw were woven to form the actual screen. Similar screens are still in use today in Egypt.

The houses which have just been described belonged to different types of settlements, villages and towns. The towns were walled, as we know from the South Town at Naḳāda, where Petrie excavated part of the fortification (without, unfortunately, recording any details about it), and from the little model of a city wall found in grave B 83, S.D. 33-48, at Hu[3] (pl. XII, 1 and 2). This little model is in many respects most instructive, even in its fragmentary state. All that is preserved are parts of two walls meeting in a rounded corner. On one a rectangular battlement is left, and at the outside a reinforcing buttress. The height of the wall without the battlement is 10 cm. The real city wall which the model copies cannot have been much higher than 5 ft., for the little men behind peep over it. These watchmen are naked and unarmed. The walls are perpendicular, and this, I think, indicates that they were built of bricks, and not of a sort of *pisé*. The little model proves that at the time of its manufacture walled settlements existed in Upper Egypt. It is perhaps not too fanciful to imagine that it represents the home town of the person in whose grave it was found. The town must have been built on a rectangular plan, and the brick wall which surrounded it—if brick it really was—was smooth and not recessed, though provided with buttresses outside. Petrie dated grave B 83, in which he found the model, to S.D. 33-48. This covers nearly the whole of Naḳāda I and a good part of Naḳāda II. In Vol. I (p. 43) it is suggested that the period of its manufacture might perhaps be the time of transition from Naḳāda I to Naḳāda II, as those may have been unruly years. Grave B 83 is only partly published. It was disturbed. Those of its contents illustrated on pl. VI of *Diospolis Parva* perhaps point rather more to Naḳāda I. On the bigger one of the two vases, which alone are figured, a large-horned sheep in the style of the white-cross-lined pottery is engraved, which resembles the sheep on the vase from Naḳāda, t. 1644.[4] The grave also contained several of the small clay animals which are suggestive of Naḳāda I. If we could put the model of the city wall as early as Naḳāda I, perhaps towards the end of the period, it would indicate that walled settlements already existed then in Upper Egypt.

I have stressed the fact that the model from Diospolis Parva, grave B 83, represents the enclosure of a rectangular city, as opposed to oval or circular towns which must also have existed. On the obverse of the Nar-Mer palette showing him as King of Lower Egypt we see him in the bottom panel as the Strong Bull who destroys the town of his enemy. What is left of the town after the furious attack of the king is part of an oval (or perhaps circular) city wall, which like the one on the little model has bastions at regular distances from each other.[5] Inside the wall the name of the town, represented by the sign of a two-handled bag, is all that is depicted. Towns with

---

[1] *Pre-dyn. Cem. at El-Mahasna*, p. 2.   [2] *Bad. Civ.*, p. 45.
[3] *Diosp. Pa.*, p. 32, pl. VI.   [4] Vol. I, pl. VIII, 5.
[5] See also, for oval and rectangular walled settlements, the tablets of Nar-Mer (oval) and Aḥa (rectangular): Petrie, *Royal Tombs*, ii, pls. X and XI.

a similar system of fortification could also be built on a rectangular plan, as is shown by the palette with the destruction of the towns on one of its sides. They have inside their walls not only their names but also a number of rectangular buildings. The only real city wall which Petrie found at Nub. t belonged to a rectangular construction. From his perfunctory description and from the little map it seems that some of the houses were outside it (fig. 17).[1] The houses must have been as near to each other as were those which Garstang excavated at Hierakonpolis. No street can be discerned at Nub. t like the one described at Hierakonpolis, but only a pavement of cobblestones of unknown purpose.

In the very few instances where the excavators have given us some ideas about the general layout of the villages they found, a circular plan seems to have been adopted. The settlement at Abydos is described as "roughly circular" with a diameter of about 30 m.[2] This seems surprisingly small considering the corn-parching kilns, one of which contained 23 large vessels. No traces of fortifications were noticed, but we would not expect them in a village. Hearths were on the south side of the settlement. This sounds as if all the hearths had been together on one side of the settlement, which would be a remarkable arrangement.

At Mustagidda, near the cliffs in area 2200-3500 [3] Brunton found the remains of a village which he thought was Badārian. Around a deposit of ashes, which in some places was as much as 36 cm. thick, the grain pits were arranged in an irregular circle. Inside this he found groups of pots, mostly cooking-pots still standing in layers of ashes. No hut constructions of any kind are mentioned, and the grain pits do not seem to have been associated with any particular hearth; they rather give the impression that, like the grain kilns of later date, they may have been communal property. This would explain why they are the only more or less solid buildings which the village seems to have possessed. What the people used as shelters we can only guess. Were they made of bundles of papyrus like the buildings imitated in blue faience tiles under Djoser's pyramid? Homes built of bundles of papyrus stuck into each other and tied together must have suggested to the ancient Egyptians something very strong and reliable, for the *Djed* pillar, which is a column made of such bundles of papyrus, was for them the symbol of stability and permanence. In spite of this, it seems that such constructions have left no trace of their existence.

The archaeological remains discussed lead to the conclusion that probably since the period of Naḳāda I, and certainly since Naḳāda II, the inhabitants of Upper Egypt had developed an urban civilization. I do not think that the few rippled sherds which Brunton picked up at Hierakonpolis justify the assumption that towns go back to the Badārian age; we should need more material to prove that, and our ignorance about the settlements of the Badārians forbids us to make any far-reaching assumptions. All we possess are the few indications which Brunton registered, and the temporary camping-ground which Caton-Thompson excavated below the hut-circles at Ḥammāmīya.

It seems rather surprising that we have no absolute certainty about the use of bricks even during Naḳāda II times. This is probably due to our lack of investigations in the field and not to any ignorance of this building material on the part of the predynastic Egyptians. It cannot be doubted that they erected walls of rough stones, at least as foundations of their buildings. As long as we have no systematic excavations of any of the predynastic town-sites, our knowledge

---

[1] *Naq. Bal.*, p. 54, pl. LXXXV, bottom right.   [2] Peet, *The Cemeteries of Abydos*, II, p. 1.
[3] *Mostag.*, p. 15.

is bound to be vague. Equally, we cannot say anything definite about the palaces of the kings or chieftains, or of the temples of the gods. All the hypotheses brought forward so far are only fanciful reconstructions without the firm basis of an actual building anywhere. Whether the little shrines depicted on the boats of the decorated pottery were housed in more permanent temples when on land seems open to doubt, as we find them beneath trees on these vases without any form of stronger structure for their protection. The earliest representations of sanctuaries on the tablets from the tombs of the kings and the great ones of the first dynasties allow for different interpretations, especially in regard to the building material, and so do the pictures of the *itrti* chapels which are in some way connected with the god Min.

The only excavated building which has been claimed as belonging to an early dynastic sanctuary is the curious structure below the temple of Hierakonpolis.[1] It was roughly circular, as far as could be ascertained, and had a diameter of about 25 m. The structure was only partly preserved. The excavator, Green, describes it as a mound of clean white sand cased with rough stones. This casing, which was only one block thick and retreating towards the top,[2] was built of natural fragments of sandstone. Green enumerates several different older archaeological layers into which the mound was built, but gives no drawing either of the strata or of the pottery found in them. It is therefore difficult to check his dating to "somewhere at the beginning of the First Dynasty", though he may well be right. Nothing was found in the white sand. About the use of such an erection, only guesses are possible. It looks as if it were the substructure of something, perhaps a small temple, and I think the explanation of it as being perhaps the earliest sanctuary at Hierakonpolis is the one most widely held. Be this as it may, it certainly is another monumental building built of rough stones. And though, as with the rough stone tumuli and pyramid at Naḳāda, its exact date is open to discussion, we can at least be reasonably sure that it cannot be later than the first few dynasties.

It is very much to be regretted that the two settlements, one in the Delta, the other in Lower Egypt, which have most recently been excavated and to which so much work was devoted—namely Merimda and Ma'adi—are not yet properly published. It seems clear even from the preliminary reports that Merimda was a rural community, while Ma'adi, which seems to extend over a very large area, was a town.

The huts at Merimda were either circular or oval (fig. 18). As they belong to the higher strata, they are probably early dynastic.[3] In construction those found in the top layer are much like the huts found in the villages of Ḥammāmīya and Badāri. They had a similar substructure of mud without an opening for a

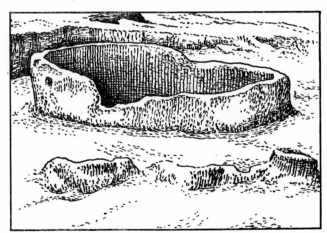

Fig. 18 Oval hut at Merimda.
After Junker, *Vorberichte* in *Anz. Wien*, 1933.

door, and it is interesting to note that the substructures were sometimes made of bricks. Post-holes were found at opposite sides of the structures, which led the excavators to assume that two

[1] Quibell and Green, *Hierakonpolis*, I, pl. IV. [2] Quibell and Green, *Hierakonpolis*, II, p. 3, pls. LXV, LXXII.
[3] See Appendix to Vol. I, revised edition.

upright poles were joined by a horizontal one over which a large mat was laid to serve as roof. As the floors of the huts were subterranean, tibiae of hippopotami were used as steps and indicate where the entrances must have been. Vases buried up to their mouths in the floors were thought to be a primitive drainage system[1]; but, not having been perforated, they cannot have been very efficient. Wind-screens like those from Ḥammāmīya also existed. Two lanes, along which the houses were loosely strung out, belonged to the top layer. Huts and granaries seem to have lain next to each other, giving the impression that the site was devoted to small farmsteads.

Maʻadi, which may have begun when Merimda was still in existence, but would have outlasted it, is thought to have been a town. Of it we know even less than of Merimda. No city wall was found, nor any indications of streets. Besides the one house plan already mentioned,[2] some irregularly-shaped subterranean pits were found surrounded by post-holes, the use of which is not obvious. Badawi thinks they were houses[3] and finds a resemblance to underground domed huts, because they have slanting walls.

To sum up the main results of this enquiry into predynastic Egyptian building for the living as well as for the dead we find that they have been both negative and positive. To take the graves first: we saw that the development aims at a proper rectangular pit with enough room for the ever-growing funerary furniture; there is no development from the circular and oval to the rectangular pits, for all of them occur together from Badārian times onward. The development aims at strengthening the walls of the pits by means of matting and sticks or wooden planks, so that the dead should have better protection. The constructions of planks are the ancestors both of wooden coffins and of the wooden wainscoting of the First Dynasty tombs. The lining with matting would have inspired the painting of matting on the walls in the tomb of Hesi-Ra or in one of the tombs of the First Dynasty recently discovered by Emery.[4]

Mud plaster was used to reinforce walls and roofs, but no brick-lined tombs are so far known from predynastic times. The construction of separate rooms for the furniture tends to drive the actual burial-chamber to a lower level. Though the graves must have been marked by some sign above ground, no such sign has yet been found anywhere.

About the forms of the Badārian houses we know little, though the remains of their settlements are fairly frequent in the neighbourhood of Badāri. The houses seem to have been circular, at least in some instances, as were their granaries, which, in the one observed instance, were arranged in a circle round the village. The first securely-dated huts are those from Ḥammāmīya, which belong to the later part of Naḳāda I and the earlier part of Naḳāda II. They are circular and have foundations of mud mixed with stones and a superstructure of wattle-and-daub. The circular huts under the temple of Badāri would be of the same date, and it may be that the rectangular house was also. At least one of the round ones had a foundation-wall built of rough stones. A similar technique was used for the Third Dynasty houses at Hierakonpolis. These were one-cell rectangular houses provided with walled-in courtyards which abutted on to a

---

[1] Junker, *Vorbericht*, III, p. 46.
[2] See above, p. 132.
[3] A. Badawy, *A History of Egyptian Architecture*, p. 17.
[4] In his excavations at Saḳḳāra, 1954. Quibell, *The Tomb of Hesi* (1913), pls. VIII and IX.

narrow street. The rectangular house model from El-'Amrah, which is of Naḳāda II date, and perhaps also the rectangular foundations from Ma'adi, may represent similar buildings.

It is certain that by Naḳāda II times Upper Egypt had developed an urban civilization, and it is likely that this reached back to Naḳāda I, for at Nub. t as well as at Hierakonpolis white-cross-lined sherds were found in the town ruins. At Hierakonpolis the city wall is later than the predynastic period, and we do not know whether an earlier one existed. At Nub. t Petrie found part of a predynastic city wall built of small bricks, the two walls which he recovered meeting at a right angle. That round or oval as well as rectangular cities existed we know from Nar-Mer's palette and from the palette bearing a scene showing the destruction of the cities, as well as from some of the small labels found in early dynastic tombs. The walls were fortified by square buttresses, one of which is shown on the little model of a city wall from Diospolis Parva.

There remains a word to be said about the opposition, expounded by the supporters of the Delta hypothesis, of "the peasant civilization of Lower Egypt" as having been in contrast with "the nomadic civilization of Upper Egypt", because that hypothesis is based on the form of graves. "Hill-tomb and cemetery are Upper Egyptian and the sign of nomads, house-tomb and inter-ments in houses are Lower Egyptian and the sign of the farmers." [1] I am at a loss to see on what this view, which is upheld by Scharff and Ricke, is based. No "house-tombs" or "hill-tombs" are known anywhere in Egypt from predynastic times, and I find it difficult to comprehend why the few burials in or between huts in the upper strata of Merimda should be characteristic of a peasant civilization. Where the earliest Merimdans buried their dead or what type of houses they had is not known, for neither houses nor graves belonging to them have been excavated. It also seems to me most odd that the large predynastic cemeteries of Upper Egypt should prove that their builders were nomads. Nor do I find any reason why the large tombs of the First Dynasty, with their complicated recessed façades, should be considered as typical of Lower Egypt as opposed to those of Upper Egypt. The beginning of the dynasties is a period when Sumerian influences were particularly strong in Egypt. The façades with the multiple niches were evolved by the Sumerians to decorate the outside walls of their temples.[2] When this design was taken over by the first Egyptian kings for their tombs, it seems to me to indicate that these large tombs were looked upon as temples rather than as houses. No house with a similar façade is known to me from Egypt or Mesopotamia. If these tombs are to be explained as replicas of the palace of the king, it seems to me necessary first of all to show that such palaces ever existed.

The substructures of the large tombs of the First Dynasty with their burial-chamber lower than the rooms for the funerary furniture, the wooden wainscoting of their walls and the painted pattern of matting, are an enlargement of the predynastic graves, a development which can be understood from the earlier habits (pl. XII, 4). Many and rich graves have been excavated from predynastic Upper Egypt. The material found in them, especially in those of the Naḳāda II period, is similar to that from the First Dynasty graves. The most important gods are common to them. No graves in cemeteries, no tomb furniture, no gods are known from the poor settlements of Lower Egypt. The excavations in Lower Egypt on which so much work was done are published either badly or not at all. They seem very poor foundations on which to base far-reaching conclusions.

[1] A Scharff, "Das Grab als Wohnhaus", *Sitzungsberichte der Bayerischen Akademie der Wissenschaften*, 1944-46, Heft 6.
[2] A. J. Tobler, *Excavations at Tepe Gawra*, II, pl. XXXIX, a.

CHAPTER VII

THE LAST CHAPTER

ENOUGH material has now been discussed to justify an attempt at assessing our knowledge about predynastic Egypt, and to enable us to draw a few conclusions.

The overwhelming impression which emerges is how little we know and how slender are the foundations on which even this knowledge rests. The reasons for this are manifold. The work of our pioneers, Flinders Petrie and his school, Reisner and de Morgan, most of them excavating about half a century and more ago, has not been followed up by modern excavations made with all the help modern technique can give, and with every grain of information extracted which the material may conceal. The lack or the inadequacy of publication of excavations in settlements cannot but make all our views lop-sided. To these drawbacks must be added the fact that the objects recovered, which have been in our museums for decades, have hardly been studied at all, and also that most of the articles and books of more recent date rely on older publications with insufficient illustrations, and do not go back to the original material. In view of all this, the poor results achieved are not surprising.

The greatest lacuna in our knowledge is about the nature of Naḳāda I. Like the Badārian it seems to belong to the African sub-stratum of ancient Egyptian civilization, which, always strong, gives Egypt one of its enduring qualities. When did Naḳāda I begin, and in what relationship did it stand to the Badārian? Only hypotheses are possible. Nor do we know many of its special achievements, because so much of it is so intermixed with Naḳāda II that we cannot disentangle it from the later period. These are only a few of the still unsolved problems in connexion with Naḳāda I. We see somewhat more clearly how it came to an end.

The new element which enters with Naḳāda II makes itself felt down to the everyday life of the people and alters their habits. Again, our lack of excavations does not allow us to see whether there was a difference in the plans of their towns and houses from those of Naḳāda I. All we have to go on is the change in pottery and flint work that took place. I think that the change in the flint-working from the bifacial to the blade technique shows more than anything else that a new ethnic element must have entered the Nile Valley. Whilst until the beginning of Naḳāda II flints in graves are rare, and only the beautifully-flaked knives and fish-tails were deposited in them, we now find in some graves dozens of little blades quite unknown before. As we saw, the older stock of the population never became quite accustomed to the new fashion, and by and by the old bifacial technique crept back for quite a number of tools, especially knives.

That these Naḳāda II invaders came from somewhere in western Asia few doubt, and they most likely account for the Semitic roots of the ancient Egyptian language. Since they left no written documents behind in the country from which they came, only guesses are possible as to their ultimate origin. For the time being north Syria or its neighbourhood seem to me the most likely place. They had been in contact with the Sumerian civilization, but perhaps not in direct contact. Some of their stone and pottery vessels are near cousins of those which Mallowan found at Arpachīya, though for the time being the difference in date between Naḳāda II and that of the

Assyrian civilizations, as given by Mallowan, are an obstacle of the most puzzling kind. If we could locate the original home of the Naḳāda II people somewhere in or near north Syria, it would explain the strange fact that they had a comparative abundance of silver, which does not exist in the Nile Valley or its near neighbourhood. No really close parallel to their specific type of vase-painting has as yet been discovered anywhere, though, as we saw, the motifs they use would not argue against a Syrian origin. There is no reason to assume that their connexion with their homeland was ever broken. On the contrary, the more they made good in Egypt, and acquired riches, the more we must reckon with new influxes from the old country.

It has even been possible to trace a few pieces in the Egyptian graves of that time which are authentic exports from Asia.[1] This trend reaches its climax during the earliest dynasties, but, in contrast to what happened at the beginning of Naḳāda II, the Sumerian influx does not reach the common necessities of life. It is to be seen in the vases, perhaps with some precious contents, the seal-cylinders and script, mace-heads with decorations in relief, and, most impressive of all, the recessed façades of the Sumerian temples copied in the superstructures for the tombs of the kings, queens, and the great men of their courts.

But none of all this reached the humbler people. There is little change in the common pottery. The painted and the black-topped vases die out during the first dynasties, but the coarse, the polished-red wares and the black remain. The flint industry takes a decided step back to the bifacial technique. This may show that the African element also was strengthened during this time, and that the growing riches of Egypt attracted new immigrants from the south as well as from Asia. The whole of the country seems to have been in the grip of some lively movement, a period of invention and discovery. Again and again in the course of these researches we came to a point where it was impossible to decide whether a type of pottery or tool, a grave or an ivory, could be assigned to the end of Naḳāda II or to the beginning of the dynasties. There is no hard and fast line which could be drawn to separate the two. The political unification of the Two Countries, in itself more likely to have been a gradual process than a sudden achievement of the mythical king Menes, does not correspond to a sudden change in civilization. There was no abrupt break with the past.

In the economic field the character of the country and its river had a decisive influence, and was put to a better use during Naḳāda II. Egypt was and is a predominantly agricultural country. Grain and cattle were the basic sources of food, supplemented by the good fish the river provided, and perhaps to a lesser degree by the prey of the hunter. Besides this, Egypt and its neighbourhood possessed raw materials for the primitive industries—clay, flint, copper, gold and an assortment of useful and beautiful stones.

However, though the Nile provided each year the fertile mud on which the crops could grow, and therefore allowed an intensive use of the soil without exhausting it, at the same time it made private possession of the land virtually impossible. No boundary stone, no fence could withstand the annual flood, and without the science of land-measuring the farmer could not rediscover the borders of the plot he had cultivated the previous year. This seems to have led to a communal working of the soil. From Badārian times onwards we find granaries well preserved even when the huts of the population have utterly disappeared. The granaries are usually grouped together somewhere on the outskirts of the settlements and not near the individual huts, a fact which

[1] Cf. Vol. I, pp. 42 ff., also fig. 36, 1 and 2.

points to their being common property. Only Merimda makes an exception, for there the granaries and huts make up small farmsteads. We do not know how far back the grain-parching kilns go, but they also suggest communal use. With their dozens of large receptacles they seem far too great for the needs of a single family. We do not know how this communal property was administered, nor do we know whether the cattle also were owned in common.

It seems likely that this primitive communism goes back to Badārian times, and that when the invaders of Naḳāda II arrived they found a developed social system of land administration based upon it. Who was at the head of this we can only guess. It seems to me probable that we have to reckon with a king, a *nśwt*, at the head of the community, as we have no indication of any other governing body. He must be sought among the owners of the most important graves with the richest furniture. Some of the excavators have mentioned and described these graves, though none has discussed what position the owner occupied in the community. We have seen that these graves were often those of women,[1] and we therefore have to ask, whether the *nśwt* was perhaps originally a woman? The position of the queen and of the hereditary princess was of great importance in dynastic Egypt, and from time to time a queen in her own right ascended the throne of the pharaohs. Meryt-Neith of the First Dynasty, with her *sereḫ* surmounted by the sign of Neith, may well have been a reigning queen, and the same is true of Queen Khentkawes of the Fourth Dynasty. These are not more than indications, and more work will have to be done before we can be reasonably certain. But we have to take into account the possibility that at least some of the early rulers may have been women. Whether their sovereignty comprised the whole of Upper Egypt from Badārian times, or at least from Naḳāda I onwards, we do not know. It is quite possible that the unification of Upper Egypt was an achievement of the Naḳāda II people, just as later on they created the united kingdom of all Egypt. If they are to be credited with the introduction of irrigation and of a system of canals, they must have had power over at least the larger part of the country, for otherwise this would not have been possible.[2] Not only does the digging of canals demand a concentrated effort of many; we must also remember that a canal has to lead from some point of the Nile to another at a distance, and this presumes the sovereignty over both ends. If my assumption is anywhere near the truth and the king in predynastic times (or the queen as the case may be) was the head of a community that by the nature of the country knew no private property in the soil, then it was the king's prime duty to organize the sowing and the reaping, the safe storing and the distribution of the grain. There are some later indications which may imply that the king was looked upon as a supreme lord of the land. One is the fiction that the king was the owner of the whole of the country of Egypt. I do not know of any dynastic period during which this was factually correct, but it might reflect earlier circumstances. Another is the *heṭep dj nśwt* formula in the tombs from the early Old Kingdom onwards: "An offering which the king gives." As Junker has pointed out,[3] this is the formula which originally stands at the beginning of the offering-list: thousands of beer, bread, oxen and wine. As long as there was no private property in all these commodities it was indeed the king who had to provide them, and though in some instances even later the king did provide them, the formula also stands in those tombs where they were provided from the owner's private farms. We may remember in this connexion that even in much later periods the king's coronation was connected with the

---

[1] pp. 123 f. above.   [2] See above, Vol. I, p. 46.
[3] H. Junker, *Giza*, II, pp. 43 ff.

festival of the god Min and that he had to reap some grain before the god. The ceremony of "*Ḥwt Bḥsw*", the driving of the calves, also points to a society in which the king was in charge of the agricultural tasks. It is a ceremonial threshing of corn, originally performed on the threshing-floor. It was done by four calves of different colours, conducted by the king in the presence of the harvest god, originally Min, with whom the officiating king was equated.[1] The festival also had a pastoral character, and the king is called "Sovereign of the *wsb* cattle". This seems originally to have been Anubis, a god, either jackal or dog. It is tempting to associate him with the burials of *canidae* which we have met since the Badārian period, and the small ivory amulets.

The earliest representation of the rite so far known dates from the Pyramid temple of Sahure of the Fifth Dynasty. The story of Joseph, even, who stored the grain during the good years so that it might be distributed in times of need, may be a distant echo of the ancient obligations of a king of Egypt.

That a common exploitation of the soil was apt to yield better returns than a small farmer could achieve seems obvious, and would have increased the riches of the country, and this in turn made secondary industries possible. That the mining and flaking of flint had become an industry, as opposed to home production, during Naḳāda I has already been mentioned in the discussion of Egypt's flint industry.[2] It was also shown to be likely that the production of gold goes back to the same period. For this I adduce no more than hints. In the first place there is the name of the capital Nub.t, "The Gold". Secondly, the existence of gold would help to explain why the Egypt of Naḳāda I should have attracted people from Asia, first to trade with it and then to take possession of it. More evidence is needed to lift these ideas out of the realm of working hypotheses.

During Naḳāda II the new industries of copper and stone work must have added both to the riches of the country and the prestige of the king. It is during this period that we find actual imports from the countries of Asia. Also, the few Egyptian stone vases which have been found outside Egypt in Marsa Matruh[3] and in Crete,[4] as well as in Byblos may belong to this period or to that of the early dynasties.[5] Since such exports are so very rare, it seems more likely that Egypt paid for its imports from abroad with something else, and gold seems to me the most quite. This, unfortunately, will be very difficult to trace, especially as we do not know whether the export was in the form of finished goods or of the raw material: if the latter, of course it would be likely impossible to find. Whether trade was a monopoly of the king is one of the many questions which deserve further investigation, just as much as his position in connexion with the different industries, especially that of gold production.

That the king must have been the great war lord also can only be surmised. Weapons in predynastic graves are rare. For the earlier periods it is mainly a few arrow-heads which show what weapons were in use, and they may indicate hunting rather than fighting, just as do the harpoons. We have no mace-heads from Badārian times, and they do not exist in Naḳāda I

---

[1] A. M. Blackman and H. W. Fairman, "The Significance of the Ceremony ḤWT BḤSW in the Temple of Horus at Edfu", *JEA*, 36 (1950), pp. 63 ff.

[2] See Chapter II.   [3] See Vol. I, p. 44.

[4] See Vol. I, pp. 44 ff.

[5] The squat stone vases found in Crete and Byblos are almost certainly dynastic.

unless we accept the disc-shaped objects as true weapons. If there were clubs of wood, they either were not put into the graves or have not survived, and it is an open question whether the throwing-sticks were not rather castanets. The pear-shaped mace-head formed part of the pharaoh's official armament all through Egyptian history, and it is first found in graves during the Naḳāda II period. Daggers, though known, were very rare. All this goes to show that the warlike functions of the king were not his main characteristic, at least not after death. The Nar-Mer palette, which shows the king at war, was dedicated in the temple of the warrior-god Horus, and not in a tomb.

But though we find no weapons in the most important graves of predynastic times, we find other objects which will throw some light on the position of a predynastic Egyptian king during his life and perhaps in death also. These are the many objects of magical significance which go far to show that the powers attributed to a king went beyond his physical prowess. Most of these objects had some connexion with fertility rites, and the king (or queen) must have been credited with influence over the fertility of men, the soil and cattle from a very early time onward.[1]

This brings us to the religious aspect of the Egyptian kingship, which is perhaps its most interesting side. We have seen that already in Badārian times there are indications of the cult of the great fertility-goddess in Egypt.[2] In a grave of Naḳāda I period there was a vase decorated with her image,[3] and two other pots with her arms and breasts were found in burials of the period, one in the grave of the lady of the hippopotami from Diospolis Parva,[4] the other, also from Diospolis (t. U 179), is from an otherwise unknown grave.[5] I have also suggested that the pairs of ivory tusks, one hollow and one solid, were connected with some fertility magic. They also belonged to the more important tombs. It is possible that some of the other magic objects discussed [6] may have served in ceremonies which were to assure fertility. It seems likely to me that the women or men who carried out these ceremonies were chosen as the leaders of their communities in other than strictly religious aspects also, because they were credited with special influence on the fertility-goddess. They were the kings or *nśwt*,[7] whatever this Egyptian word may originally have meant. The great goddess, who also was a cow, must have been one of the most important if not the most important deity of predynastic Egypt. We found her sign, the cow horns and the arms, not only on vases but on slate palettes, combs, pins and the little tags found so often in threes and probably used in some magical rite. Her position among the gods is reflected in the position of women in the country of Egypt. But she is not alone; to her belongs a male divinity, who is her son and lover. He would have been venerated since Naḳāda I and probably earlier. I think he is the one represented on the two white-cross-lined vases with the dancing scenes.[8] Unfortunately, both these important pieces were bought and are without provenance, which considerably diminishes their value as evidence and makes it impossible to date them more precisely than to the time of Naḳāda I or the beginning of Naḳāda II. However, as I think there is no reason to doubt their authenticity, I may be allowed to draw some conclusions

[1] Cf. G. A. Wainwright, *The Sky Religion in Egypt*, pp. 6 ff.   [2] See pp. 65 ff.

[3] Cf. Vol. I, pl. III, 1-4.   [4] See above, p. 73; Vol. I, p. 31.

[5] The vase is in the Ashmolean Museum, Oxford; I could trace no other object from t. U 179, and the grave itself is unpublished.

[6] See above, pp. 60 ff.

[7] *nj-sw.t* belonging to the *sw.t* plant is the explanation given by the *Wörterbuch*.

[8] Cf. Vol. I, p. 64, fig. 14.

from them.   The one at University College, London,[1] shows a woman and a man performing a
dance.   A line joins the two.   The man, who is by far the larger, has feathers or twigs stuck in
his hair.   The woman, her hair flying wildly, is without arms.   A similar dance is shown on the
other vase now in Brussels, but there are two males and six women dancing round them.   Again
the size of the males and the decorations they wear in their hair shows them to be the most
important figures.   The women with the flying hair are armless.   Some are connected by lines
with a man.   I would like to identify the two dancing men as one and the same god attended
by women, and the whole scene as some fertility rite.   It seems to me likely that the same god
is represented on a decorated vase from El-'Amrah, t. b 225, dated "between S.D. 46 and 63",
but probably nearer to the earlier than to the later limit.[2]   The vase, which is 30 cm. high
(pl. XIII, 4 and 5), has two boats, one carrying the standard with the two concentric curved objects
which I take to be the horns and arms of the cow-goddess, and, above, a group of two men and a
woman.   The figure in the middle is an ithyphallic man with curly hair and two feathers or twigs
stuck in it.   He has a pair of castanets in one hand.   On his right a woman dances the cow-dance
with her arms raised and her hands nearly touching her head; on his left is a smaller man, also with
castanets.   The woman is the tallest figure and has a huge, perfectly round head.   On the other
boat, which carries the standard of the mountains, the same woman with a small man who lays a
hand on her shoulder stands on one cabin, and on the second cabin of this boat another man plays
the castanets.   It seems to me that on this vase the connexion between the curly-haired man
with his feathers (is he already "high of feathers" ?) and the fertility-goddess is obvious.

Another decorated vase with pictures belonging to the cycle of the fertility-goddess was bought
and hence is without provenance.   This magnificent specimen is in the Metropolitan Museum of
Art (pl. XIII, 1-3).   The pot has three lug handles each of which is surrounded by necklaces of
wavy lines.   Between them and filling the main part of the vase are three boats, each with many
oars and a large branch at one end.   In the centre of each are the two erections which may
be chapels.[3]

On the most important boat one of these is provided with a small addition, either an ante-
chamber or an entrance passage.   Fastened to it is the same emblem as on the El-'Amrah pot,
two double concentric curves which do not quite meet at the top.   As has been said before, this is
one of the most common emblems in these representations.   On the building with the ante-chamber
a sort of tent is erected, unless it is meant to be the interior of the chapel.   In it the sacred marriage
is consummated between a large woman with a huge, completely circular head and a little man
the size of whose head is a fraction of that of the woman's.   There is no doubt that she is the
dominating figure, and therefore the symbol attached to the building must belong to her.   This
goes far to prove that the double curves represent the horns and the arms of the fertility-goddess.
Only the holy couple is represented on this boat; nobody is allowed near the spot where the
sacred mystery is performed.

The scenes on the two other boats are different.   On one the emblem which I have called
the Z-sign is attached to one of the cabins and out of it grows a branch.   In front of it is a row of
three women holding each other by the hand, and on the other chapel a larger woman dances by

[1] *Preh. Eg.*, pl. XVIII, 74.
[2] *El Amrah*, p. 23, pl. XIV, D 46.   The vase is in the British Museum.
[3] Cf. Vol. I, p. 13.

T

herself, her arms raised above her head. I would like to connect this scene with those on the white-cross-lined pots and the El-'Amrah vase, whereby I would suggest that the man is replaced by the Z-symbol with the branch. This I, therefore, think must be the emblem of a male deity. Whether the row of women below the boat has some connexion with the ceremony on board is unknown. There are four of them. The largest one, and the only one where the hair is indicated, lays her arm on the head of her neighbour, who grasps the arm. The two other women with folded arms are unconnected. Below the middle of the boat is a symbol consisting of two parts. One of these is rectangular, and is just possibly the same as one from the white-painted Brussels vase.[1] The other, surrounding the rectangle like an arc, ends in two signs which somewhat resemble the ring encircling the mysterious word *bš* [2] on which the vulture stands in the inscriptions on the two large vases of Khasekhem. Counterbalancing the row of women on the other side of the symbol is a row of birds. These are separated from each other, and two feathers stick out of their backs.

Between the boat with the Z-standard and the next is another dancing woman with raised arms. In this last boat, and on the chapel next to her, stand three persons. The largest person, who is in the middle, is a woman who lays her left hand on the head of a smaller woman. On her other side is a little man, who carries a crook in his right hand while with his left he holds the centre figure round the waist. This, to my mind, is the first divine triad so far known in Egypt, and it consists of mother, father and daughter. The woman, as her size and central position indicate, is the most important personage. The crook in the hand of the man may reveal his identity, for it is the same crook which on the slate palette from El-'Amrah is stuck through the sign of Min.[3] On the other chapel stands a man holding what I think is a pair of castanets. It is to his cabin that the standard is attached, and it is not easy to decide what standard it is meant to be. It looks somewhat like a pair of horns with perhaps the bird in the middle which we have met frequently on pins, combs and tags, and as palettes, but it may be something entirely different. It is not even easy to decide whether the standard belongs to a male or female divinity. Perhaps with the great goddess herself in the boat this may be one of her less usual symbols. On the remaining parts of the vase many of the animals and symbols are known from other decorated pots, but of the meaning of most of them we are ignorant. They are of minor importance compared with the main representations of this vase.

Apart from the sacred marriage, the triad is of the greatest interest. Though we do not know the intermediaries, it is the beginning of a motif which is at its most glorious in the triads from Mycerinus's Valley Temple.[4] There about a dozen were found, each composed of the great goddess with her cow horns of archaic type who in Mycerinus's time is called Hathor. With her is the king and a minor deity representing different nomes, a triad of gods. On two of the sculptures Hathor sits in the middle and puts her arm round Mycerinus, showing that she is his wife. On the others the king has usurped the middle position, which is in keeping with his standing at the height of the Fourth Dynasty. He has become the greatest god. Here too Hathor is represented as his wife.

This close connexion with the Great Mother, I think, shows one of the roots of the Egyptian kingship. He is the lover—and son—of the fertility-goddess, the Ka-mutef (bull of his mother),

---

[1] Vol. I, p. 64, fig. 14.
[3] See above, p. 89.

[2] Quibell and Green, *Hierakonpolis*, I, pl. XXXVIII.
[4] Reisner, *Mycerinus*, pls. 38 ff.

and as such has supreme influence over the fertility of the country. He is Min, the strong bull, of the Nar-Mer and the battlefield palettes, whose tail forms an integral part of the king's insignia of state. No other statue of a divinity was found in the precincts of the Mycerinus pyramid with the exception of two small fragments of a jackal that may have been the decoration of some object. Only the great god and his consort and mother, who are the parents of the gods of the nomes of Egypt represented by the smaller figures at their sides, had their place in the temple. It is a long way from the painting of the decorated pot in the Metropolitan Museum to the triads of Mycerinus. It seems rather doubtful whether on the vase the scene has already, as it were, descended to earth, and whether a king should be recognized in the man of the triad carrying the crooked sceptre. It seems to me unlikely that during the predynastic period the *nśwt* was more than the witch doctor of more recent times credited with special influence over the great goddess. The beginnings from which the supreme office in Egypt must have sprung prove to have been very different from those from which grew the corresponding office in Mesopotamia. On the Nar-Mer palette the more than life-sized king, himself a god and a son of the great goddess, slays his enemy single-handed. No human being is near, other than the servant carrying the king's personal belongings. On Eannatum's stela of the vultures the king is in front of the phalanx of his knights, who, led by him, subdue the enemy. He is *primus inter pares*. No such idea can possibly be upheld about the Egyptian king (pl. VII, 1-2).

The assumption that the *nśwt* of Upper Egypt did not lay claim to being a god in predynastic times rests on only a few facts. The first is the shape and the position of his tomb in the cemetery. We saw that amongst the graves of the predynastic cemeteries we could single out some that were richer and equipped with rarer objects than the others, and these I ascribed to the leaders of the community. Nothing is known that might lead us to suspect that they differed in shape or position fundamentally from those of the rest of the people, and hence that the occupant differed fundamentally from the people. But at the beginning of the dynasties we are at once confronted with a totally new situation. The enormous tombs which Emery excavated along the mountain terrace overlooking the Nile Valley at a point where once Memphis must have been are marked as something more than ordinary by their position and by the façades that were given to them. The recessed façade was imported into the Nile Valley from Sumer, where it was the exterior of a temple. Hence its use for these tombs in Egypt has made them into temples of the great god, into which he retired at death. I do not think that these Saḳḳāra tombs can have been anything else but royal tombs. Who else could have been allowed to make a temple out of his tomb but the king, and, perhaps, his nearest relatives? As a god the king could have several tomb-temples, and this would at least explain the otherwise curious fact that we have more than one tomb of many of the early kings.

I do not know why the recessed façade in Egypt is commonly called a "palace façade". Neither in Egypt nor in Mesopotamia is a palace known with such a façade as that which the Sumerians developed for their temples. Nor do I see a palace or a door in the *sereḫ*, which is first used to enshrine the royal name during the early days of the dynasties. *Sereḫ* means throne in Egyptian.[1] If the *sereḫ* were a palace or a door, it seems odd that the Egyptians should not have called it so. It is only fitting that the royal name should be shown on a throne. The *sereḫ* is not the same as the recessed façade of the tombs, and they do not represent the same object. The one is

[1] See *Wörterbuch*.

obviously what its name says, namely a throne, the other a temple. Both were introduced at a time when the Egyptian king had at last attained the status of a god.

But there is another indication that the first king of the First Dynasty was the one who arrogated to himself divine attributes. In the Turin Papyrus the predecessors of the kings of the First Dynasty are called *Šmšw-Ḥr*, followers of Horus. This to my mind shows that they had adopted Horus as their god while the former *nśwt* had followed another god. From the time of the First Dynasty onwards the king identifies himself with the god and becomes the living Horus. Emery has shown conclusively [1] that the king Ḥor-Aḥa, who is either the first or the second king of the First Dynasty—it is disputed whether he or king Nar-Mer takes pride of place—has the Horus included in his name, which must be read "Horus the Fighter". We have some indications as to the god whom Horus replaced in Upper Egypt. It was the bull. On the Nar-Mer palette on the side, where the king is identified with Horus and wears the crown of Upper Egypt, he yet dons a robe of state decorated with cow heads to which a bull's tail is fastened. As so often in Egypt, the older tradition does not die but manifests itself where we should expect the new. On the other side of the palette, where the king wears the Lower Egyptian crown, the king is still the bull to which the tail and the cow heads on the Upper Egyptian side allude. In both instances it is no longer the question of the king being a follower of this or that god; he has become himself the living god.

The bucrania which Emery found [2] deposited on a low bench around the tomb of King Djet (probably the fourth king of the First Dynasty) at Saḳḳāra confirm the evidence of the Nar-Mer palette. They show that the king of Lower Egypt was identified with the bull-god. So far Emery has found no stela at Saḳḳāra comparable with those found in the Royal Tombs at Abydos [3] in Upper Egypt. There the same King Djet on his beautiful stela, now in the Louvre at Paris, is shown as the falcon Horus. Thus, the king is the bull-god as sovereign of Lower Egypt and became the falcon-god in Upper Egypt. It seem to me likely that the early identification of Horus with Min goes back to the time when Horus had replaced him as chief royal god in Upper Egypt. At the same time he adopted the cow as his mother, an odd story even among Egyptian gods. But she was too powerful to be dispensed with, so Horus had to accommodate himself to her.

Besides these two royal gods, the king identified himself with many of the other great gods of Egypt. The best known is the sun-god Reʻ, but I know of no indication that the king as the sun-god goes back to the early period with which we are concerned. Nothing shows that Horus during this time was considered as a sun-god, and of Reʻ there is no sign. The palette, which on one side shows the destruction of various towns by the pharaoh,[4] is unfortunately mutilated, so that it shows only four of the seven gods who swung the hoe against their walls. Horus leads the gods and is represented on the first town in the upper row, but those on the three other towns in that row are now lost. The second row is headed by the lion, probably the same god whom we find associated with the Upper Egyptian sanctuary,[5] and whom the king as Sphinx represents. He is followed by the scorpion, who may be Selket. The scorpion occurs on the white-cross-lined

[1] W. B. Emery, *Excavations at Saqqara, 1937-1938. Ḥor-Aḥa*, p. 21.
[2] Emery, *Great Tombs of the First Dynasty*, II, pl. VII.
[3] Vandier, *Manuel*, I, 2, p. 725, fig. 482.
[4] See above, pp. 102-3.
[5] C. de Wit, *Le rôle et le sens du lion dans l'Égypte ancien*, p. 194.

and the decorated pottery,[1] and was frequent among the objects of the great deposit of Hierakonpolis.[2] That we know the scorpion only as a goddess would not hinder the king from identifying himself with her. He was also "the two ladies". Can this be another indication of the matriarchal strain with which we have been confronted already? On the last town the pair of falcons known as "the two lords" do their destructive work. These two have been called Horus and Seth,[3] but are more likely Horus and Min. We have nothing to prove that Seth was identified with Horus at this time, nor can we be absolutely sure that he was among the royal gods. On the large mace-head from Hierakonpolis he is shown twice on the perches from which the Rekhit birds are hung by the necks, together with Min and, perhaps, one of the hill-gods, possibly *Tep-Dwat*, and others which are now lost. If, and it is possible, we have to see the king in all the gods on these standards, then Seth is one of them. The little group of four animals from Naḳāda, t. 721 (pl. VI, 6-8), consisting of two falcons, a lion and what I think can only be the Seth animal,[4] show him among the royal gods and different from the two falcons. His position, however, as compared with that of Horus and Min, seems to have been a minor one, until under King Peribsen of the Second Dynasty he replaces Horus.

The discussion of the religious aspect of kingship during predynastic and protodynastic times demonstrates the predominant position which the king held or tried to hold in the beliefs of the ancient Egyptians. It tends to obscure for us what must have been the more personal and humbler aspects of ancient Egyptian religion. The Great Mother and her son, who are also the cow and the young bull, have always remained among the foremost gods of Egypt. She must have appealed to people regardless of her connexion with the king. Apart from her eternal rôle as the Great Mother, she had relations with the tomb and the dead, and *ex-votos* to her were deposited in graves. The slate palette from Gerzeh,[5] where her head is adorned with stars, shows how early she became Queen of Heaven. Her standard is the most frequent one on the boats of the decorated pottery. It is certainly not a nome ensign. Whether Min was her son and lover from the beginning cannot be decided. We badly need a corpus of Egyptian painted pottery which would unite all the existing scenes from both the white-cross-lined and the decorated wares. To me it seems as if the curly-haired god with the feathers (which after all may be twigs) is not the same as the bull Min, with whom the goddess is later associated. Her boat is generally accompanied on the pots by one or two others, of which one at least carries the standard of a male god.

The standards of male gods so carried are not always the same, and though I can think of several explanations for this, none can be proved. The Z-sign (fig. 19) is the most frequent, and from the vase in the Metropolitan Museum seems to belong to a male god. Whether this may be a simplified or primitive form of the sign for Min can only be decided when we have discovered what the Min-sign stands for (fig. 20, a and b, fig. 21). The Min-sign itself occurs

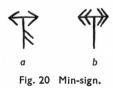

a   b

a   b

Fig. 19 Z-sign.   Fig. 20 Min-sign.   Fig. 21 Min-sign and Z-sign.

[1] E.g. *Corpus*, pl. XXIII, 66M; *Diosp. Pa.*, pl. XVI, 78 b and c.
[2] Quibell and Green, *Hierakonpolis*, pl. XVIII, 15 and 16, etc.
[3] Sethe, *Untersuchungen*, 3, p. 31.
[4] See above, p. 75.
[5] See above, p. 90.

—if we are to follow Petrie[1]—only in late contexts. In *Diospolis Parva*, p. 16, pl. IV, it is classified as the earliest. In one instance, where a vase from Ballas is decorated with four boats,[2] two carry the Z-sign, one the three hills, and the fourth the Min-sign, which speaks rather against such an identification. Whether I am right in seeing two different gods represented by the standards either with two (fig. 22) or with three or more (fig. 23) mountains remains to be proved. I should like to assign the two mountain standards to *Tep-Dwat*, the one on his mountain and those with three or more to *Nb. Ḥaswt*, the lord of the deserts.

Fig. 22 The mountain sign.   Fig. 23 Sign of the desert or hilly country.   Fig. 24 Neith sign.

We are on somewhat safer ground with the crossed arrows of the goddess Neith (fig. 24). On a remarkable vase from Diospolis Parva[3] one of the cabins carries this ensign. Two women dance on its roof, holding each other by the hand while the other hand is laid on the hip. This is, as far as I know, a unique posture, and I wonder whether this represents a dance in honour of Neith in contrast to that of the cow-goddess, where the hands and arms are held high to symbolize horns. The other boat on this vase with the Z-standard has a single man dancing on or behind the cabin. Neith's sign is rare as compared with that of the cow-goddess, the Z-sign or the different hill signs. We know very little of her and her myth and can only infer that the crossed arrows indicate a goddess of the hunt. Though she appears on none of the major monuments of the early dynasties, yet most of the women's names preserved on the private tombstones from Abydos[4] are compounded with hers, and in the case of Mer-Neith, whom I suspect to have been a queen in her own right,[5] the Neith emblem tops the *sereḥ* in which the royal name is enclosed. It is perhaps worth noting that the Neith emblem does not occur anywhere in Lower Egypt in predynastic times, not even as an emblem of the boats on the decorated pots of Harageh, Gerzeh or Abuṣīr el-Meleḳ, where we find the double curves of the Great Mother, the Z-sign and also the Min-sign. As far as we can see at present, she belongs to Naḳāda II, and we should remember that the Red Crown which she wears in dynastic ages was first found on a sherd in a Naḳāda grave.[6]

Horus on the crescent moon is the only other god of the later Egyptian pantheon still to be mentioned. His standard is rare, and probably late. Newberry mentions the throwing-stick as occurring on three vases as the cult-object of a god Methen mentioned in the Pyramid Texts.[7] I know of only one vase—one at University College, London—which has a boat of which the emblem can possibly be a throwing-stick. If Newberry is right, then we have a god who seems to have vanished during later periods. It seems possible that the standard on a vase now in the Metropolitan Museum represents two uprearing snakes (fig. 25).[8] The motif is repeated on each side of the standard, and there the snakes—if they are snakes—seem to stand on a line.

[1] So in *Preh. Eg.*, pl. XXIII, 31, 32.   [2] *Naq. Bal.*, pl. LXVI, 8, Q 100.

[3] *Diosp. Pa.*, pl. XX, 11.   Now in the Ashmolean Museum, Oxford.

[4] *Royal Tombs*, II, pls. XXVI-XXVIII.

[5] See above, p. 142.   [6] See Vol. I, p. 37.

[7] Percy E. Newberry, "Some Cults of Prehistoric Egypt", *Ann. Arch. Anthr.*, vol. V, p. 135.

[8] Metropolitan Museum of Art, no. 11.150.33.

It is quite possible that other gods may be represented on pots hidden in some museum and never published. However, the fact that Seth occurs nowhere is most surprising and strongly speaks against his having been a god of some importance before the rise of the dynasties.

Of the signs for which no acceptable explanation has been offered so far, the one which seems to be composed of four pairs of horns is the most frequent (fig. 26). The horns curve inwards like those of the cow-goddess and are attached, one in each main compass-direction, to what sometimes looks like a box, sometimes like a line, and sometimes simply like four curves without any support.

It is a great pity that the painted vases with the ensigns carried on the boats, our main source for the oldest gods, have never been studied properly, and that Newberry's little article written in 1913, out of date and incomplete, is still the only serious study of this most revealing evidence for the gods of predynastic Egypt. If I am right in my suggestions, and the emblem of the double curves is that of the great goddess (fig. 27), the Z-sign that of the male god or of a male god associated with her (fig. 19), we may conclude, as our investigations in other directions have often led us to believe, that these two were the main deities of predynastic Egypt. These two emblems are by far the most frequent on the boats, and they were found on vases from Lower as well as from Upper Egypt. This would show that the main goddess and god were the same for both

Fig. 25 Two snakes (?) sign.   Fig. 26 Unexplained sign.   Fig. 27 Sign of the Great Goddess.

parts of the country, and that, far from being local gods, they were universal. They were, indeed, universal not only in Egypt, but, as far as we can see, throughout the ancient East.

It is even more difficult to decipher the scenes which occur on the decorated pottery without being connected with boats, and especially to decide whether the animals represented must be looked upon as divinities or as animals connected with them. It would be rash to deny that they often are. The snakes, the scorpions, the crocodiles and perhaps even the rows of flamingoes will have to be explained in that way. We must, however, also reckon with sympathetic magic finding an expression in these paintings. If we remember the fragment of the vase from Badāri [1] in the form of a hippopotamus with the boat, the hunters holding their harpoons, and the large number of spare harpoons painted on its back, one can hardly deny that such a scene of a successful hunt is meant to purvey the same good luck for the next actual hippopotamus chase. The same idea occurs on a white-cross-lined vase from Alawniyeh.[2] It is one of the rare oval, four-legged dishes painted on the inside. Two main scenes are executed opposite to each other. One consists of two hippopotami facing each other, and a man whose harpoon has hit one of the animals from behind. Above the two animals there are branches, and between this scene and the one on the opposite side there are some signs, the meaning of which is not known, though one may recognize some waterlines. A woman and a man dancing with raised arms may give a religious character to the whole picture, and indicate that the acting persons are more than human. Especially is this so as only one huntsman and one harpoon are shown, scarcely enough for a mere mortal to

[1] *Bad. Civ.*, pl. LIV, 15.   [2] *Maḥâsna*, pl. III.

attack two hippopotami with.[1] But even though the picture may describe a myth, its possession may have meant to the owner the assurance of good luck for a dangerous undertaking.

There is not much more we can deduce from the pictures of the painted vases. Much of their symbolism is a closed book to us. Tree worship there was, as the trees with the small chapels underneath show. Such a holy tree is pictured in a much more naturalistic style on the great mace from Hierakonpolis.[2] Most of the vases with paintings of animals and human beings come from graves, especially all those which are well preserved. That similar vases were in use in the houses is proved by Caton-Thompson's finds in the little village at Ḥammāmīya. There she excavated decorated sherds with animals and also with men. Whether these were put to everyday use or were reserved for special occasions can only be guessed.

Some of the animals which occur on vases of both styles have also been found buried in the cemeteries [3] from Badārian times onwards. They were the cow or bull, the antelope or goat, and perhaps the sheep, and a canine, either jackal or dog, all of which must have been credited with divine powers.

The special care and the amount of valuable furniture which the predynastic Egyptians lavished upon the graves is considered to be a proof of their belief in a life after death, a life that closely resembled that in the land of Egypt. All our later evidence confirms this assumption, but, human nature being what it is, this is scarcely the whole story. The fear that the dead might return and revenge himself by inflicting misfortunes on the living who had not buried him properly or neglected the necessary offerings must have been deep-rooted and helps to explain why such a considerable amount of a person's fortune was given to the dead. From the end of the Old Kingdom onwards we have written proofs for these beliefs, and I do not think we shall go far wrong if we attribute them to the earlier period also. The latter part of the Old Kingdom is a time when many of the old traditions were first written down. Such are the Pyramid Texts, which, though we only possess them from inscriptions of this period, yet include much that is far older than that. The particular documents which attest the belief in the power of the dead to influence the fate of the living are the "Letters to the Dead".[4] They are generally addressed to a deceased relation, who is supposed to take the side of the aggrieved and help him or her against the machinations of a malevolent dead man.

There is one evil in particular against which it seems likely that the predynastic people tried to guard themselves through soliciting the help of the dead. It begins to emerge from our evidence that the dead man was credited with having in some way influence over the fertility of the living, their cattle and the soil. The *ex-votos* of women-figurines and of groups of cattle recovered from graves all point that way. They were to remind the dead person of what was expected of him. Whether the dead themselves had that power, or whether they were supposed to be near the eternal source of life, and therefore able to influence the great goddess herself, cannot be decided, but it seems to me that the latter is the more likely. We have seen in the course of our investigations that the objects which seem to have had some magical significance were not found evenly distributed in the graves of a given cemetery. They were only recovered from the graves which were outstanding in other aspects also, and which, therefore, I have ascribed to the leading women

---

[1] See T. Säve-Söderbergh, "On Egyptian Representations of Hippopotamus Hunting as a Religious Motif", *Horae Soederblomianae*, 1953.   [2] Quibell and Green, *Hierakonpolis*, I, pl. XXVIc, 8.

[3] See above, pp. 127-8.   [4] A. H. Gardiner and K. Sethe, *Egyptian Letters to the Dead* (London, 1928).

and men of the community. It has been suggested that they owed their position to a special connexion with the fertility-goddess. These witch doctors, or whatever else they may have been, evidently took their power of influencing the fertility-goddess with them into their graves. Perhaps, also, they were thought to enter into her kingdom at death. If, therefore, the survivors did not want to risk barrenness and famine, they had to provide for a decent burial and those offerings which in their view were their due. From the First Intermediate Period a letter to a dead person has survived which confirms the opinions just expounded, even though it comes from a very much later age.[1] In it a son complains to his father that he has as yet no male offspring, and asks him to intercede with his mother so that a child be granted to his wife. I think that as the dead man himself is not asked to help, but merely to intercede with "his mother", it is clear that she was the potent one, and that, most likely, she was not his earthly mother but the great goddess herself. We would have liked to know where this letter written on a pot was found, for it does not seem likely that it could have been deposited in the grave immediately after death. From the tone of the story it seems much more probable that it was written some time after the death of the father. Was it laid together with the offerings in front of the false door of the grave, or was it perhaps put into the grave of someone who was just being buried and therefore in a position to deliver it direct?

All this goes far to show that the graves and the cemeteries played a much more important role in the religion of the predynastic Egyptians than that of a mere resting-place for their deceased. A good part of their religious observances must have centred upon them. There is some evidence which makes it likely that ceremonies took place there either at the burial or at certain other times. Petrie, when describing grave t. 5 at Naḳāda,[2] speaks of eight large jars stacked at the north end. Such jars are, he says, typical of Naḳāda II burials and were always filled with ashes. Only the very poorest graves lacked them. Nothing was found in these ashes except some bits of broken bones of animals. "No trace of human bone occurred, nor were any of the human bones in the burials ever calcined or discoloured. . . . We learn, however," he goes on, "that a great burning took place at the funeral, and the ashes of the vegetable matter, and even the burnt sand beneath it, were gathered up and buried in the grave." These ashes must have been the remains of great sacrifices offered to the dead, and the cost of these together with the expenses of the grave and its furniture must have been a substantial drain on the possessions of the living. To me it seems likely that they were offered not only from a sense of filial piety to make life after death pleasant for the deceased, but also from fear of the consequences which might arise if these obligations were not carried out as they should be. All this points to the chthonic character of the predynastic Egyptian religion, still unaffected by the veneration of the sky which emerged at the end of our period with the sky-god Horus, and even less by sun-worship and a heavenly hereafter which was adopted much later. For the predynastic Egyptians the seat of the gods was the underworld, to which the dead descended; a belief which was never wholly superseded in ancient Egypt.

Though the position of the king and the religion, as far as we have ascertained, both stress the rural character of the predynastic community, it had long since ceased to be wholly rural.

[1] Gardiner, "A Letter to the Dead", *JEA*, 16, pp. 19 ff. Baumgartel, "Tomb and Fertility", *Jahrbuch für Kleinasiat. Forschung*, I, pp. 56 ff.
[2] *Naq. Bal.*, p. 19.

Probably from Naḵāda I, but certainly from Naḵāda II onwards, a number of the predynastic Egyptians lived in towns. The industries they had developed—pot-making, flint-flaking, stone-vase manufacturing, etc.—were in the hands of specialists. A lively trade took place not only with the people in their immediate neighbourhood but also with others much farther afield, as the imported pieces from the Sumerian world testify.

In Egypt, just as in Hither Asia, an urbanized society had been evolved. Whether this extended outside Upper Egypt we cannot say, as no predynastic towns like Naḵāda, Hierakonpolis and probably Koptos are known from Lower Egypt. This may be due to lack of excavations, or it may not. The three cemeteries of Harageh, Gerzeh, and Abuṣīr el-Meleḵ and the predynastic finds in the Fayum do not create an impression of very rich or advanced communities. A consideration of the archaeological material leads us to wonder if Herodotus was not right after all when he says that Menes founded Memphis and made the country, which had been swamp, habitable for humans. No doubt, about the beginning of the dynasties things did happen in that neighbourhood. Apart from Memphis and its necropolis, there are Tarkhan, and above all Helwan, a cemetery of great importance which, when once properly studied, will shed much new light on this fascinating period. Ma'adi also, once it is published, should provide much-needed material to enlarge our knowledge.

So far nothing that has been published from Lower Egypt points to a superior and individual civilization in these regions. We have seen how deeply rooted the culture of the early dynasties is in that of Naḵāda II. Administration and constitution, religion and art, town and house plans, and, last but not least, graves and cemeteries, all can be traced back to institutions already extant, or at least foreshadowed, in Upper Egypt during predynastic times. None of the characteristic features of early dynastic Egypt can be found in communities in Lower Egypt apart from those which belong to the orbit of Naḵāda II; and Naḵāda II is not a Lower Egyptian creation. It is a symbiosis of two civilizations, the one African, the other Asian, the one reaching the Nile Valley from the south, the other from the east, through the Wadi Ḥammāmāt. It was this symbiosis that created the new unity which is early dynastic Egypt.

If we try to enumerate the typical Lower Egyptian characteristics that are not found earlier in Upper Egypt we are hard put to it to find even a few. Of the great gods of Egypt perhaps Ptaḥ is Lower Egyptian. He first appears at Tarkhan, where his image is scratched on a stone bowl, presumably as the god of the quarries there. He is not a royal god at the time, and does not appear on any royal monument of the first dynasties. In age he cannot even compare with Horus, although even he is a latecomer. The importance of Lower Egypt begins with the dynasties, when Sinai became of interest as the home of the copper and turquoise mines and as an overland connexion with Palestine and Asia.

For the understanding of the earliest dynastic Egyptian cultures Naḵāda II is the key. The beginning of the dynasties was not a cultural but a political event. It helped to intensify a civiliz-ation which had made it possible, but from which it is not divided by a hard and fast line. We may be able one day to fix the date of the first pharaoh of the First Dynasty, though his hold over Lower Egypt would still have been precarious. But this important date does not mark the introduction into Egypt of a totally new civilization, as different from the earlier as Naḵāda II must have been from Naḵāda I. It is rather the logical development and the culmination of a trend of events the beginnings of which reached far back into predynastic Egypt.

INDEX

GENERAL

GEOGRAPHICAL

PLATE I

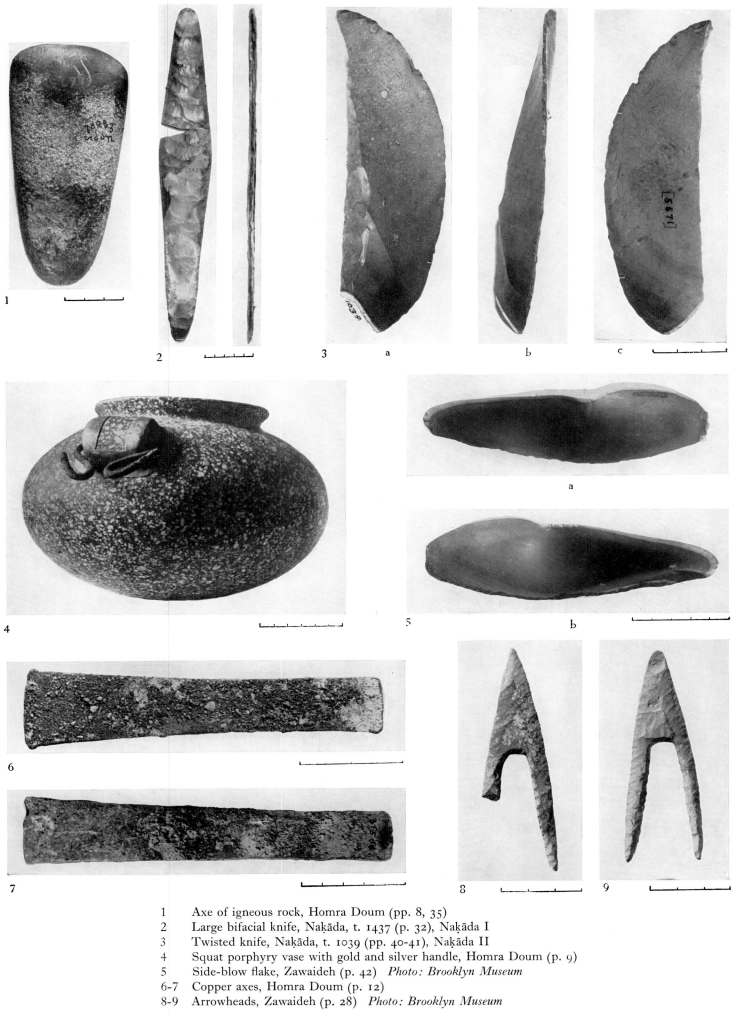

1   Axe of igneous rock, Homra Doum (pp. 8, 35)
2   Large bifacial knife, Naḳāda, t. 1437 (p. 32), Naḳāda I
3   Twisted knife, Naḳāda, t. 1039 (pp. 40-41), Naḳāda II
4   Squat porphyry vase with gold and silver handle, Homra Doum (p. 9)
5   Side-blow flake, Zawaideh (p. 42)   *Photo: Brooklyn Museum*
6-7 Copper axes, Homra Doum (p. 12)
8-9 Arrowheads, Zawaideh (p. 28)   *Photo: Brooklyn Museum*

(Scales in cm.)

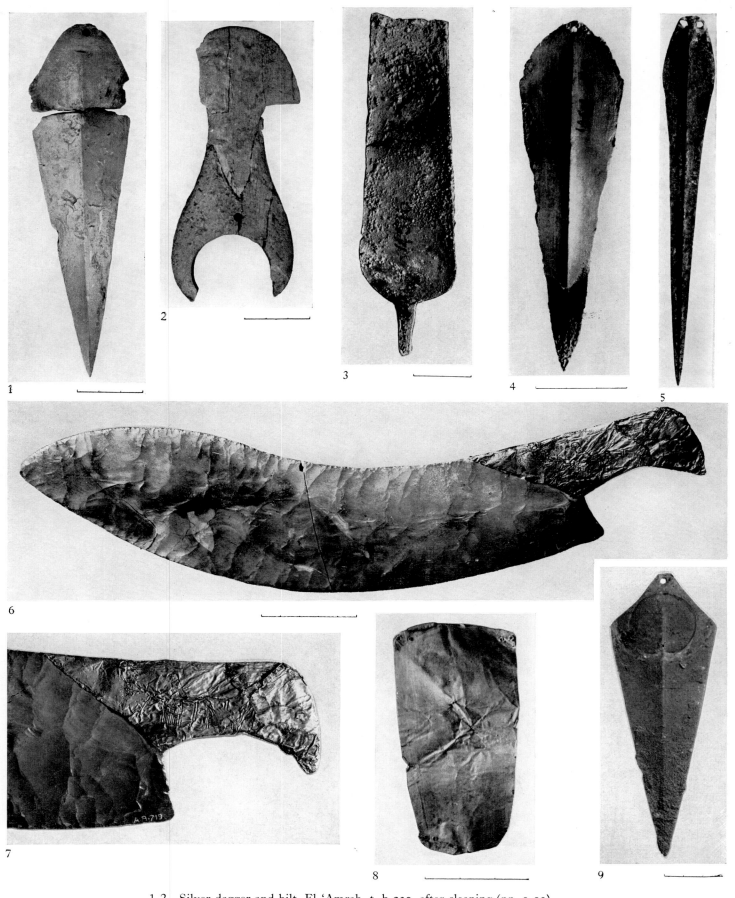

PLATE II

1-2   Silver dagger and hilt, El-'Amrah, t. b 230, after cleaning (pp. 9-10)

3   Fragment of silver knife, Homra Doum (pp. 9, 16)

4   Silver dagger, Homra Doum (p. 9)

5   Long copper dagger, Naḳāda, t. 836 (p. 10)   *Photo: Ashmolean Museum*

6-7   Flint knife with gold handle (p. 6)   *Photo: Royal Ontario Museum*

8   Gold foil with remnants of silver foil, Homra Doum (p. 9)

9   Copper dagger, El-'Amrah, t. a 13 (p. 10)   *Photo: Ashmolean Museum*

(Scales in cm.)

PLATE III

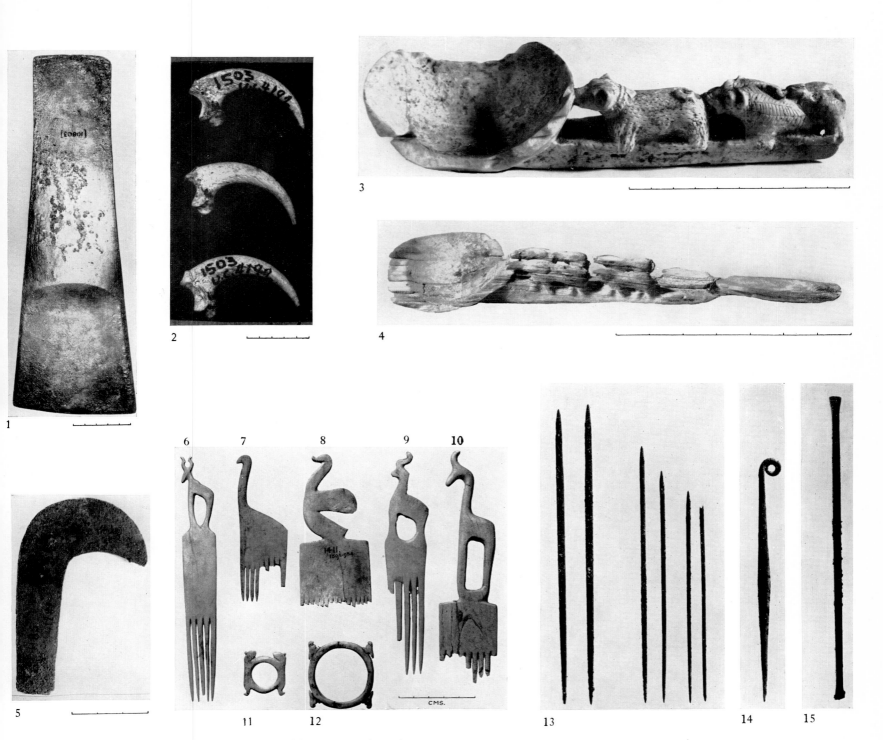

1   Hoe, Tarkhan, t. 1015 (p. 15)
2   Claws, Naḳāda, t. 1503   *Photo: Flinders Petrie Museum, University College, London*
3   Spoon, Ballas
4   Spoon, Naḳāda, t. 460 (3-4: pp. 55, 56)   *Photos: Ashmolean Museum*
5   Copper hook, El-Maḥāsna, t. H 85 (p. 20)
6-10 Combs, Naḳāda I and II (pp. 48-52)
11-12 Rings, Naḳāda, t. 1480, Diospolis Parva, t. R 159 (p. 76)
13   Sewing needles, copper, Naḳāda, t. 3 (p. 18)
14   Copper pin, Naḳāda, t. 1345 (pp. 2, 17)
15   Double-edged chisel, copper (p. 16) *6-15 Photos: Ashmolean Museum*

(Scales in cm.)

PLATE IV

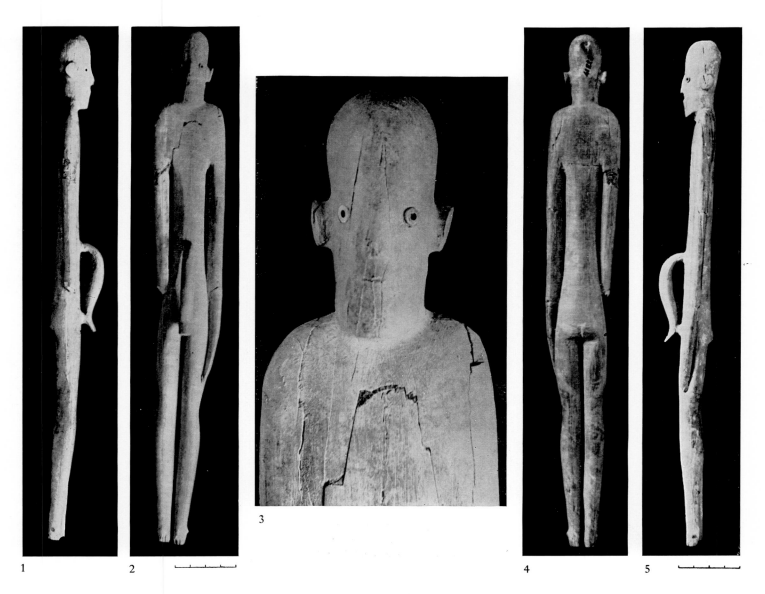

1-5   Ivory statuette, El-Maḥāsna, t. H 29 (p. 60)

(*Scales in cm.*)

PLATE V

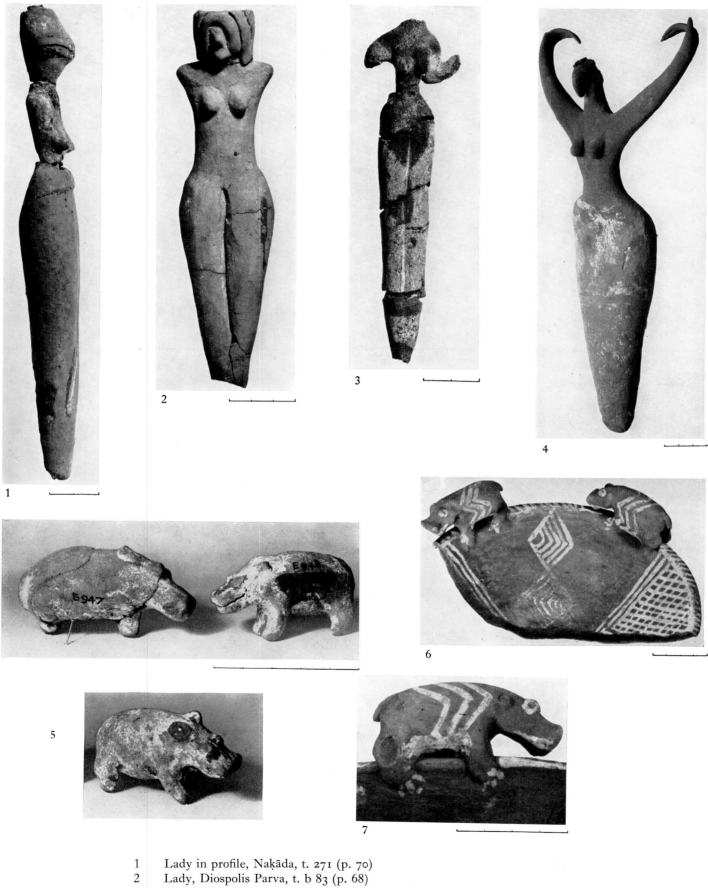

1   Lady in profile, Naḵāda, t. 271 (p. 70)
2   Lady, Diospolis Parva, t. b 83 (p. 68)
3   Lady, Diospolis Parva, t. b 101 (p. 68)   1-3 *Photos: Ashmolean Museum*
4   Dancing woman, Mohamerieh (p. 69)   *Photo: Brooklyn Museum*
5   Hippopotami, Diospolis Parva, t. b 101 (p. 73)   *Photos: Ashmolean Museum*
6-7   Details of the hippopotamus bowl from El-Maḥāsna, t. H 29 (p. 60)

(Scales in cm.)

PLATE VI

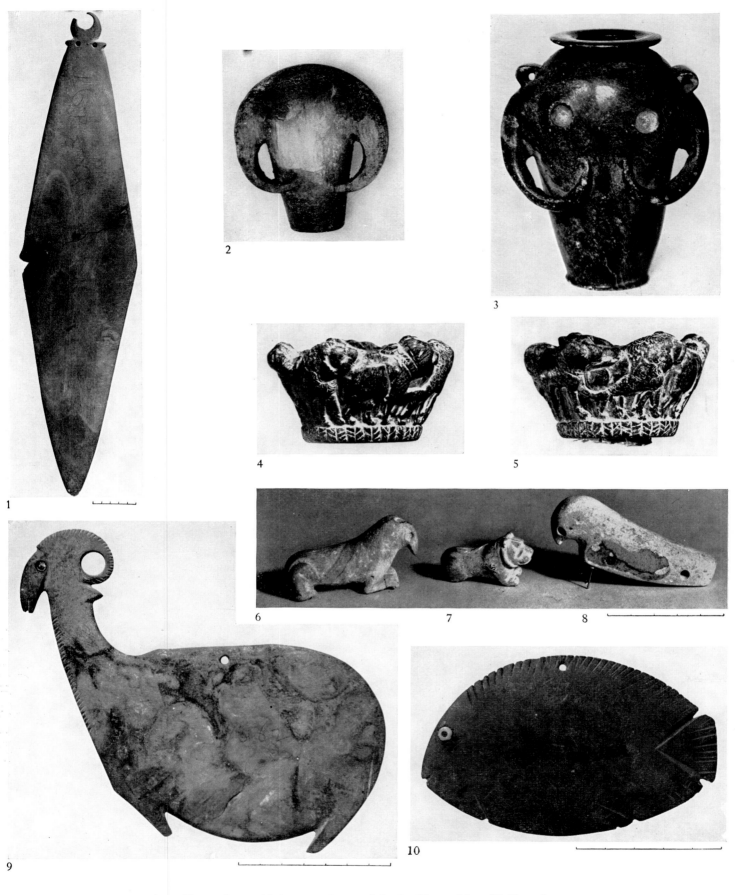

1   Slate palette with horns and ears of the fertility goddess, El-'Amrah, t. a 97
          (p. 83) *Photo: University Museum, Cambridge*

2-3   The symbol of the fertility goddess, (2) from Naḳāda, t. 1788, (3) bought (p. 74)

4-5   Small mace(?) head, Hierakonpolis (p. 120)

6-8   Three of the animals, Naḳāda, t. 721 (p. 75)

9   Slate palette in the form of a Barbary sheep, Naḳāda, t. 1562 (p. 84)

10   Slate palette in the form of a fish, Naḳāda, t. 1740 (p. 88) 2-10 *Photos: Ashmolean Museum*

(Scales in cm.)

PLATE VII

1   Nar-Mer palette: reverse (pp. 94, 96)   *Photo: Cairo Museum*
2   Stela of Eannatum of Lagash with his phalanx (upper panel (p. 96))   *Photo: Alinari-Giraudon*
3   Slain enemies from the statue base of Khasekhem (p. 101)   *Photo: Ashmolean Museum*
4   Battlefield palette (p. 100)   *Photo: Ashmolean Museum*

(Scales in cm.)

PLATE VIII

1   Slate Palette, Cairo Museum (p. 101)

2-5   Details of Nar-Mer's mace-head: (2-3) the three running men. (4) The king in the ḥeb-sed pavilion and the Horus falcon. (5) The figure in the closed palanquin and the cow and calf in the enclosure (pp. 114, 115) 2-5 *Photos: Ashmolean Museum*

(Scales in cm.)

PLATE IX

1-2 Nar-Mer's mace-head: the two most important personalities (p. 114)   *Photo: Ashmolean Museum*

1 The king in the heb-sed pavilion with the Horus falcon above

2 The queen (?) in the palanquin, above her the cow and the calf

(Scales in cm.)

PLATE X

Nar-Mer's mace-head. 1 The king's sereḫ and retinue (p. 115). 2 Standard-bearers, running men, bull, goat and numerals (p. 115). 3 The bird on the chapel (p. 115). 4 Enclosure with gazelles (p. 115) 5 Bull, goat, and numerals (p. 115). *Photos: Ashmolean Museum*

(Scales in cm.)

PLATE XI

1   Badārian tomb with hamper(?) (p. 124)   *Mostag.*, pl. VI, 8

2   Hut circles, Ḥammāmīya (p. 129)   *Bad. Civ.*, pl. LVII, 1

3   Matting lining a Naḳāda II tomb (p. 125)   *Mostag.*, pl. VI, 6

4   Door of hut circle, Badāri

5-6, 8   Hut circles, Badāri (p. 129)   *Bad. Civ.*, pl. LVIII, 1-4

7   Rectangular house, Hierakonpolis (pp. 129-130)   *Garstang, Excavations at Hierakonpolis . . . Ann. Serv.* VIII, 1901, pp. 132 ff.

PLATE XII

1-2   Model of a city wall, Diospolis Parva, t. B 83 (p. 135)   *Photos: Ashmolean Museum*

3   House model, El-'Amrah, t. a 4 (p. 132)   *Photo: British Museum*

4   Early dynastic brick-lined tomb, El-Maḥāsna, t. H 129 (p. 139)   *Cem. at El-Maḥāsna*, pl. X, 48

(*Scales in cm.*)